THIRSK & SOWERBY

THROUGH TIME

Cooper Harding

AMBERLEY PUBLISHING

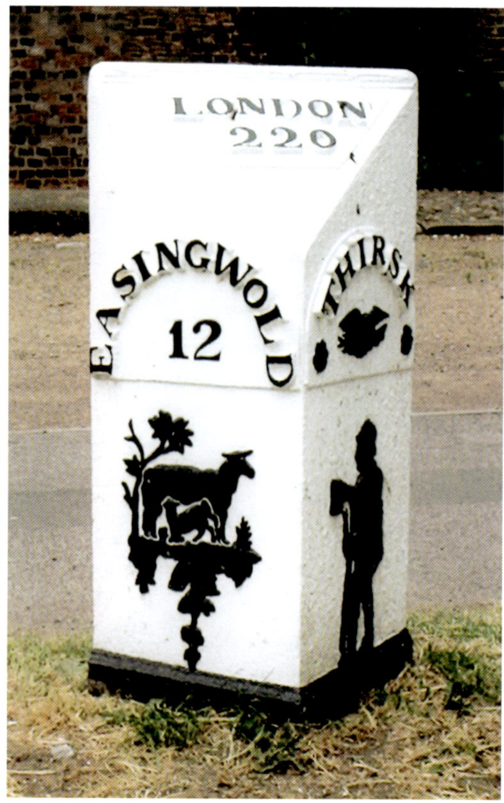

The 'Drover' Milepost in Ingramgate
This unique mile-marker shows a drover cheerfully celebrating the safe arrival of his herd.

First published 2009

Amberley Publishing Plc
Cirencester Road, Chalford,
Stroud, Gloucestershire, GL6 8PE

www.amberley-books.com

ISBN 978 1 84868 660 1

British Library Cataloguing in Publication Data.
A catalogue record for this book is available from the British Library.

Typeset in 9.5pt on 12pt Celeste.
Typesetting by Amberley Publishing.
Printed in the UK.

Introduction

The popularity of the picture postcard reached its height between 1902, when people were first allowed to write a message on the same side as the address, and the 1920s, when the 'Box Brownie' camera brought snapshots within the reach of all. It is the late Victorian period and the Edwardian years before the outbreak of the First World War that are most represented in the pictures that form the collection in Thirsk Museum, from which many of the early views have been selected for this book. The general impression is of a small market town, reasonably prosperous at the centre of a fertile agricultural district and generally content with itself. That state continued until the 1950s, when changes in the pattern of agriculture and of economic conditions meant that the old way of life was passing. By the late 1960s, Thirsk seems to have fallen into the doldrums, the main road through the town choked with heavy traffic on its way to and from the booming industries of Teesside and its cobbled Market Place a shabby overnight park for heavy goods vehicles. It was a bottleneck that drivers avoided if they could. Two things coincided to revive the town's fortunes. In 1972, the A19 by-pass was opened, relieving the town of most of the heavy through-traffic. Then the arrival of increasing numbers of tourists from the USA seeking the surgery of a certain James Herriot alerted the folk of Thirsk. The modest vet they knew as Alf Wight was in fact a best-selling author, and his fictional alter ego became the hero of a long-running TV series. Thirsk took on a new role as a centre for tourism in that part of the North Riding of Yorkshire now christened 'Herriot Country'. That phase is, perhaps, now passing, but, with the growth of a busy industrial park, investment in a ambitious Auction Mart complex and the development of new blocks of retirement apartments, twenty-first century Thirsk is an attractive place to live in. A forward-looking Town Council has worked hard to smarten the appearance of the town centre and improve local amenities. These changes are reflected in the colour photographs in this book. It has not always been easy to follow in the footsteps of the past. Thirsk was fortunate in its early photographers, Joseph R. Clarke and son in particular. Often, the view from the original spot is obscured; the tripod must often have been set up in the middle of the road and its owner clearly had access to the upper windows of buildings in the town centre, points not readily available today. The task of matching those early views has been challenging but absorbing, taking me on occasions into spots I had never visited before and walking paths I was not aware of. I hope the comparisons and contrasts made here between the old and the new will help to put both past and present in perspective.

Acknowledgements

Acknowledgements are due in the first place to the Trustees of Thirsk and District Museum Society who are the titular holders of the Thirsk Museum collection. Two former Trustees, the late Dr Peter Wyon and the late Mr Peter Hatch, deposited a number of postcards and early photographs; their wealth of local knowledge was always a most valuable source of information. I am also extremely grateful to the current society president, Ray Ballard, for putting at my disposal his extensive collection of old pictures of Thirsk and district. I have to thank Bill Bateman for photographs and very valuable details about the history of his family and the yard named after them, Bryan Cooke for a fine colour picture of the bridge at World's End, Dr R. Firth for a photograph of the flood in 2000, which inundated his Finkle Street dental surgery, and our webmaster, Tony Pereira, for a most comprehensive set of photographs taken in the saddler's shop. Mrs Dorothy Reveley has contributed photographs of the demolition of Salem chapel taken by her late father, Mr James Greenley of Sowerby, Mrs Susan Stephenson photographed the milestone near her house, and many other people have, at various times, added to the museum collection. Finally, I am indebted to Margaret, my wife, who has suffered months of domestic disruption as our home filled with files and photographs. She has been a patient consultant, counsellor and critic, for which I am grateful beyond measure!

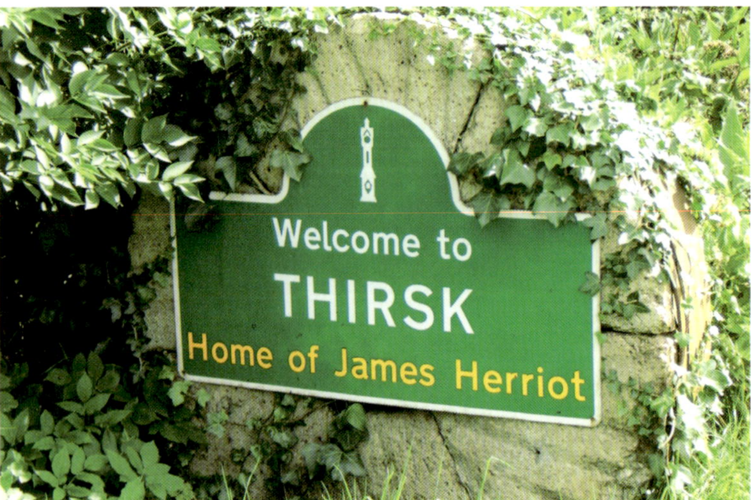

Thirsk welcomes the visitor, announcing itself home to the vet who put the town firmly on the tourist map.

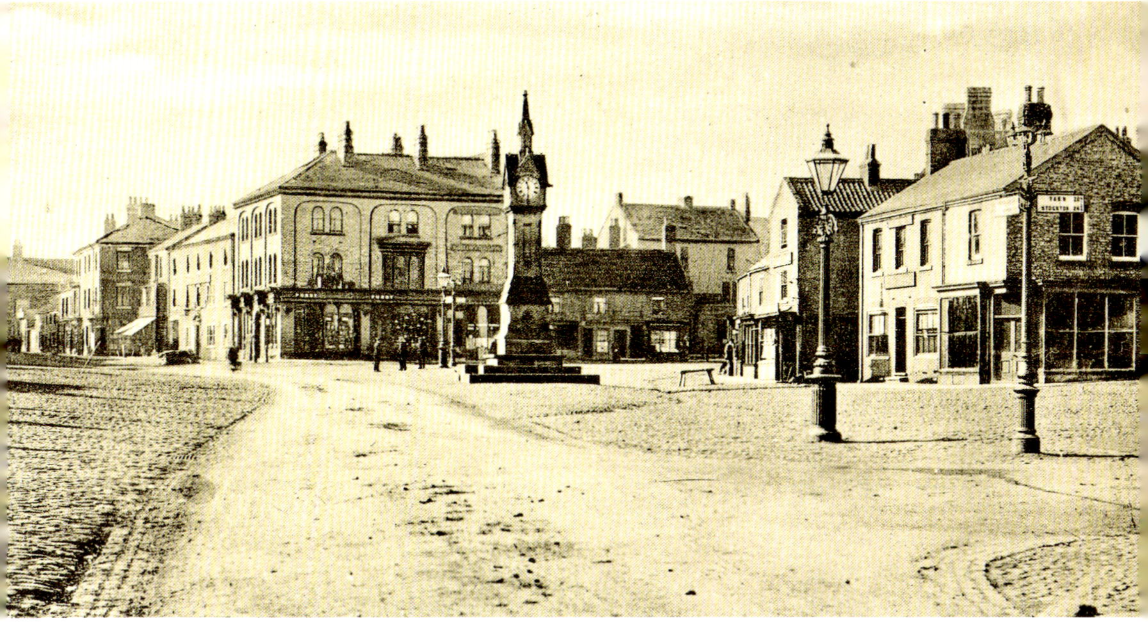

Thirsk Market Place

The Market Place lies at the heart of Thirsk, a centre for the weekly sales of produce and an arena for parades, funfairs, feasts and celebrations. The square is unusually empty in this photograph from the early 1900s, though the clock, which is on the site of the ancient market cross, shows 11.30. Electric lighting has been installed but the gas lamps are still in place. The lower picture was taken at 7.20 on a Sunday morning; the trees are a pleasant addition among the posts and signs that intrude elsewhere.

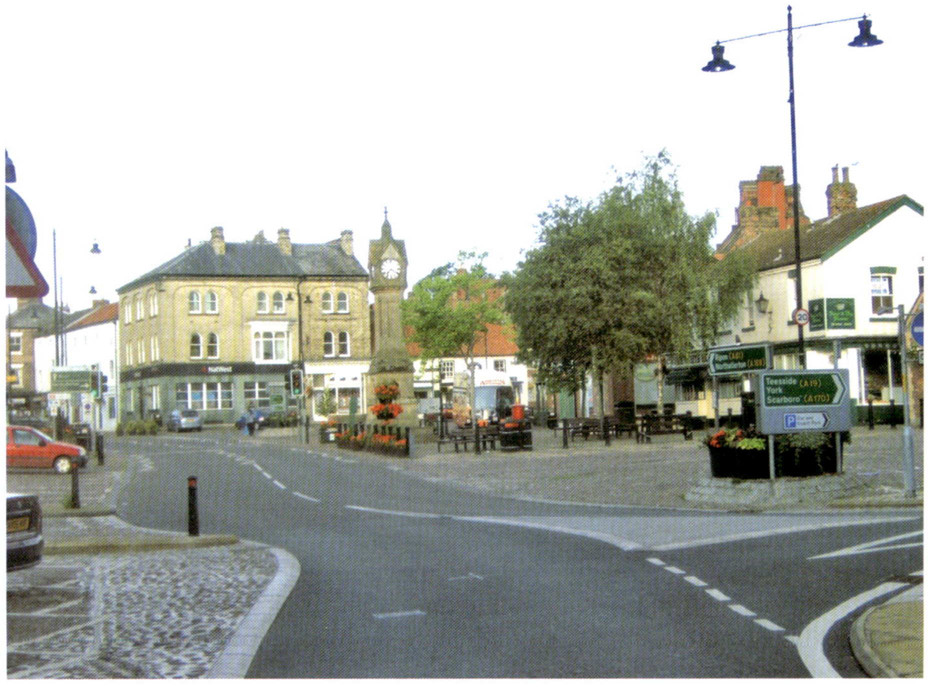

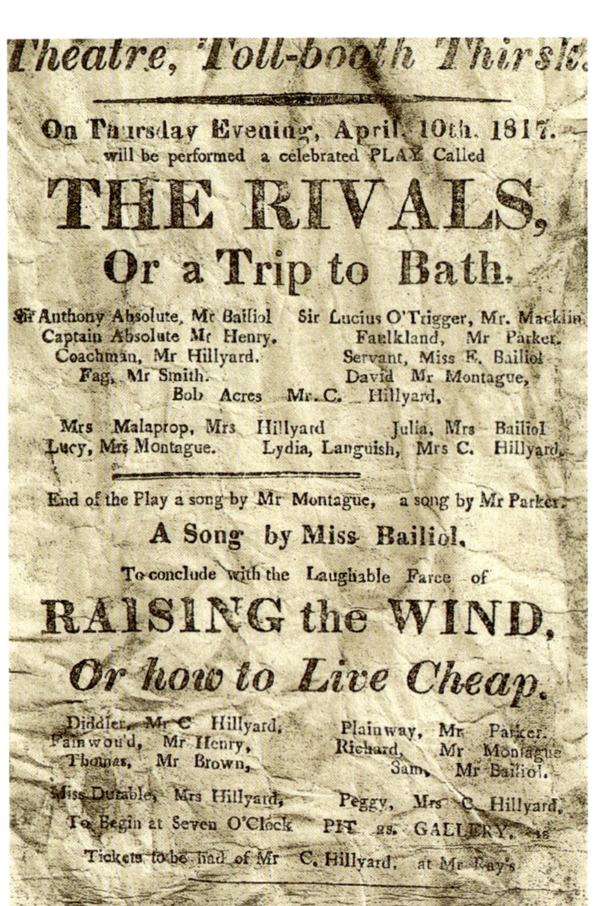

Theatre, Toll-booth Thirsk.

On Thursday Evening, April 10th. 1817.
will be performed a celebrated PLAY Called

THE RIVALS,
Or a Trip to Bath.

Sir Anthony Absolute, Mr Bailiol	Sir Lucius O'Trigger, Mr. Macklin
Captain Absolute Mr Henry.	Faulkland, Mr Parker.
Coachman, Mr Hillyard.	Servant, Miss F. Bailiol
Fag, Mr Smith.	David Mr Montague,

Bob Acres Mr. C. Hillyard,

Mrs Malaprop, Mrs Hillyard	Julia, Mrs Bailiol
Lucy, Mrs Montague.	Lydia, Languish, Mrs C. Hillyard.

End of the Play a song by Mr Montague, a song by Mr Parker.

A Song by Miss Bailiol,

To conclude with the Laughable Farce of

RAISING the WIND,
Or how to Live Cheap.

Diddler, Mr C Hillyard,	Plainway, Mr Parker.
Fainwou'd, Mr Henry,	Richard, Mr Montague
Thomas, Mr Brown,	Sam, Mr Bailiol.
Miss Durable, Mrs Hillyard,	Peggy, Mrs C Hillyard,

To Begin at Seven O'Clock PIT 2s. GALLERY, 1s

Tickets to be had of Mr C. Hillyard, at Mr Ray's

The Tolbooth Destroyed

A playbill of 1817 advertises a performance of *The Rivals* at the Tolbooth. This building stood on the south side of the square near the Golden Fleece Hotel and housed the magistrates' Court Room on the upper floor. It was here, in 1834, that the booth of a travelling showman caught fire, destroying the timber-framed hall. The drawing below shows the demolition of the ruins; the Tolbooth was never rebuilt.

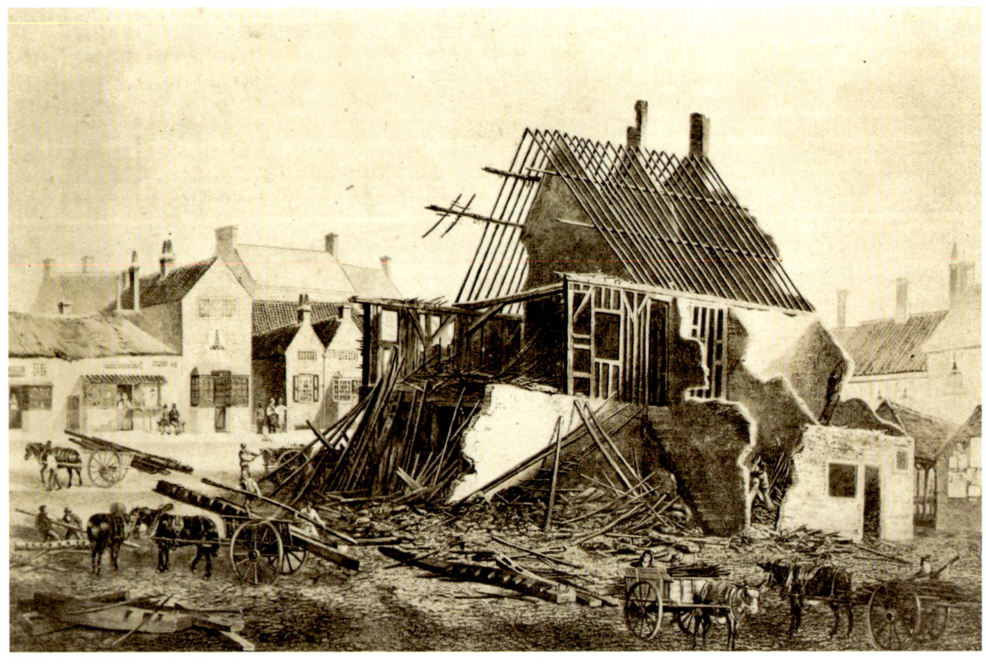

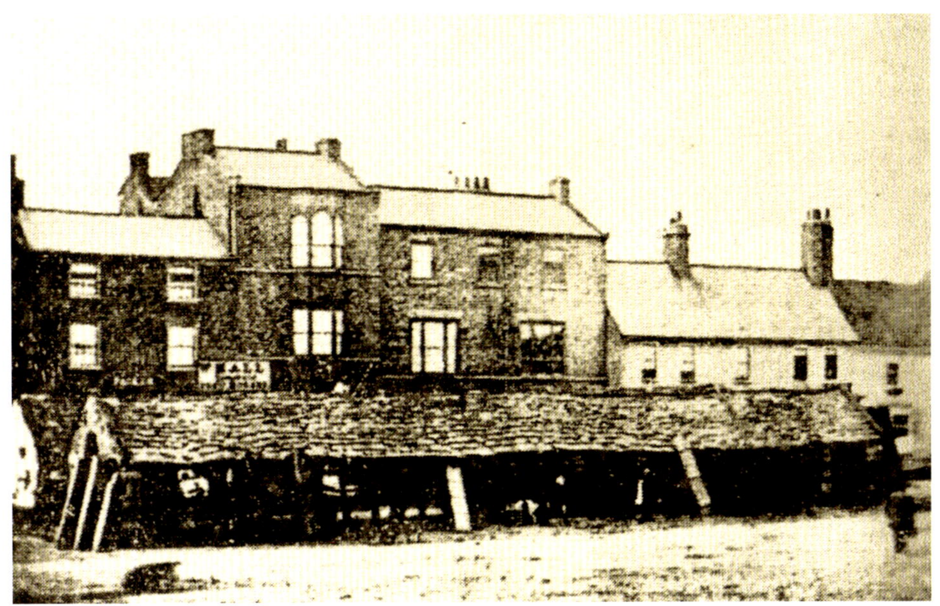

The Shambles

This very early photograph dates from the 1850s. It shows the Shambles — two rows of open-air butchers' stalls — which were then derelict and were finally demolished in 1857. An ancient by-law decreed that bulls sold for slaughter in Thirsk market should first be baited by dogs; this cruel blood-sport took place in the Bull Ring still marked out in the cobbles where the buses draw in. The inset shows the replica ring that marks the spot where the bulls were tethered.

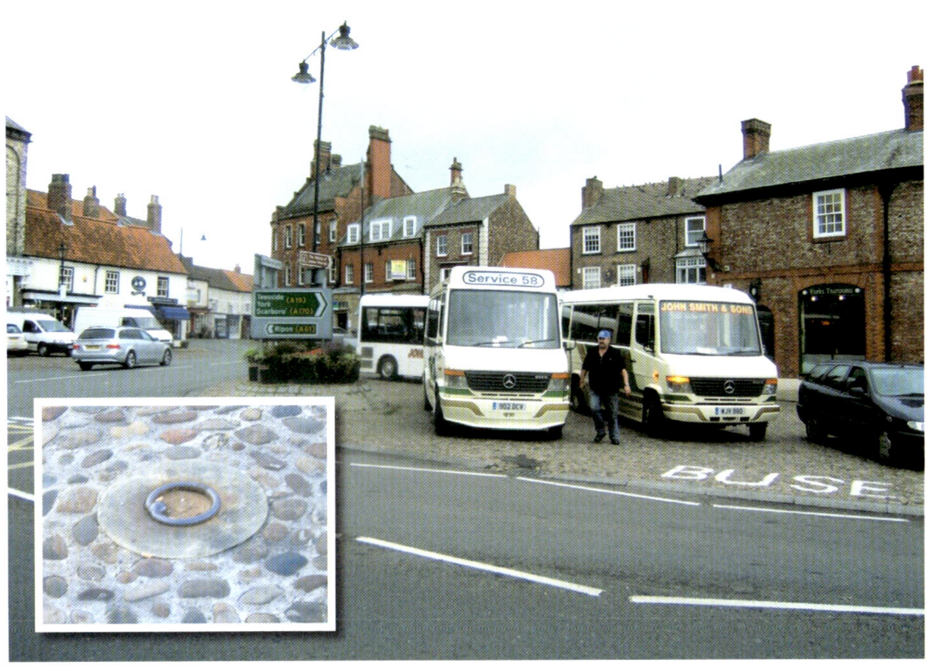

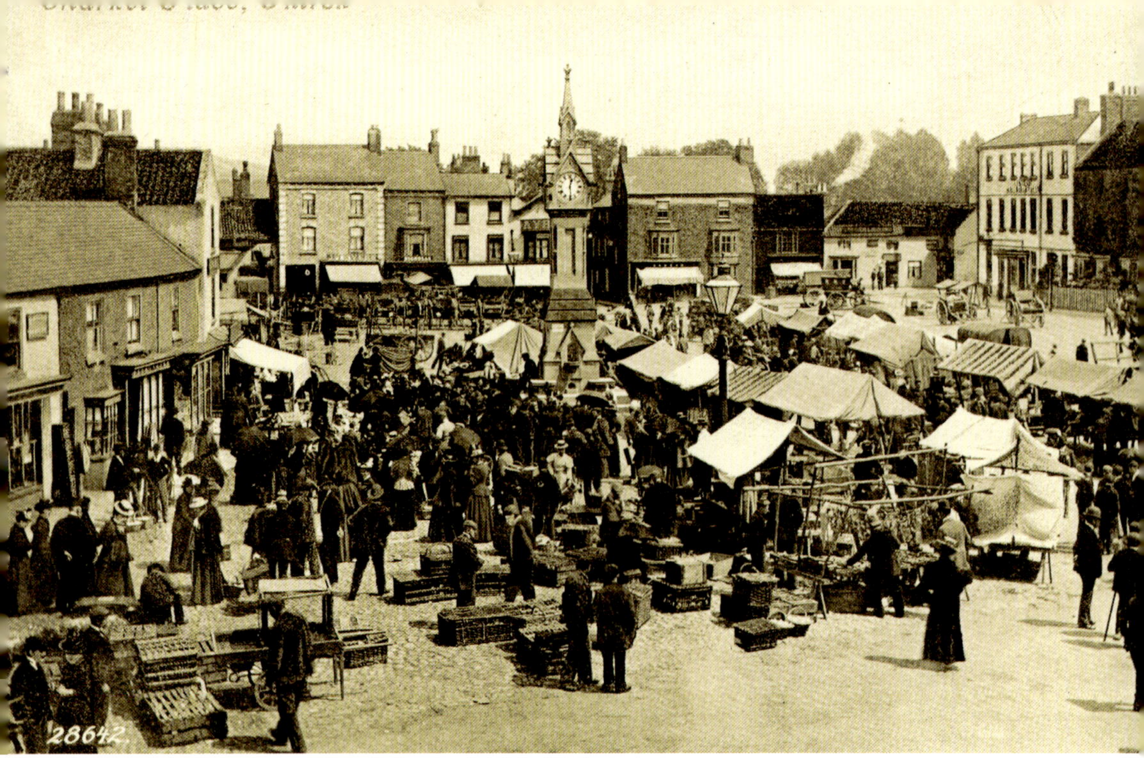

Thirsk Clock

Thirsk erected the clock in 1896 to commemorate the marriage of the then Duke and Duchess of York, later George V and Mary. This spot soon became a centre for the weekly sale of eggs, poultry and game; with dealers coming in from cities like Leeds and Bradford, business here was brisk. The area round the clock is still a focal point; now shaded by trees and furnished with benches, it is a place to sit and watch the world go by.

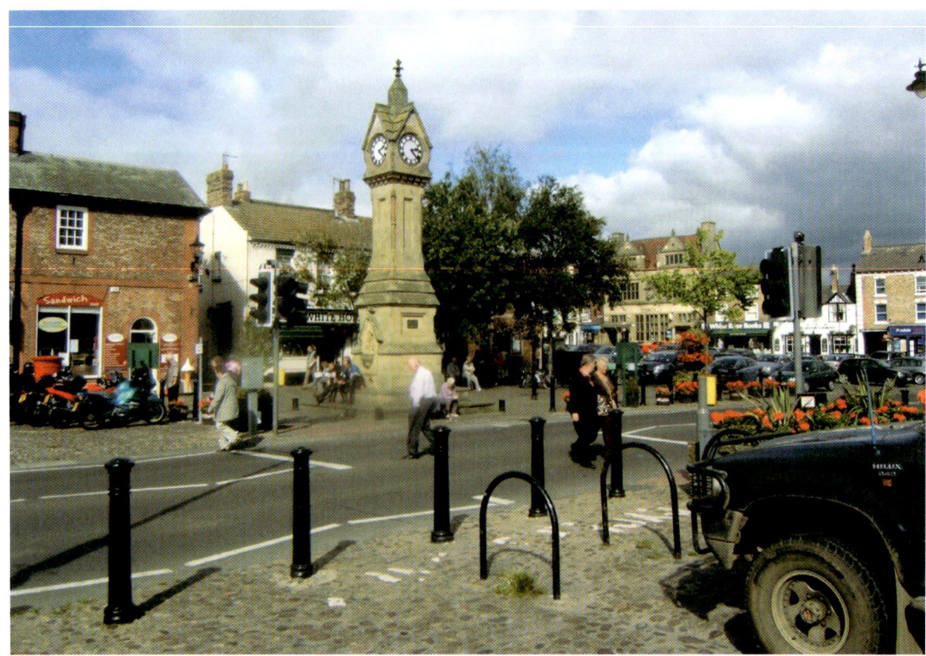

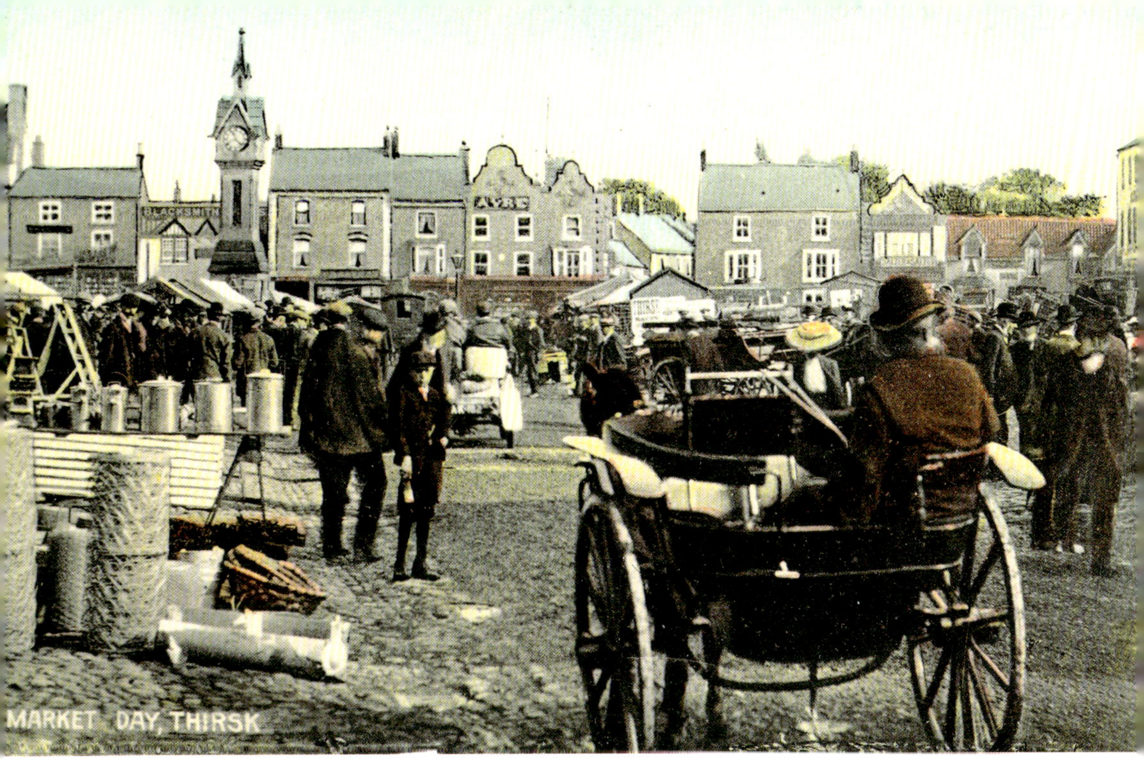

MARKET DAY, THIRSK

Market Day Traffic

A driver with pony and trap makes his way through a busy Market Place. A closer look at the picture above shows that ahead of the trap there is an early motorcar — the shape of things to come. It would be a bold person who ventured through the town in pony and trap in today's heavy traffic, though two young cyclists have chosen their moment to turn up Kirkgate.

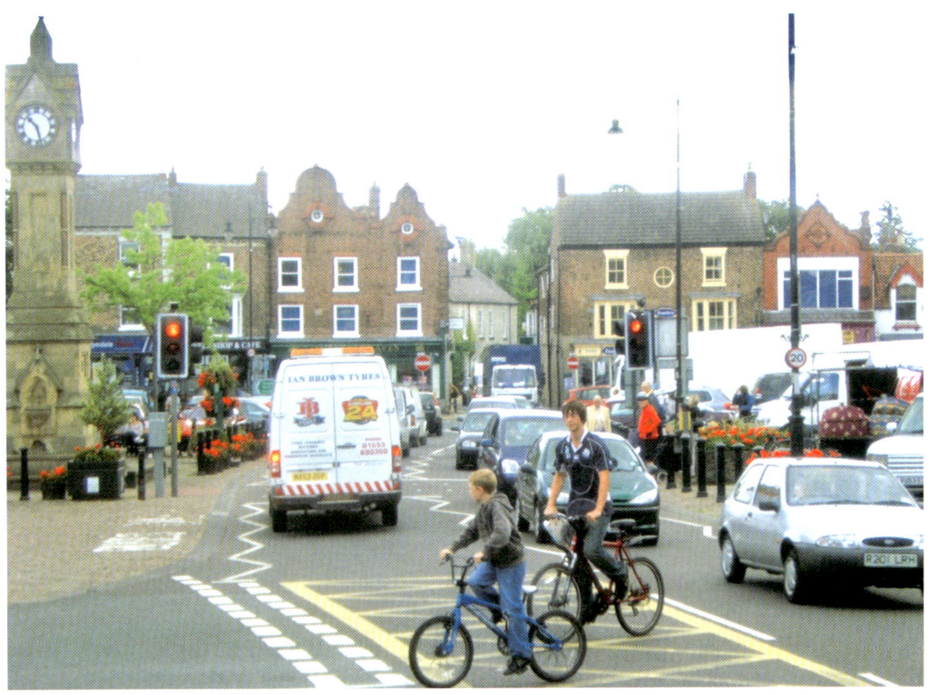

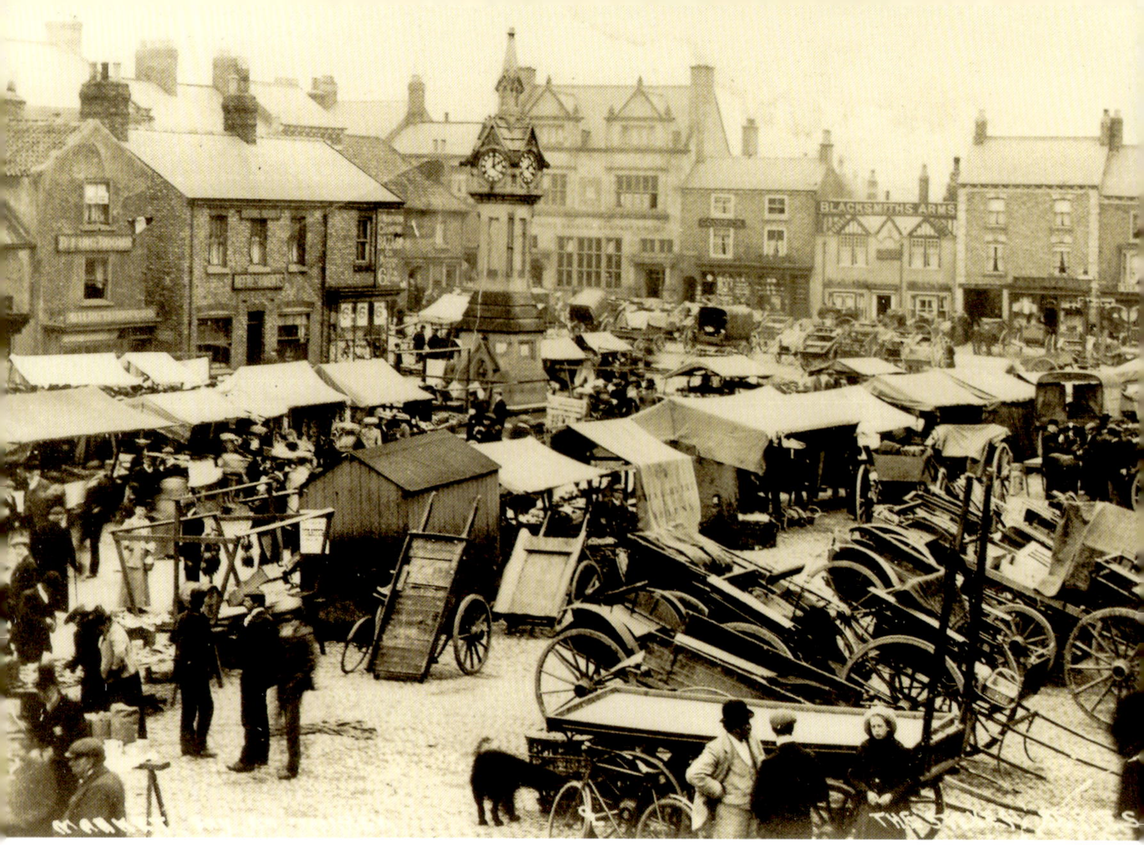

Market Stalls

The photograph above offers a back-stage view on a Market Monday. The stalls face the roadway, while the traders' carts and barrows are parked behind. The horses will have been taken round to be tethered in one of the inn yards, with fodder and water provided. The picture below shows how the stalls now face away from the traffic and the pavement is clear for folk to pass by.

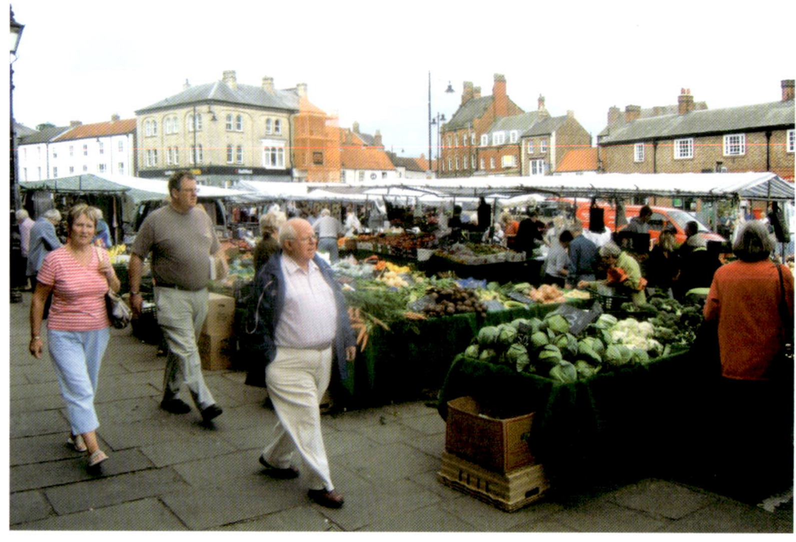

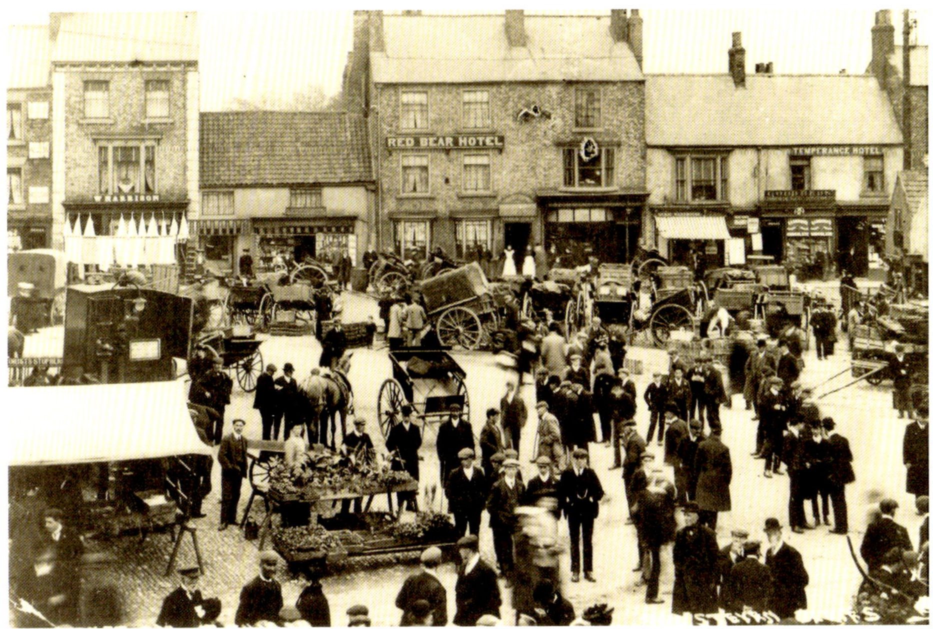

Outside the Red Bear

The Red Bear was one of four public houses on the north side of the Market Place, dating back to the early decades of the nineteenth century. In 1997 considerable feeling was aroused locally when this pub was refurbished as the Darrowby Inn with the hope of attracting custom from visitors on the Herriot trail. In the picture above, several groups of young men, some smartly dressed in bowler hat and stiff collar, are engaged in transactions of some sort. The photograph may record one of the Hiring Fairs when men presented themselves for employment for the coming year. The modern picture is a cheerful conversation piece.

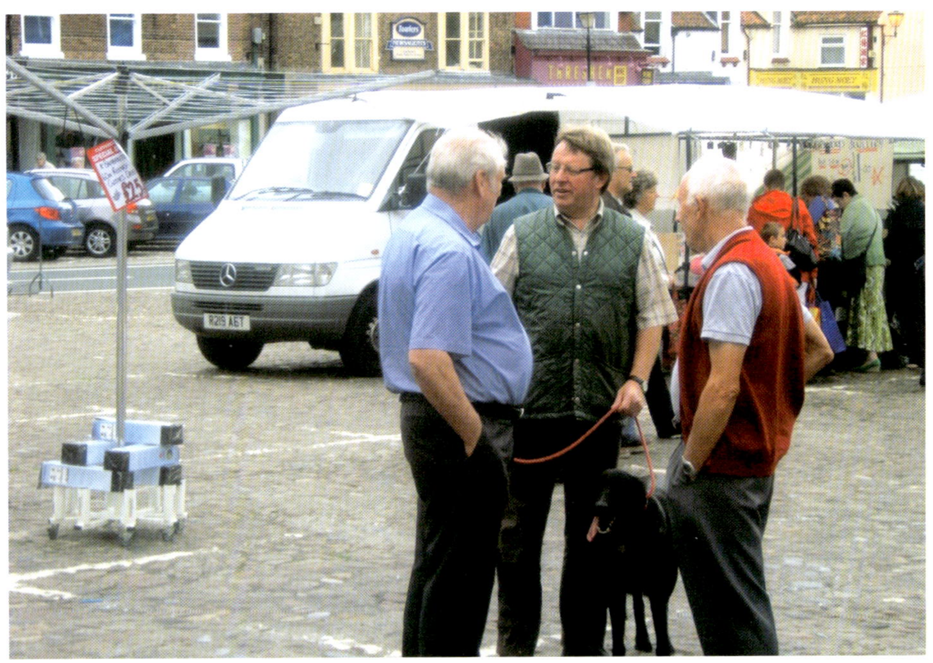

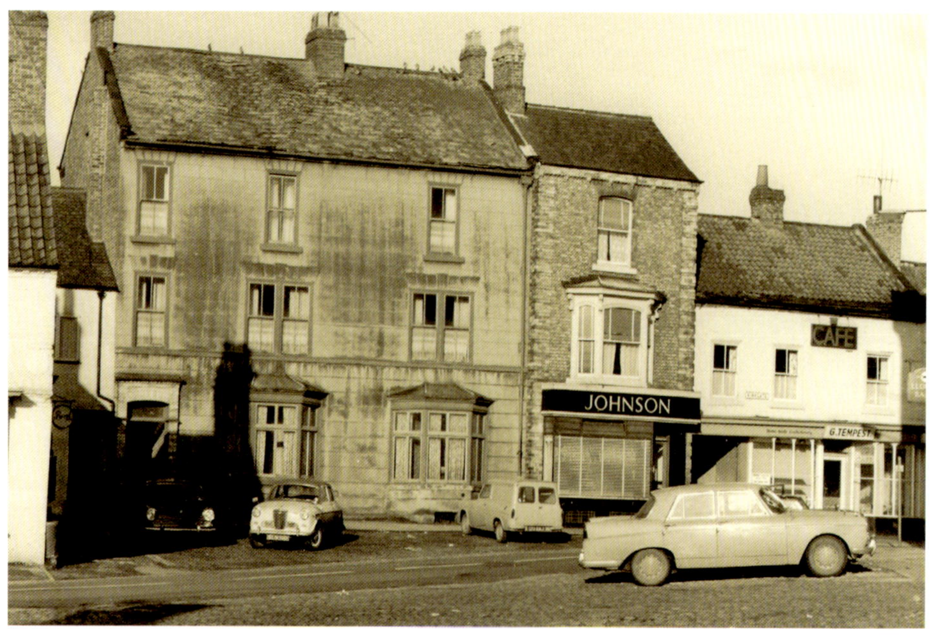

The King's Arms

This former public house stood grimy and deserted at the foot of Kirkgate as it had done for many years before this 1970's photograph. The doorway, just visible on the left, led to a yard at the rear with old cottages and outhouses, equally derelict. The building was pulled down early in 2001 and the site developed, with an archway giving access to the premises behind. The ground floor of the building, seen in the lower picture, houses the local police office.

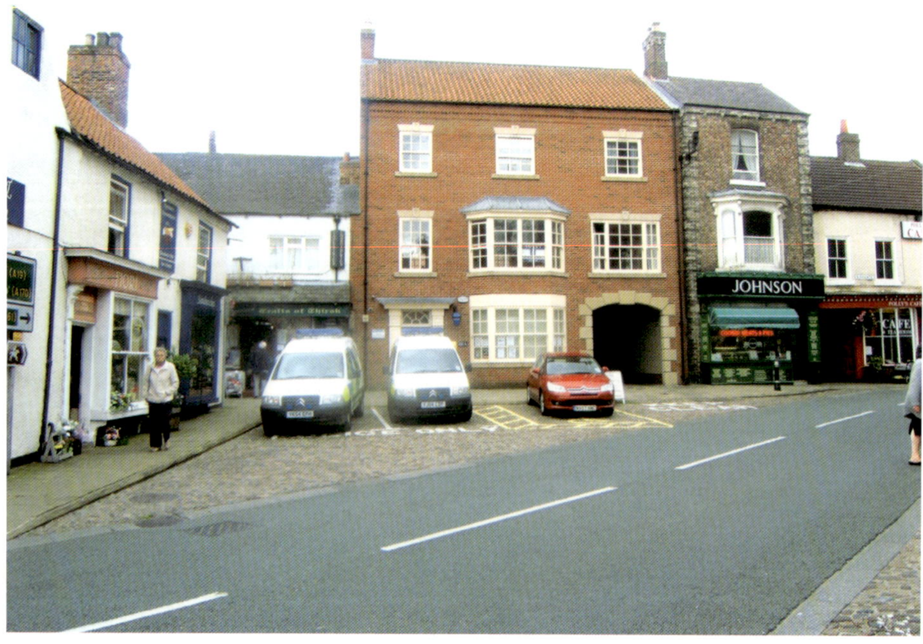

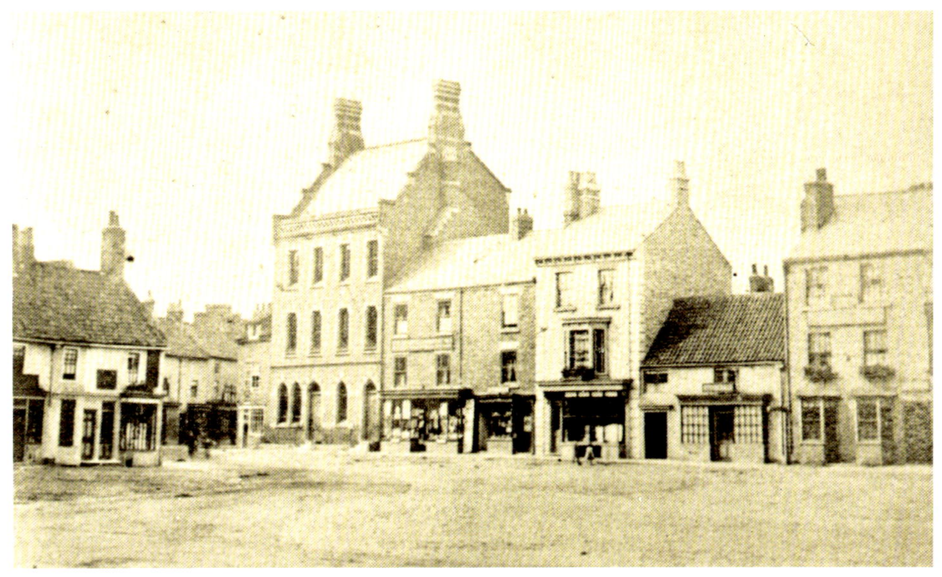

The Bank Building

The faded print here is the only known image of this corner of the Market Place showing the Bank Building, later extended to replace a little shop at the bottom of Kirkgate. Built for the Quaker-owned Backhouse's Bank in the mid-nineteenth century, it was sold to the York City and County Bank in 1873. It now houses an outfitter's shop, which has offices above, and remains the tallest building in the town. Today, Lloyds Bank occupies the site next-door, while the little shop to the right is a sixteenth-century survival, preserving the general roofline of bygone days.

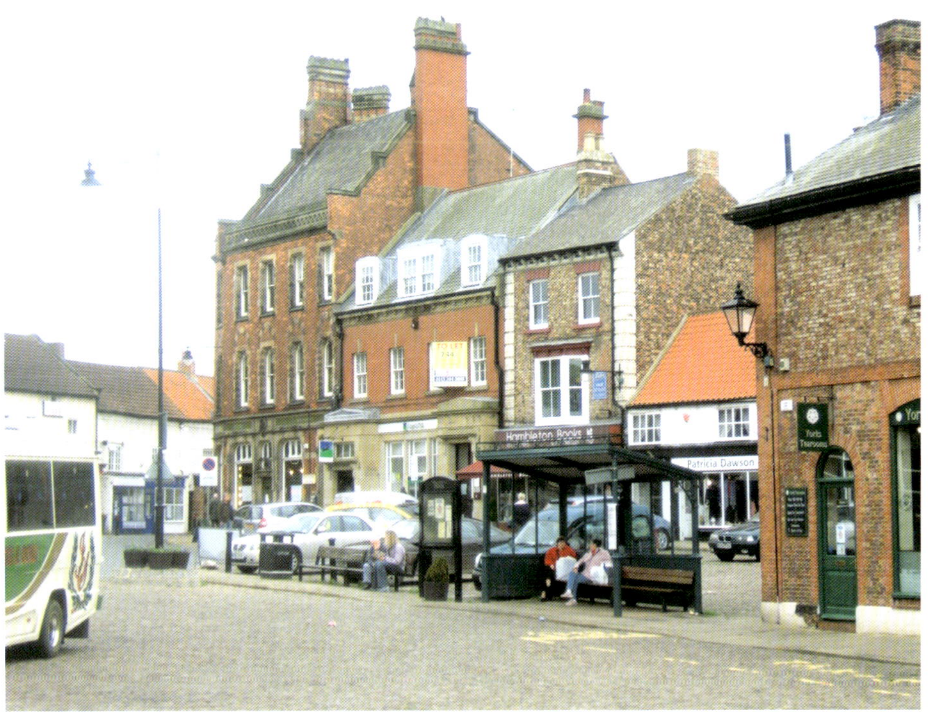

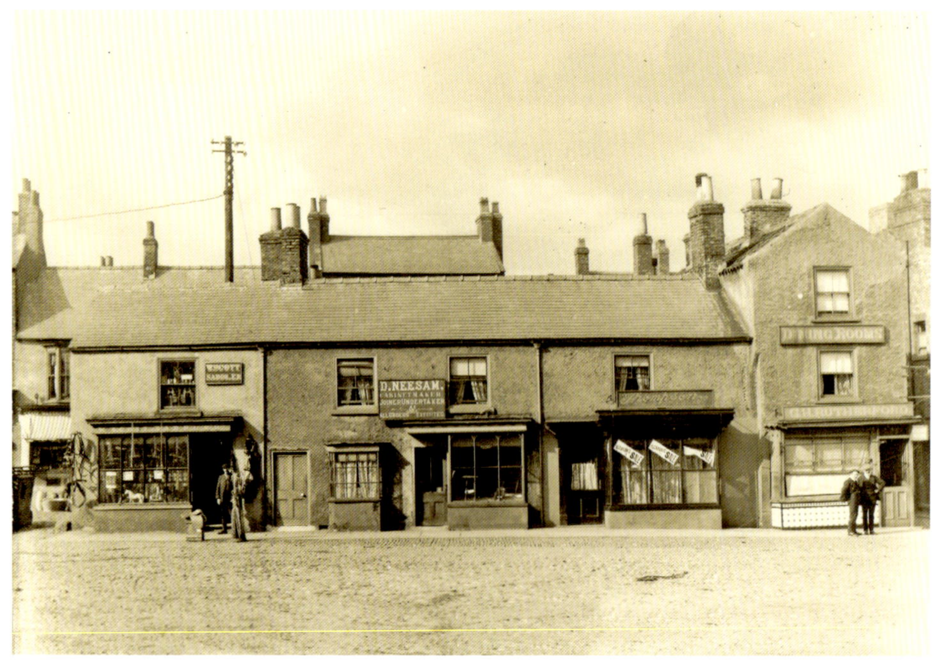

Thirsk Head Post Office 1909

Known to have been thatched at one time, the row of old shops seen in the top photograph was demolished in 1908 to make way for the Head Post Office. Its opening is marked in the lower picture by the presence of the staff, a total of twenty-seven in all, most in uniform. The six post-carts served outlying villages, and there were telegraph boys on duty to deliver telegrams at any hour of the day.

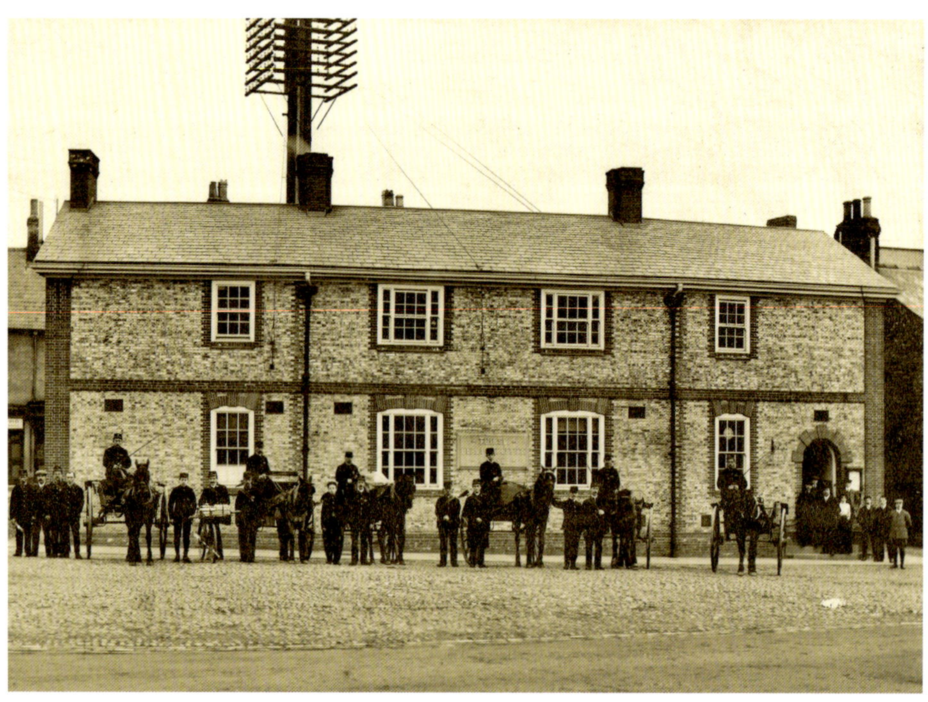

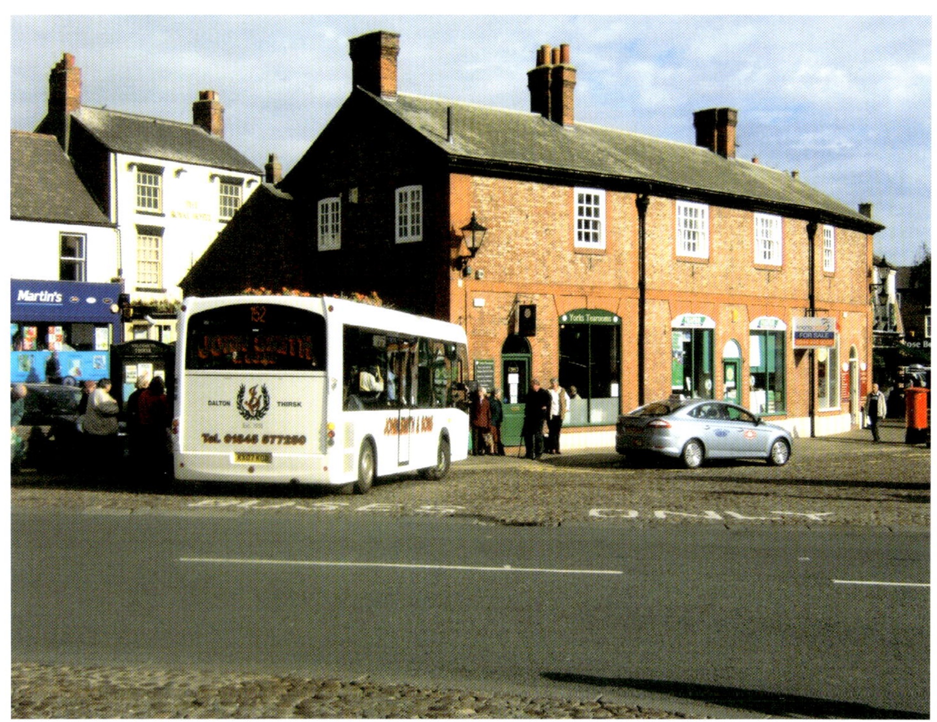

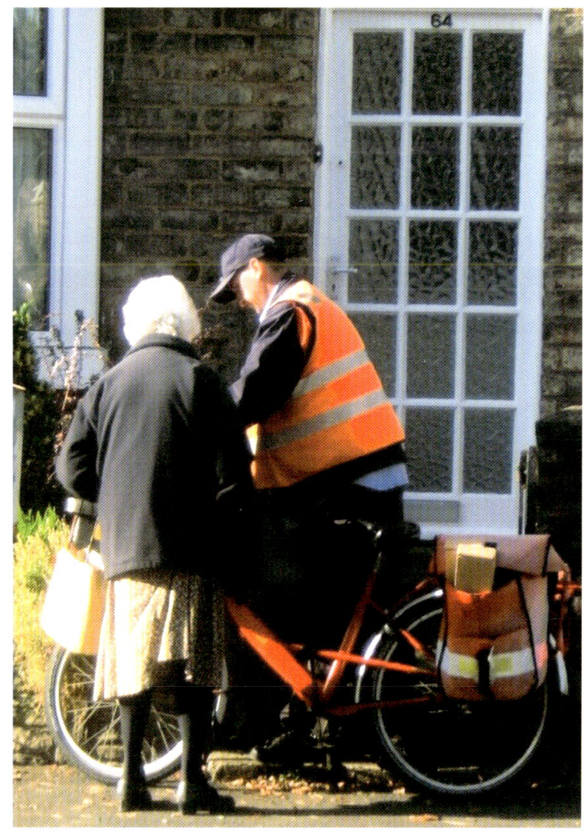

The Post Office Block 2009
Some twenty years ago the main Post Office depot was moved to the Industrial Park on the York road, while the business counter was transferred to the Co-op. The 1909 Post Office building is now occupied by a café, a snack bar and a photographer's, with other little shops to the rear. The modern postman seen in the lower picture pursues his bicycle round clad in today's informal attire.

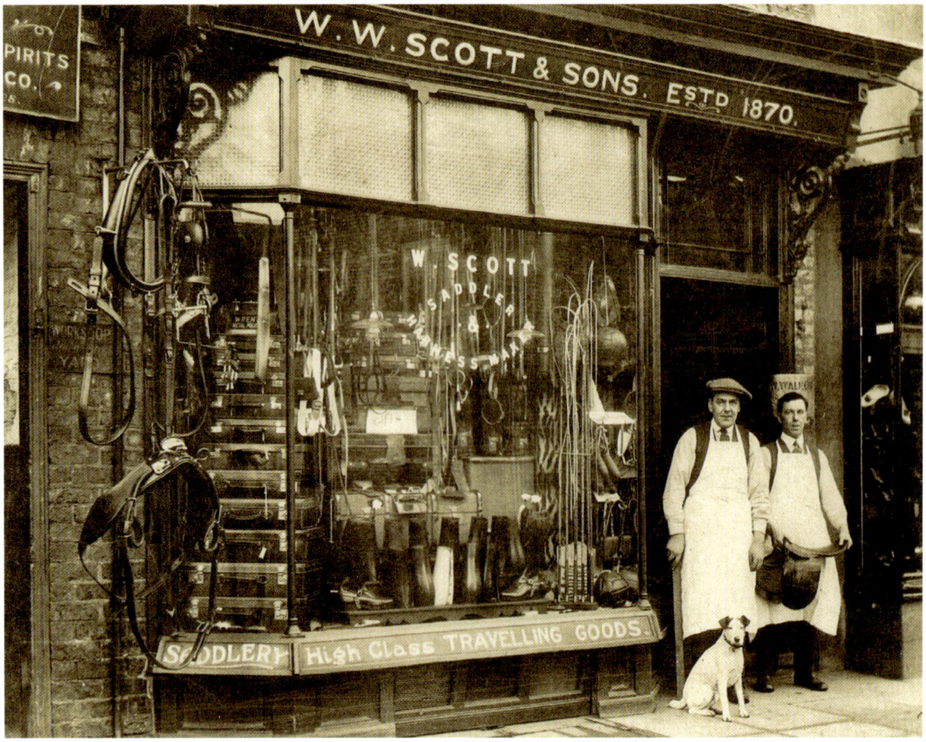

Scott's Saddler's

Scott's saddler's shop was originally in the block demolished to build the 1909 Post Office (see page 14) but moved to new premises on the north side of the Market Place. Seen in the doorway are George and William Scott, sons of the founder of the business. In the years before the First World War there were still three saddlers in Thirsk, with plenty of work to do in the horse-drawn era. By the 1990s Geoff Moore, who took over Scott's business, was the last working saddler in the area. He is seen below at work with his son Mike.

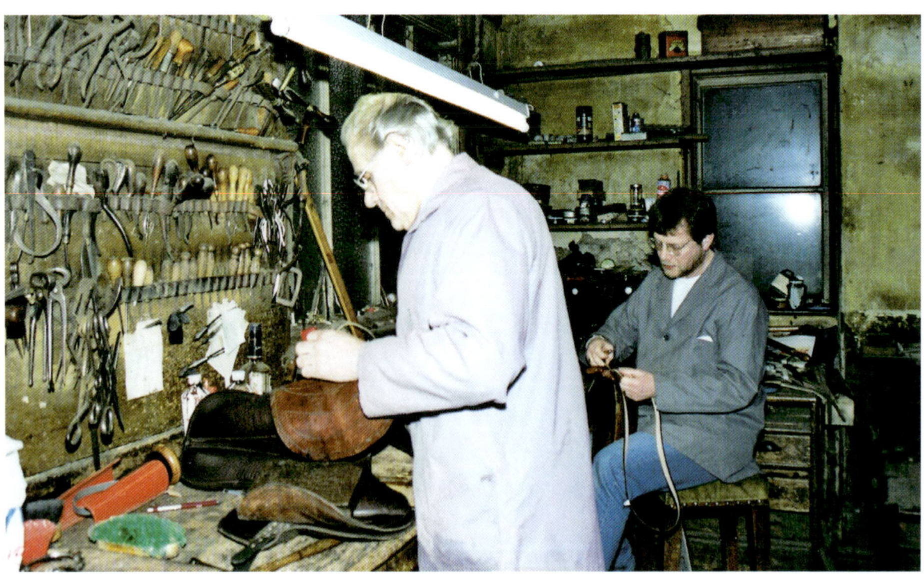

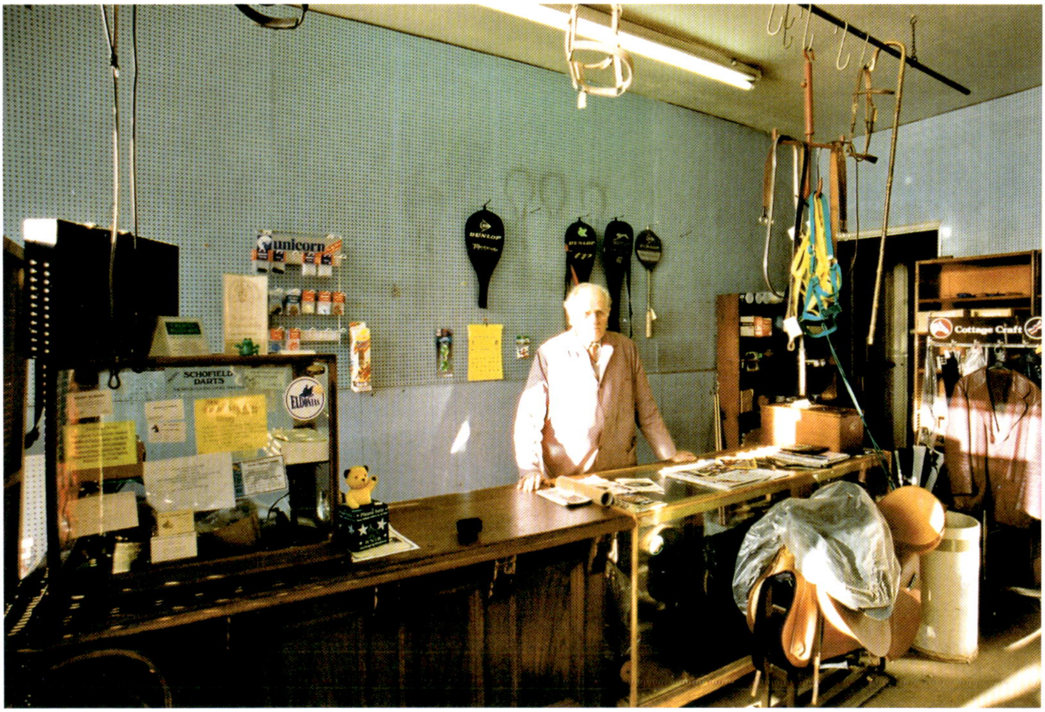

Everything Must Go!

Geoff Moore retired in 2001. He is seen again in the top picture, presiding over the clearance sale of his stock-in-trade. The shop is now home to the local Tourist Information Centre.

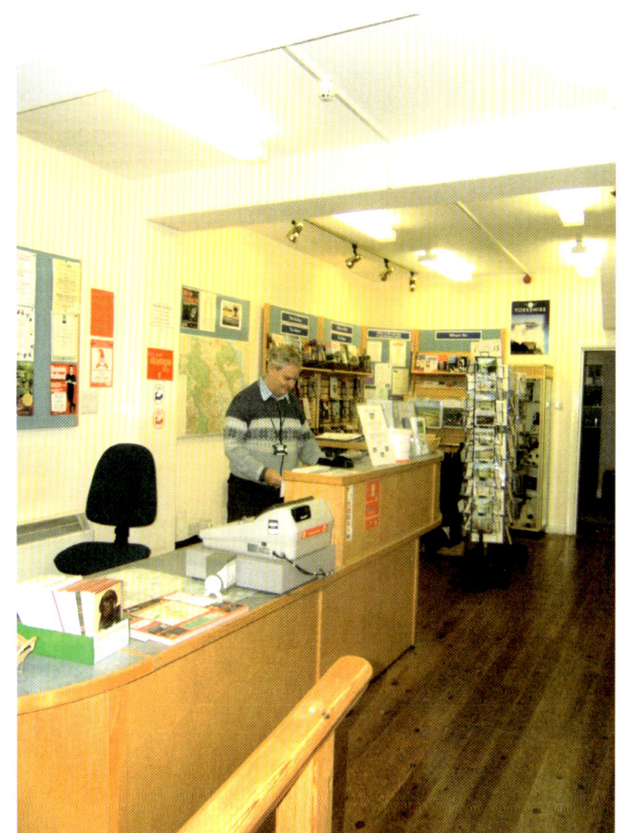

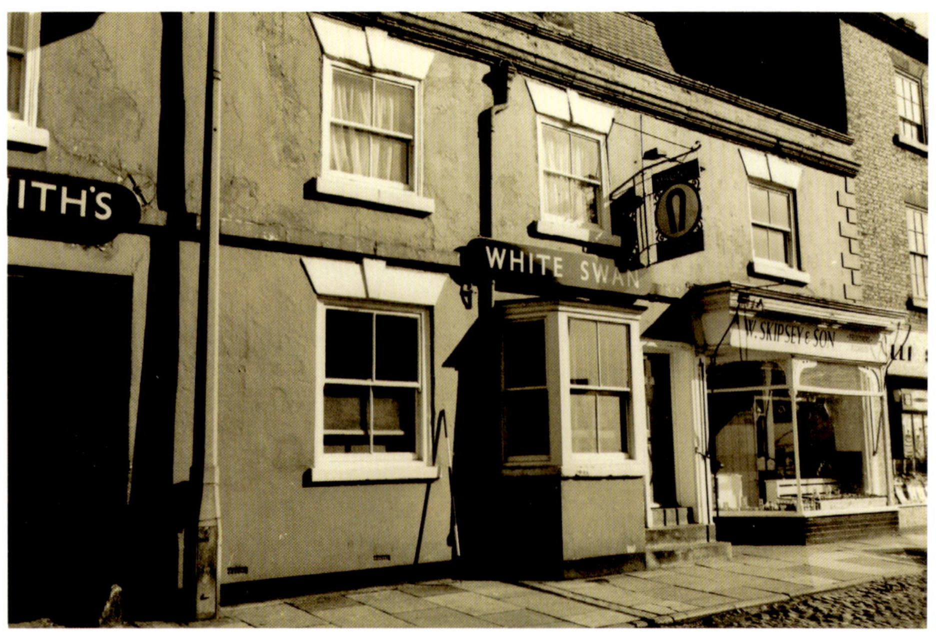

The White Swan

Another of the public houses on the north side of the Market Place, the White Swan presented a late Georgian façade to the street, though the building dates from an earlier period. By the time this photo was taken in 1970, part of the premises was shared with Skipsey, fruiterer and florist. The archway on the extreme left was the only passageway wide enough to give access for vehicles to the rear of the other shops. As the modern view shows, this building is now a hardware store; the passage is only half the original width, while Skipsey's shop is a well-frequented branch of Oxfam.

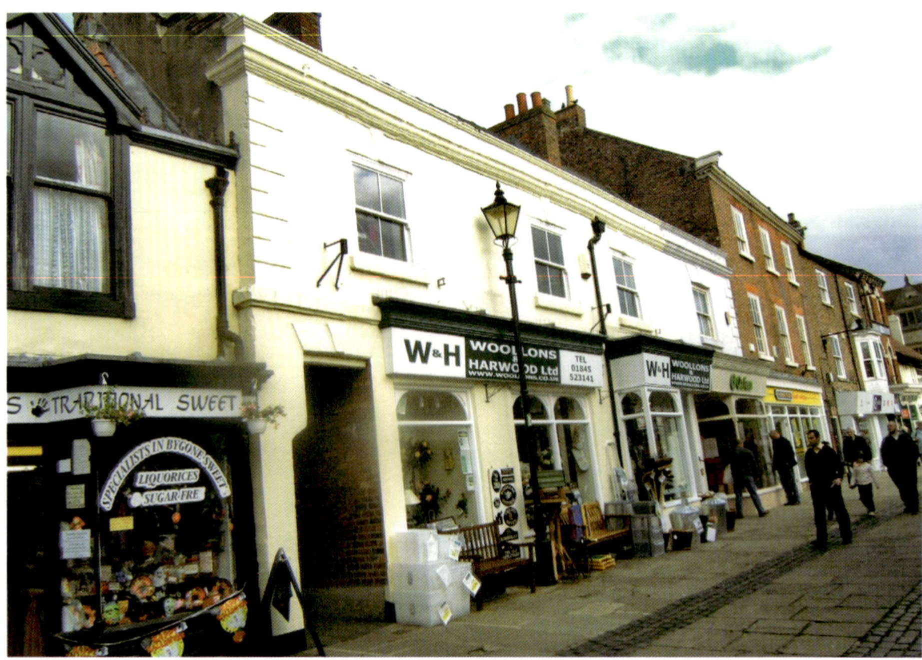

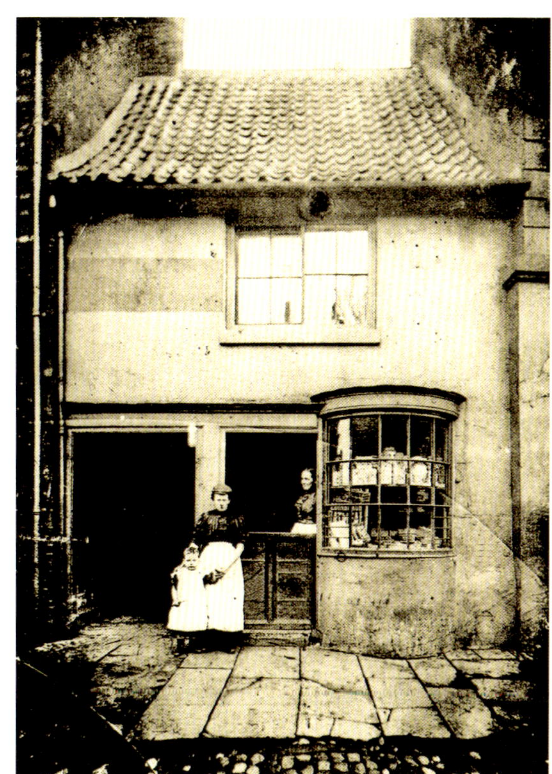

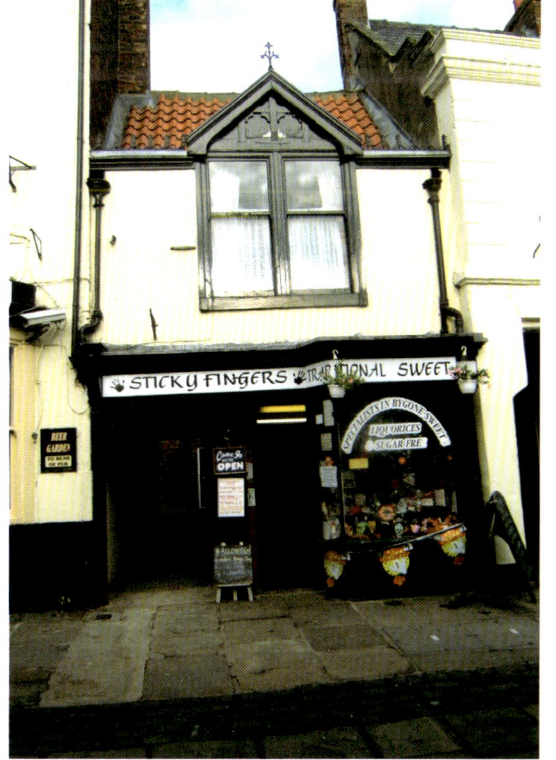

Bateman's Shop

A shop was here in 1851, but the building is much older. In 1869 William Dale Bateman took over a grocery business, which remained in family hands until the 1980s. William Bateman's wife, Margaret, stands at the shop door, while her assistant, Jane Gregson, holds a neighbour's child. William later replaced the bow window with a more modern shop-front and also raised the roof-line. The shop is now an old-fashioned sweet shop, but the yard behind is still known as Bateman's.

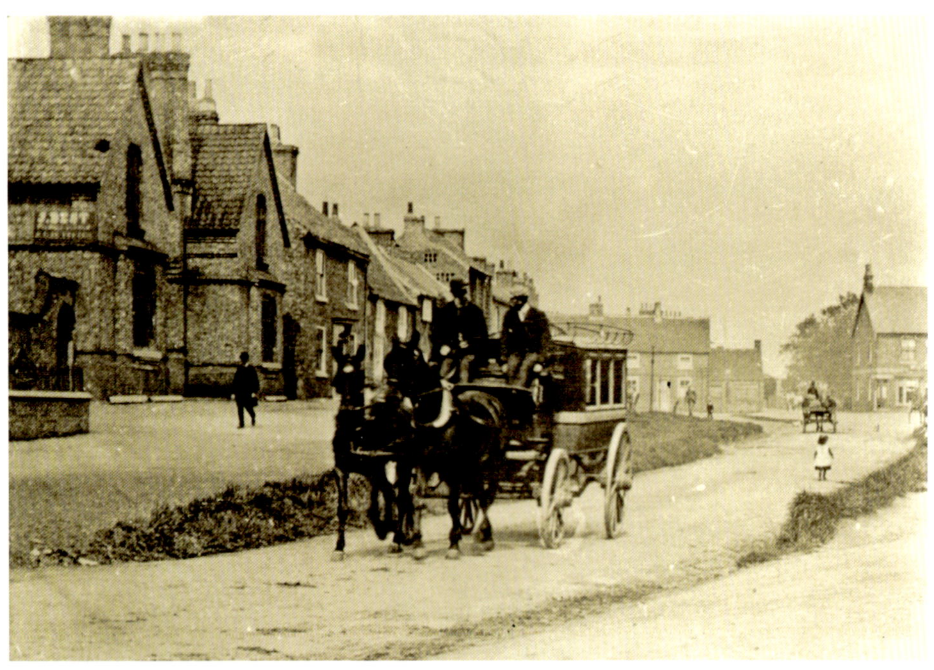

Buses in Ingramgate

Until the North Eastern Railway Company introduced a motorbus service in 1905, the horse-bus, run by the Golden Fleece Hotel, was a familiar vehicle in and around the town. It carried passengers to and from the railway station and delivered them to their homes or lodgings as required. It is seen here in Ingramgate on its way back to the Market Place. Today's bus service, the No. 58, follows the same route but keeps to the left-hand lane!

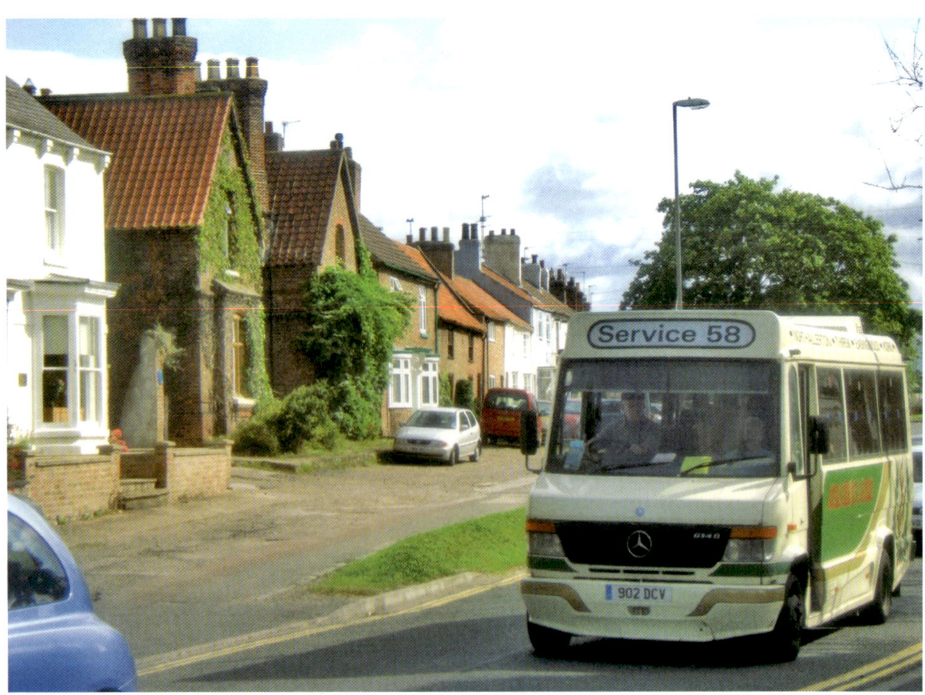

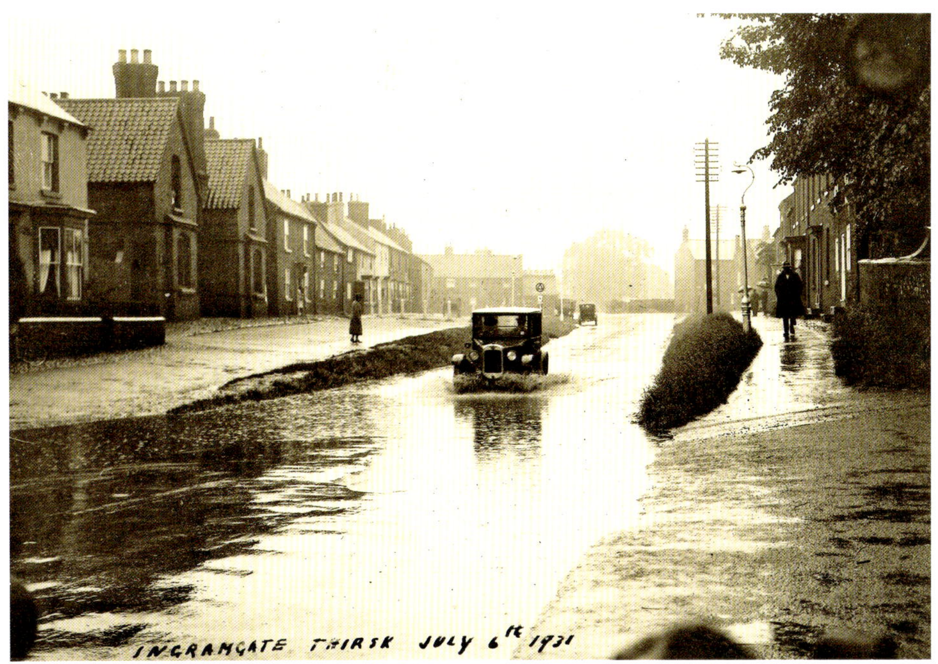

Floods in Thirsk

The Cod Beck, bridged at the foot of Ingramgate, is subject to sudden spates which, on rare occasions, flood low-lying parts of the town centre. The car in the first photo is braving the water at the foot of Ingramgate, flooded in July 1930. It was not until the serious floods of the year 2000 that the water rose to the same level, viewed here down Finkle Street towards the bridge.

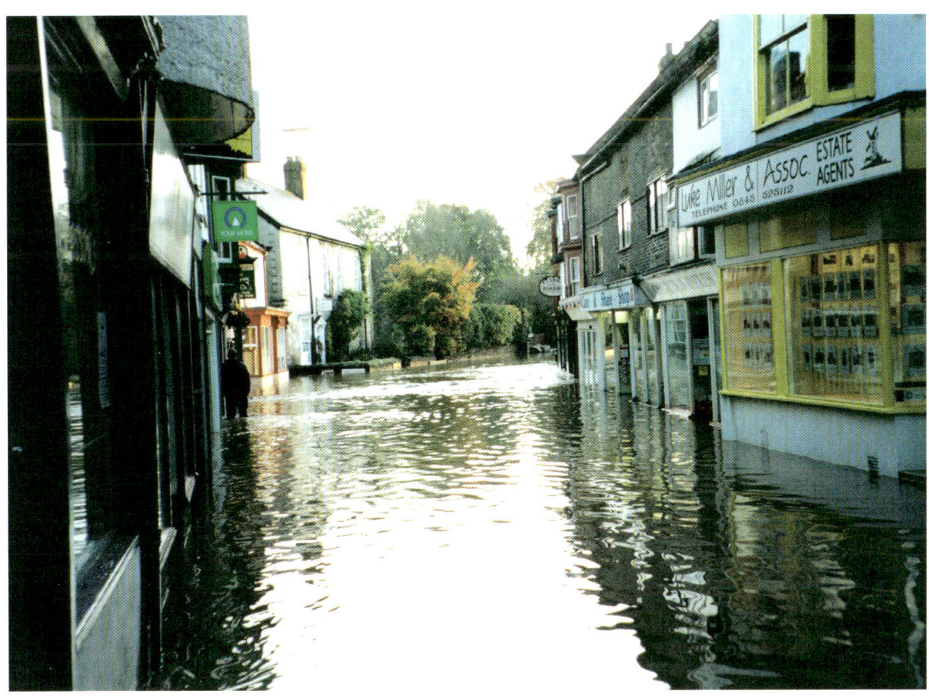

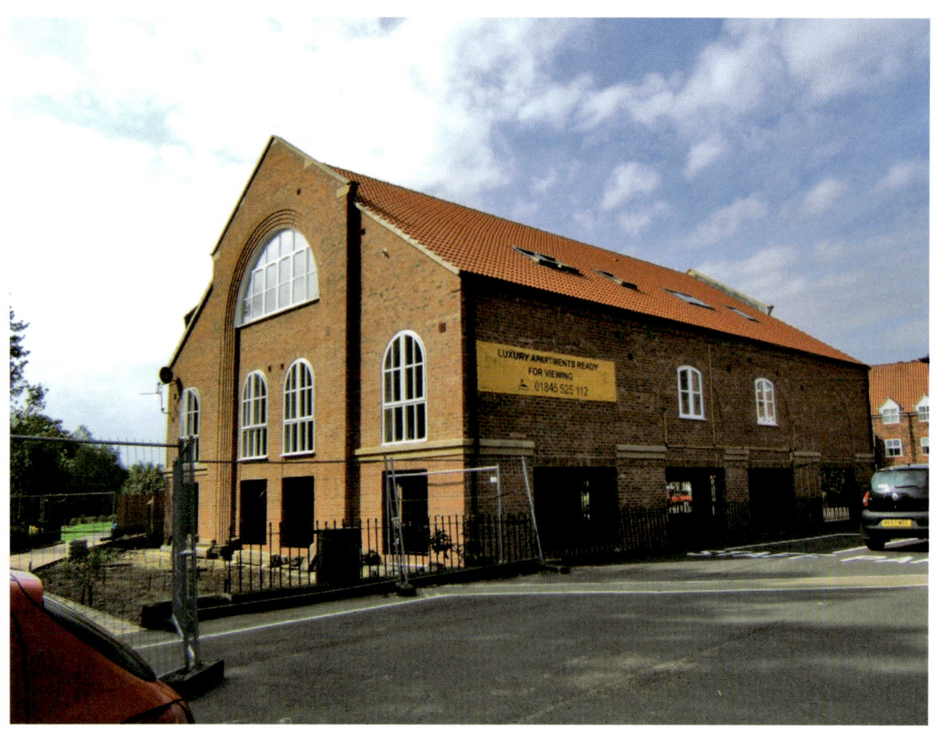

Salem House and Salem Chapel

Salem House is an imposing feature of the residential development on the site of a former nursery garden. Standing close to the Cod Beck, this block of apartments is raised on pillars to avoid flood damage. Its name, unintentionally reminding us of the school in Dickens' novel *David Copperfield*, is taken from the Congregational chapel, which stood on this spot and which has clearly influenced the unusual architectural style of the modern building.

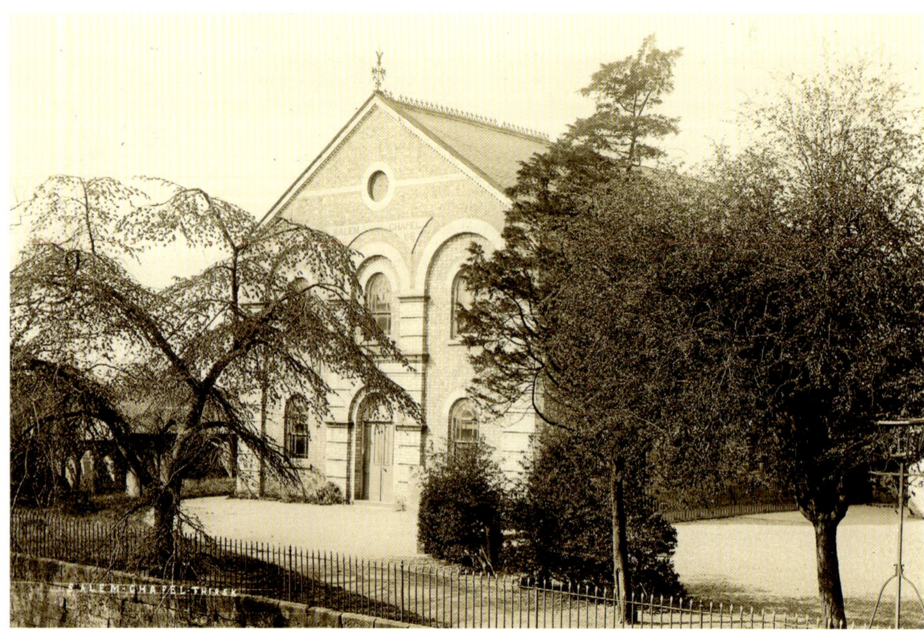

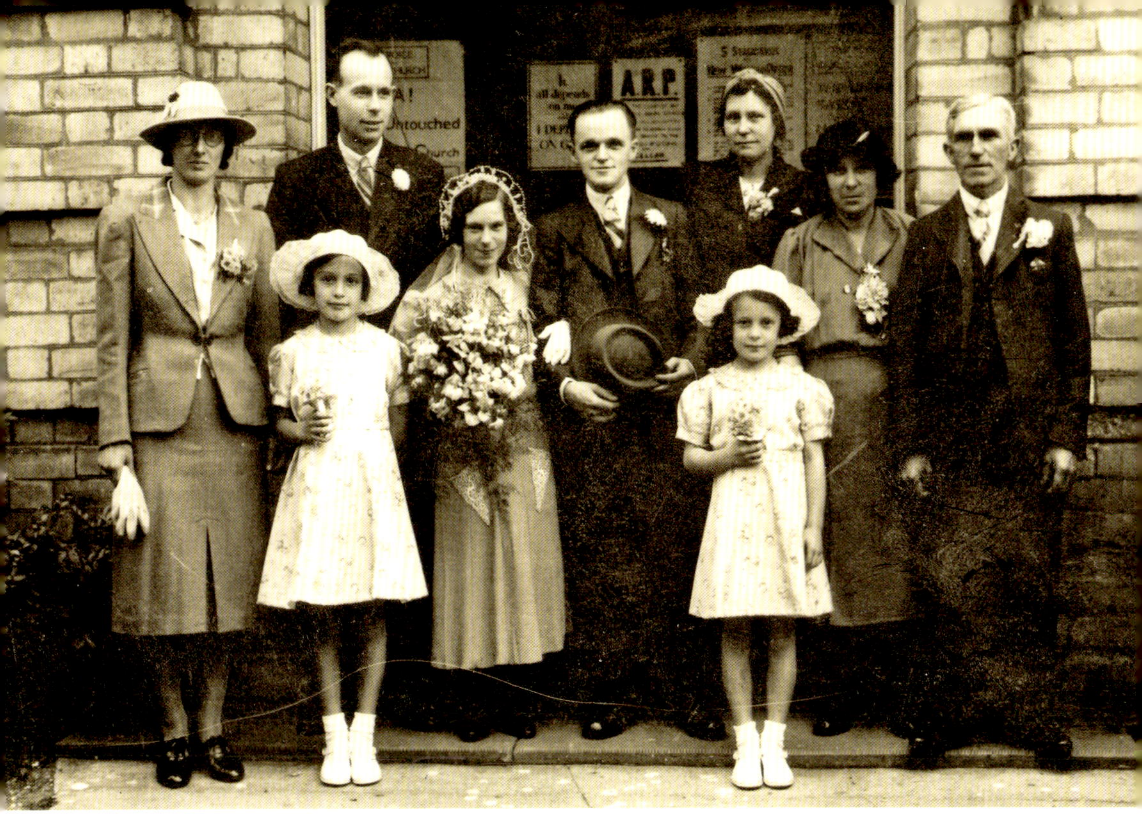

The last years of Salem Chapel

The wedding of Minnie Stuart and Arthur Brown took place at Salem Chapel on 4 November 1940. After the end of the war, however, the cost of maintaining the chapel, built in 1845, was too great for its small congregation and it was closed. It was used for storage for some years but became increasingly dilapidated until it was gutted by fire in 1988. The ruined building was finally demolished in 1991.

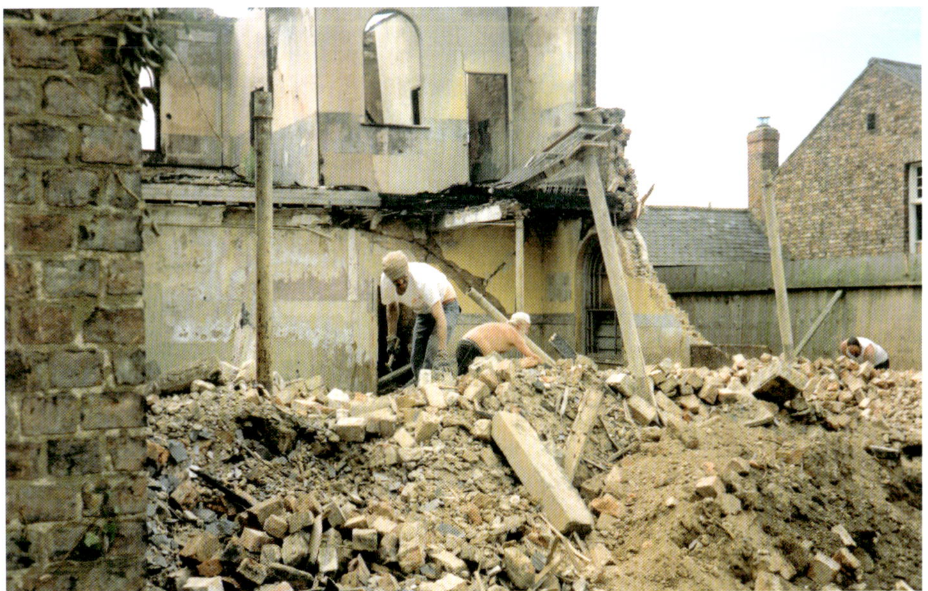

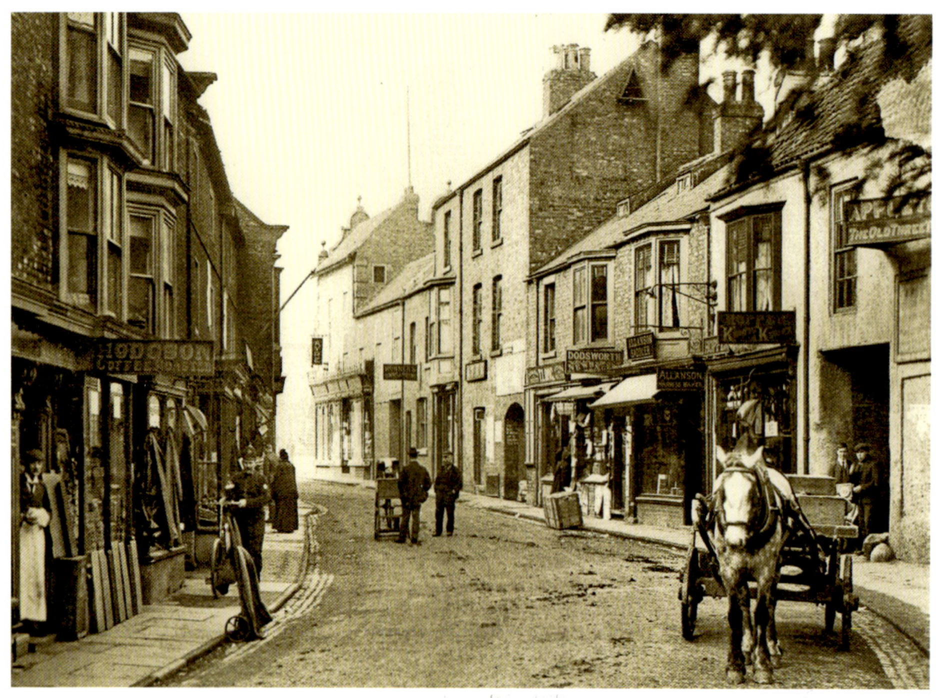

Finkle Street

This name is shared by streets in several towns in the North East and may represent an old Danish word for a corner. The street certainly swings to the left and leads into a corner of the Market Place. This layout had a possible defensive purpose, preventing a marauding troop having a clear view of what lay ahead. Finkle Street is now one-way only, and the recent photograph shows how much the pavement has been widened. The Old Three Tuns, seen on the right, has a fine timber-frame interior.

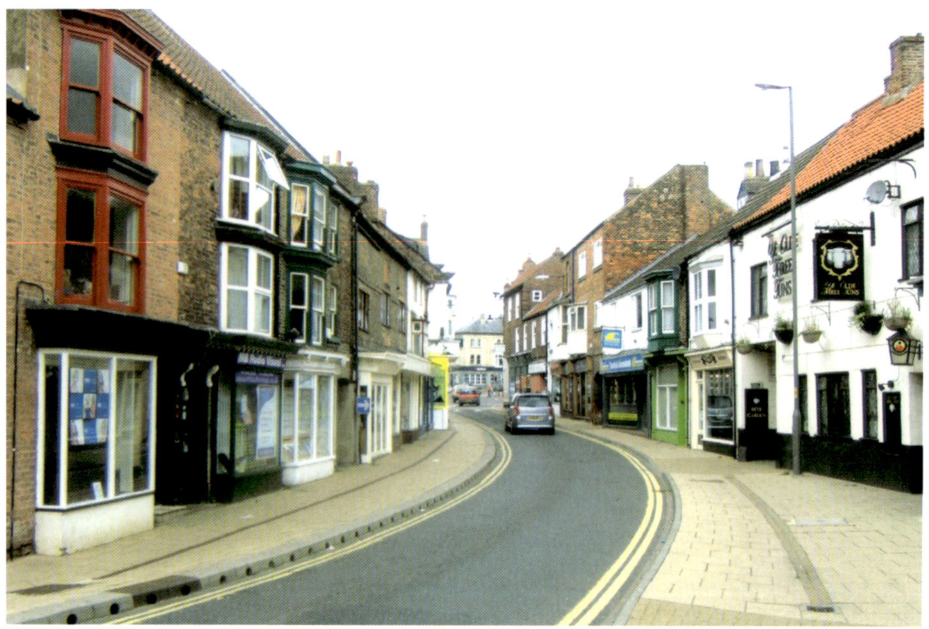

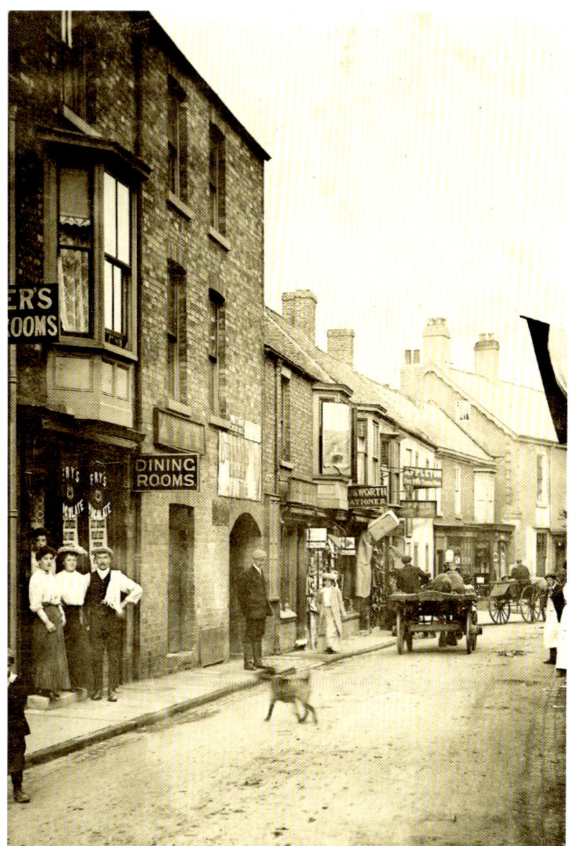

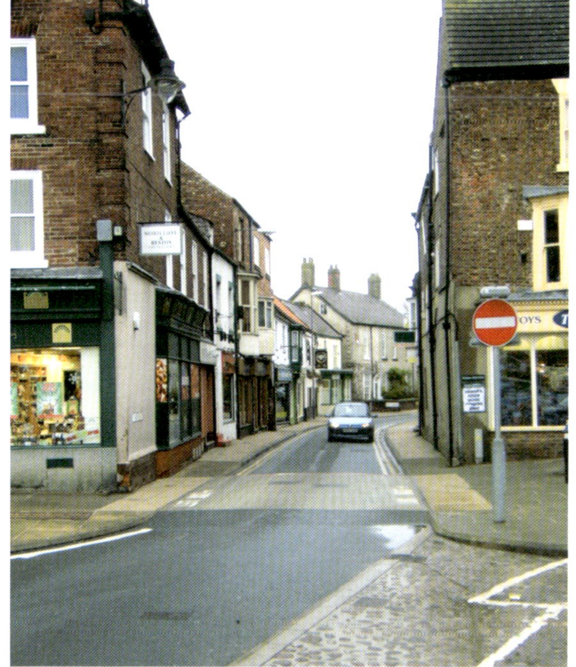

Finkle Street Again

Here we are looking down the street from the Market Place. The first picture dates from about 1906. The folk standing in the doorway are the staff of Horner's Dining Rooms, a popular eating place, especially on busy market days. Beyond them we see the warehouse for Ayre's grocery and chemist's, with a stationer's and a shoe shop further down, then the Old Three Tuns once more. The modern view, taken on a wet afternoon, offers a duller prospect.

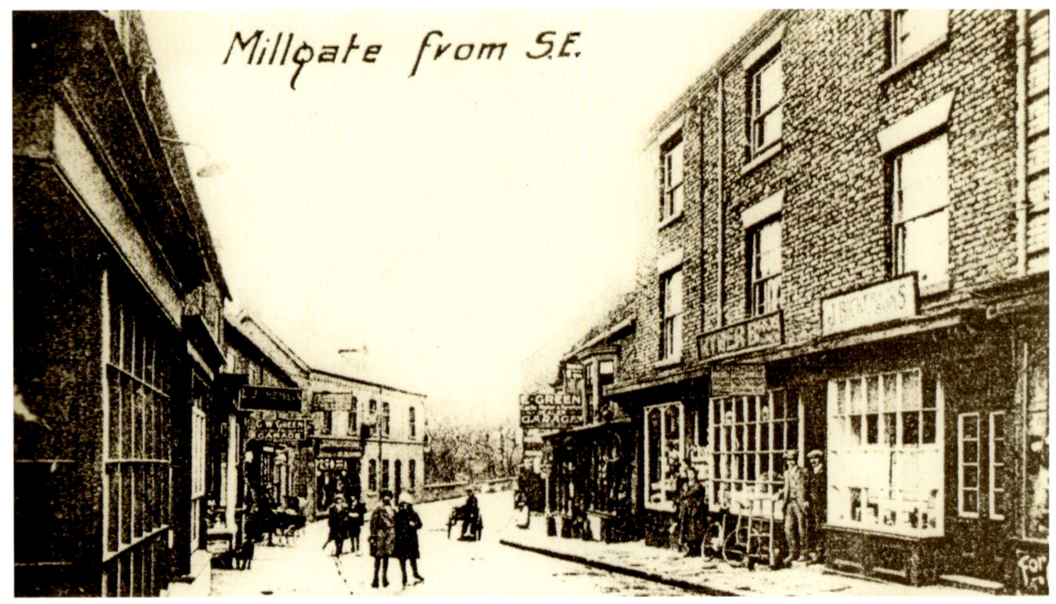

Millgate seen from the Market Place

Five other thoroughfares in Thirsk share with Millgate the old Norse word 'gate' to mean street. The town watermill stood at the far end until it was demolished in the 1960s. The upper picture is unusual in showing a street with snow. Elijah Green had a cycle and motor business on the right; his son George had a similar one opposite, where his name still appears in mosaic in the floor of the doorway. As the second picture shows, this is still a street with a variety of modest shops.

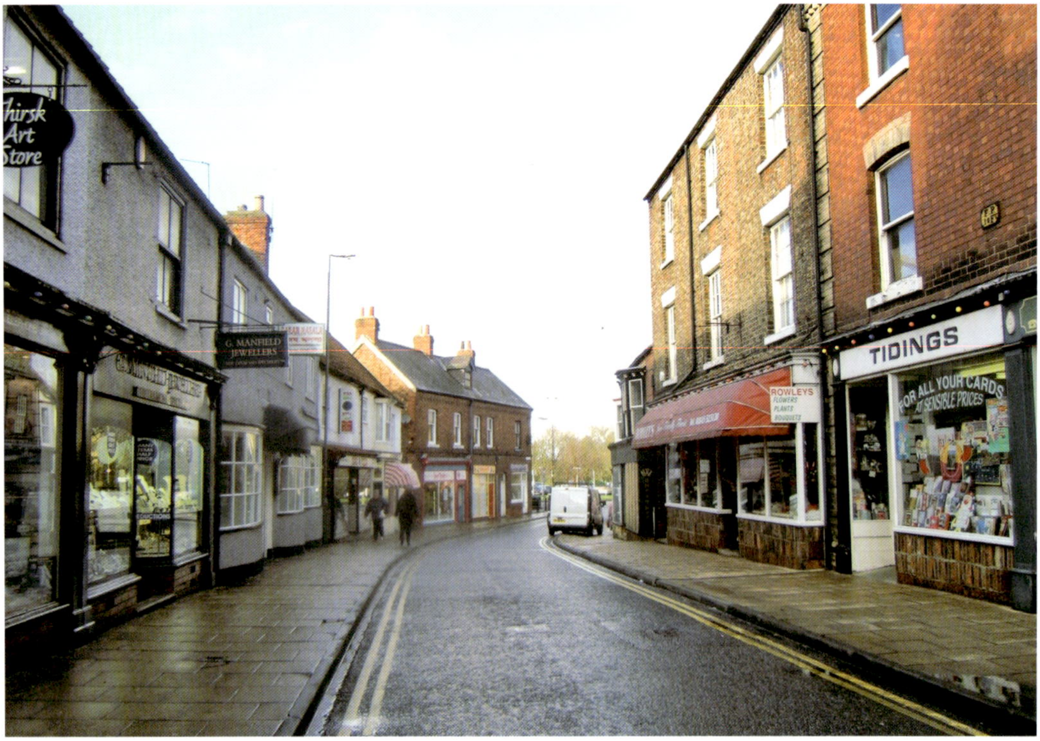

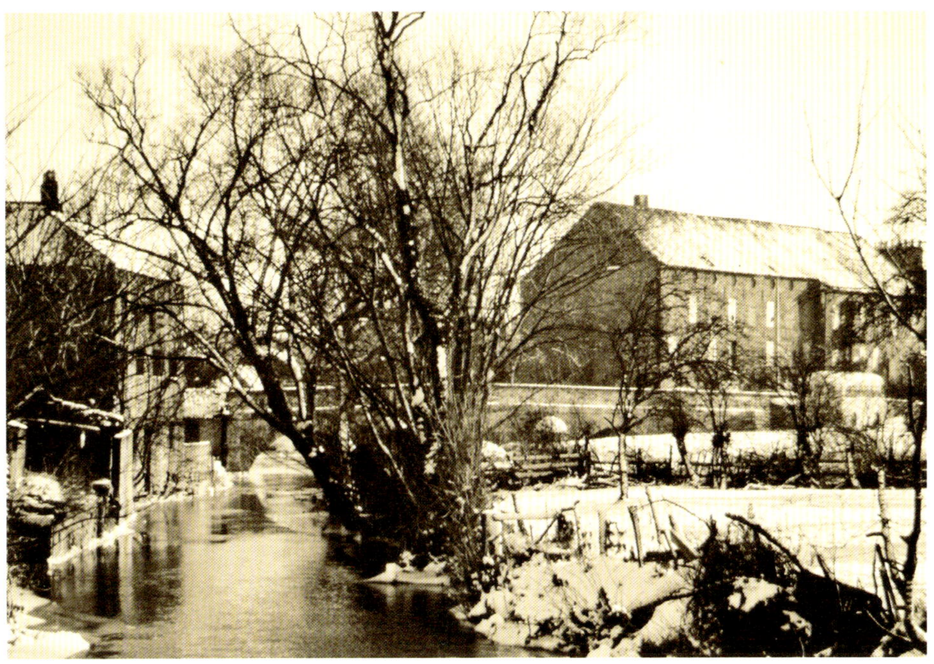

Rymer's Mill

More snow! The mill appears in the background here shortly before it was pulled down. The Rymer family had mills along the course of the Cod Beck, at Kilvington and Borrowby, together with another mill in Long Street (page 59). The site of the mill has been laid out as a garden overlooking the waterside.

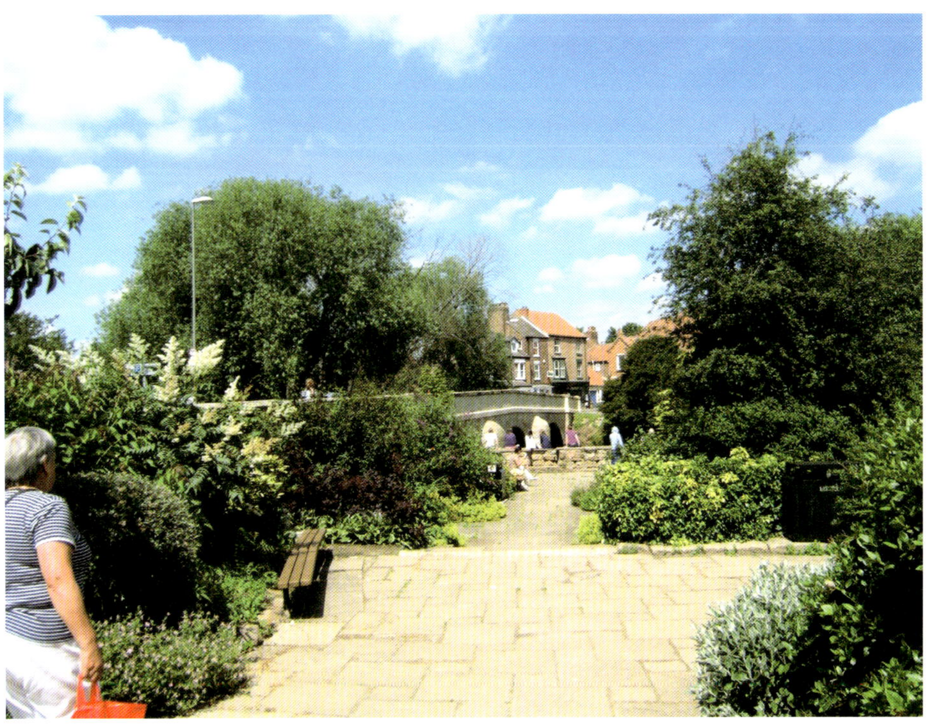

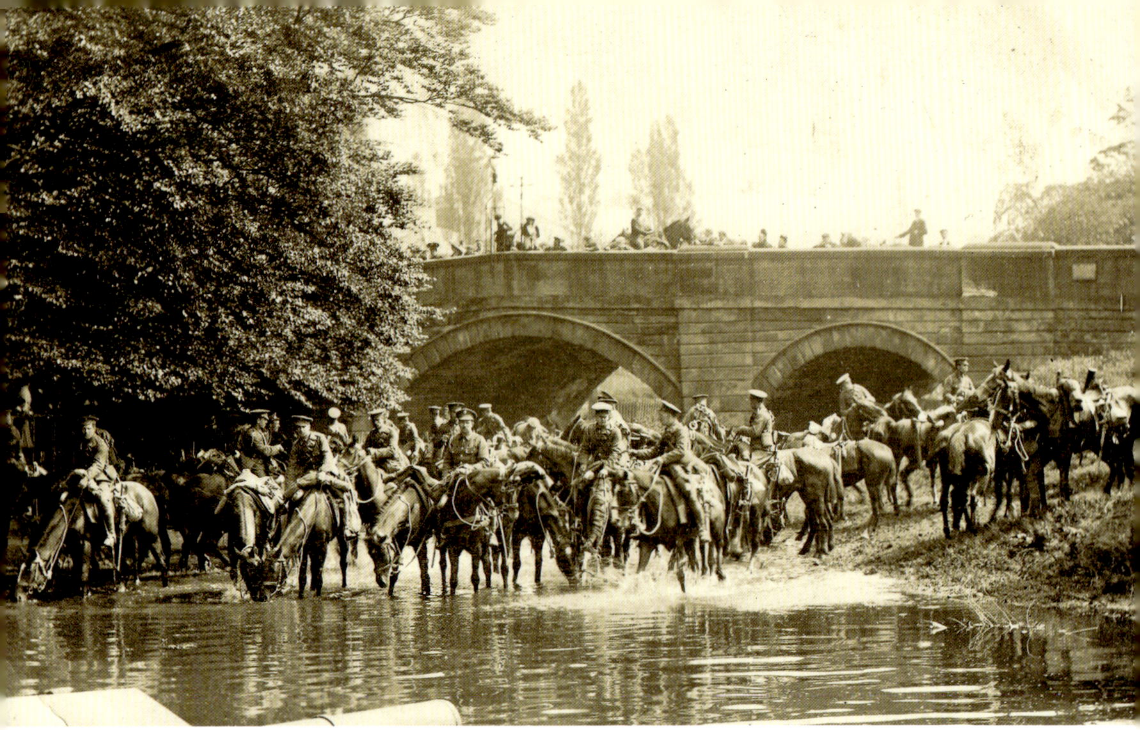

Watering the Horses — 1906

Cavalry units had an annual summer camp near Thirsk in the years before the First World War. Here, men of the 18th Hussars are watering their horses at the ford by the Ingramgate bridge. A photograph of the same spot today shows that the water is shallow here, but there is now no way down to it from the right-hand bank.

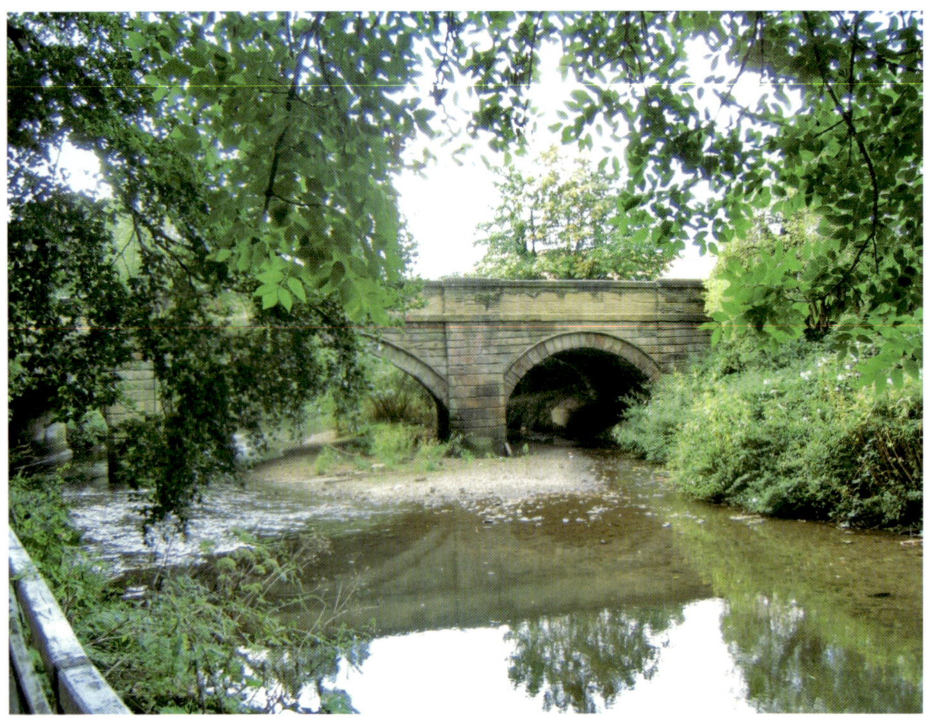

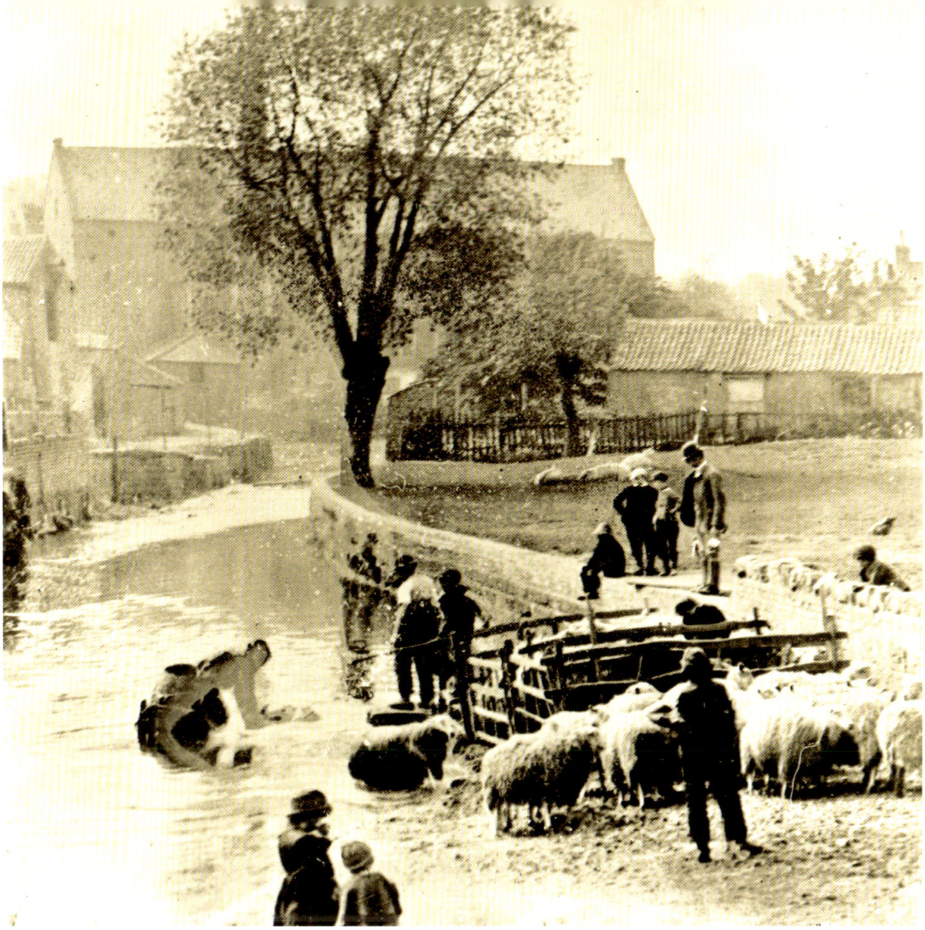

Washing Sheep in the Beck

The mill in the background here gives a clue as to the spot where a nineteenth-century photographer watched these sheep being washed. This was along a stretch of grass off St James' Little Green called Green Garth, better known in recent times as the site of Todd's yard, a builders' supply depot. It has now been given over to housing, with these apartments overlooking a shady riverside walk.

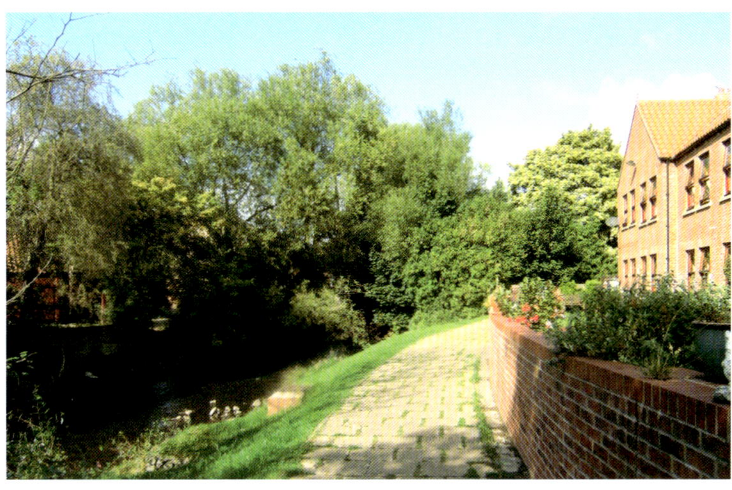

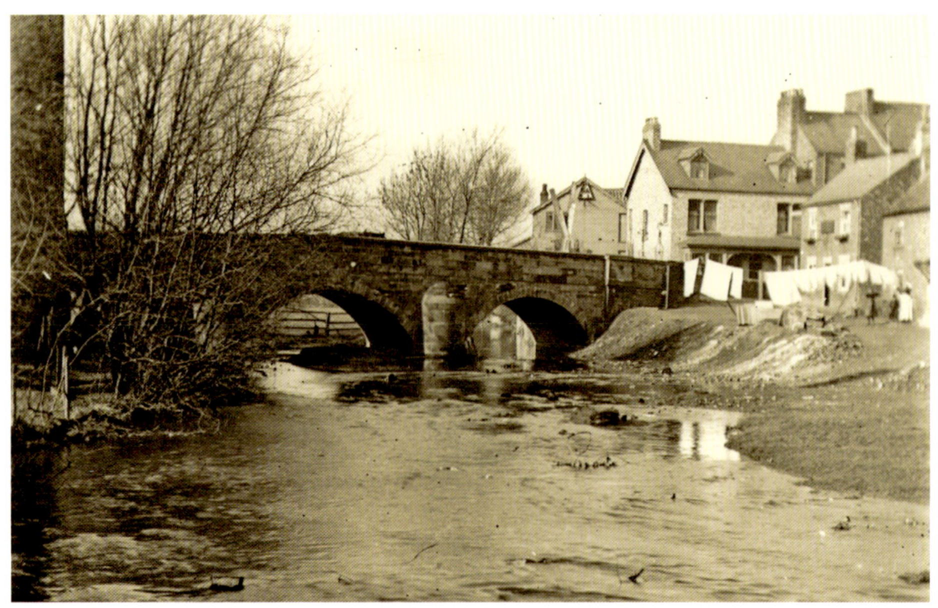

Mill Bridge and Waterside

The bridge here carries traffic from Millgate across the Cod Beck towards St James' Green. In the first picture the end wall of the mill is just visible on the left. The washing line belongs to one of the cottages that stood on the far side of the stream, known as Waterside. At constant risk of flooding, they were condemned and demolished in the 1990s, replaced by modern flats. The second picture shows the fresh stonework on the bridge where the parapet has recently been restored.

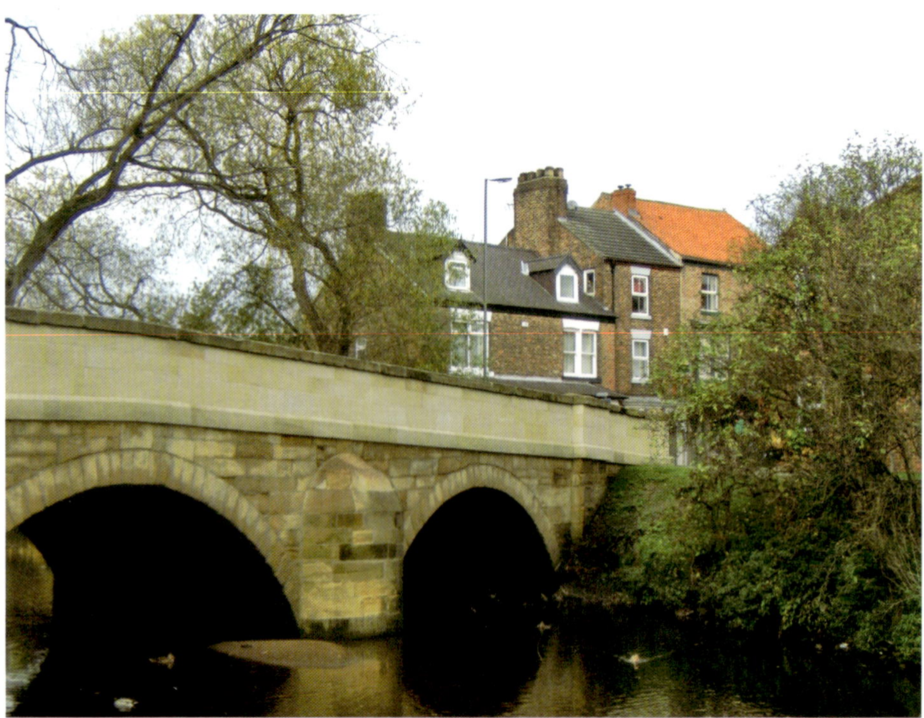

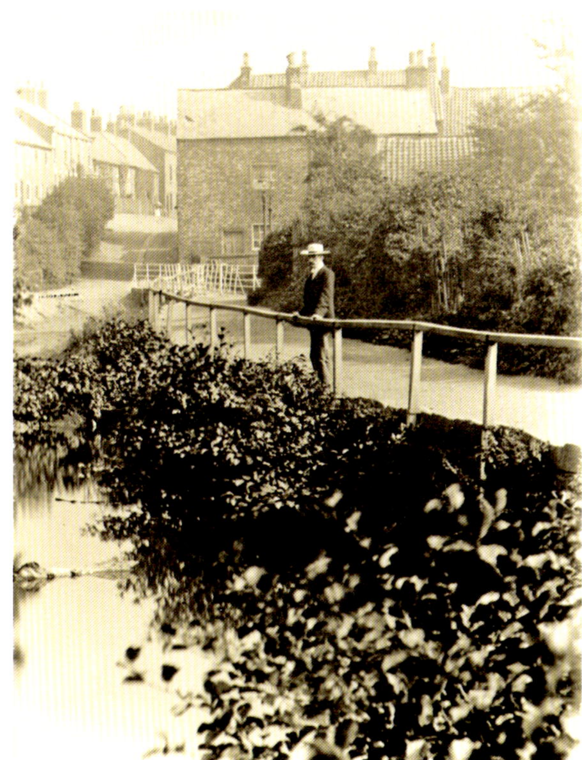

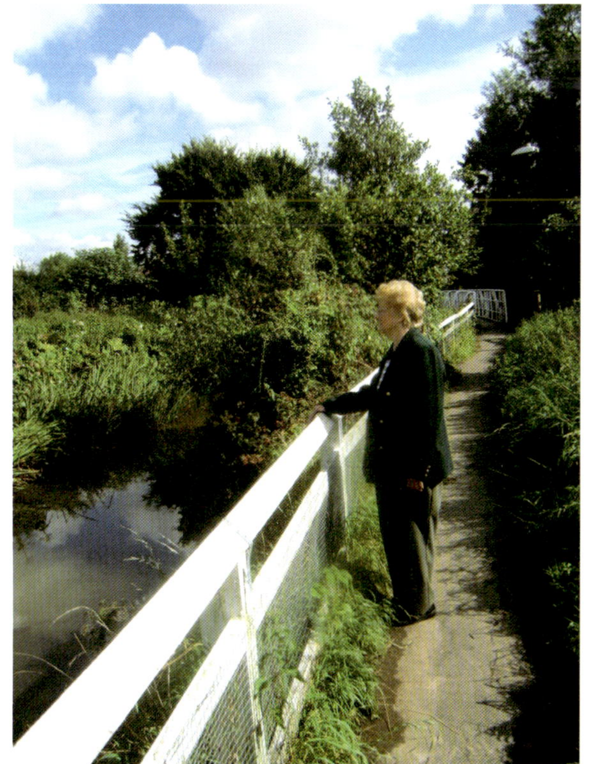

The Iron Bridge

A metal bridge, seen in the background in these photographs, carries the footpath that runs alongside the Cod Beck across to St James' Green. This walk is a good point from which to look for fish in the water or watch duck and other waterfowl along the stream. The vegetation has grown considerably since J. T. Fox took his view in the 1900s.

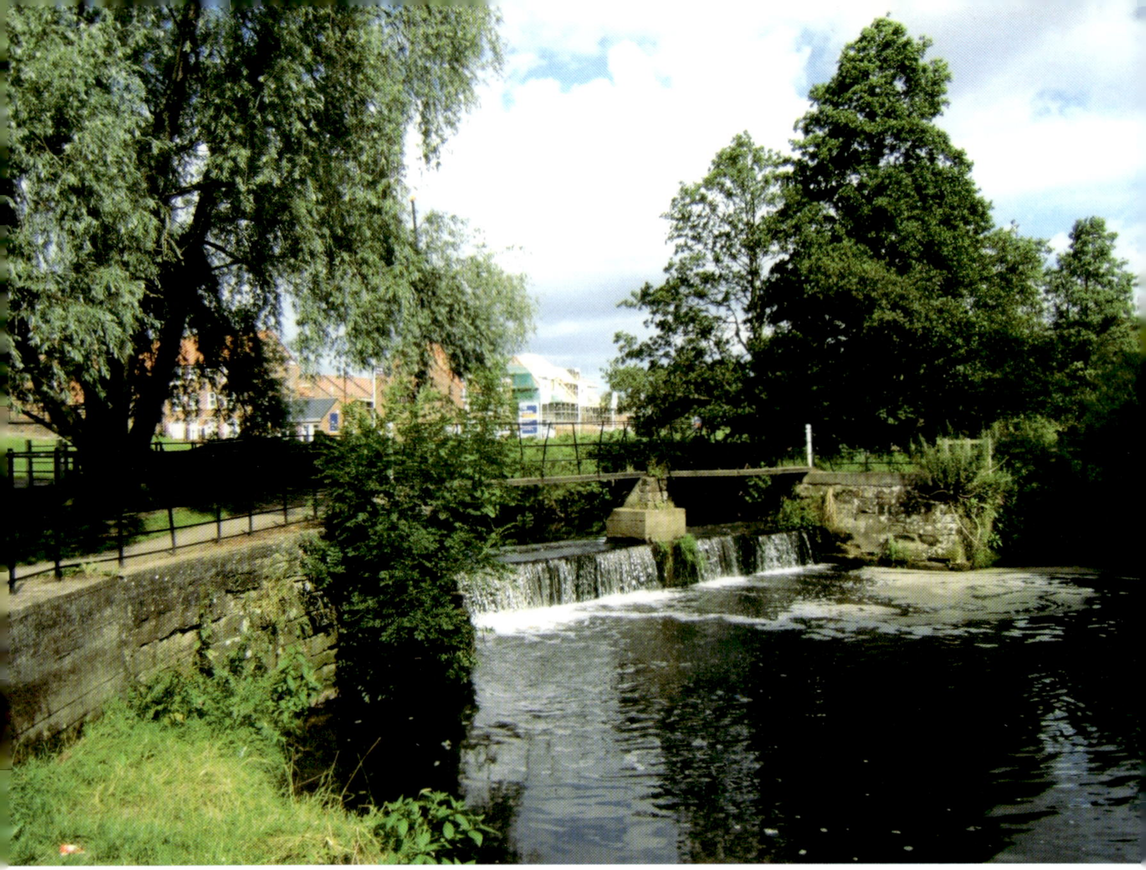

Norby Weir

This weir was built some 200 years ago to provide a head of water to drive the town mill. A mill stream carried the water alongside the road past the cottages in Norby. This waterfall was a favourite subject for postcards and remains a pleasant spot today.

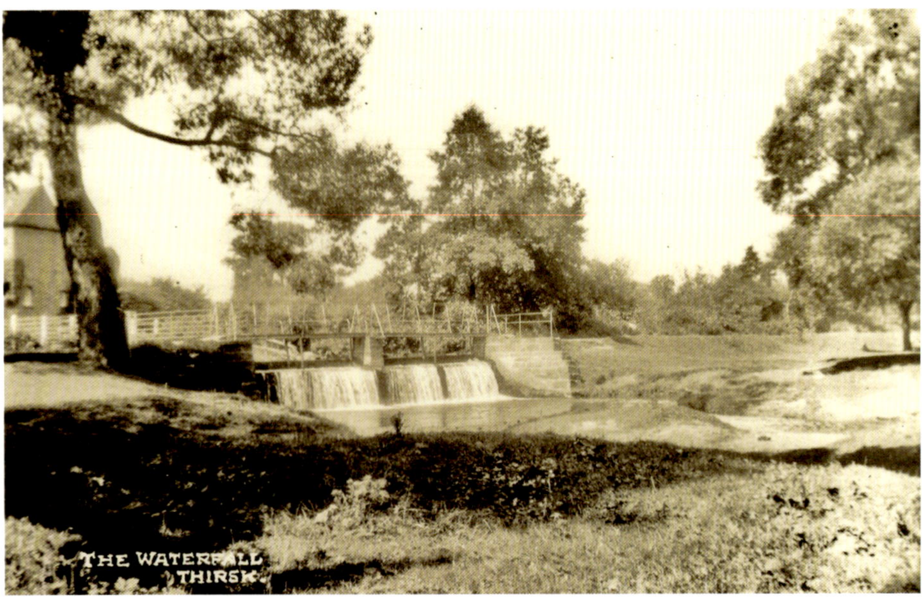

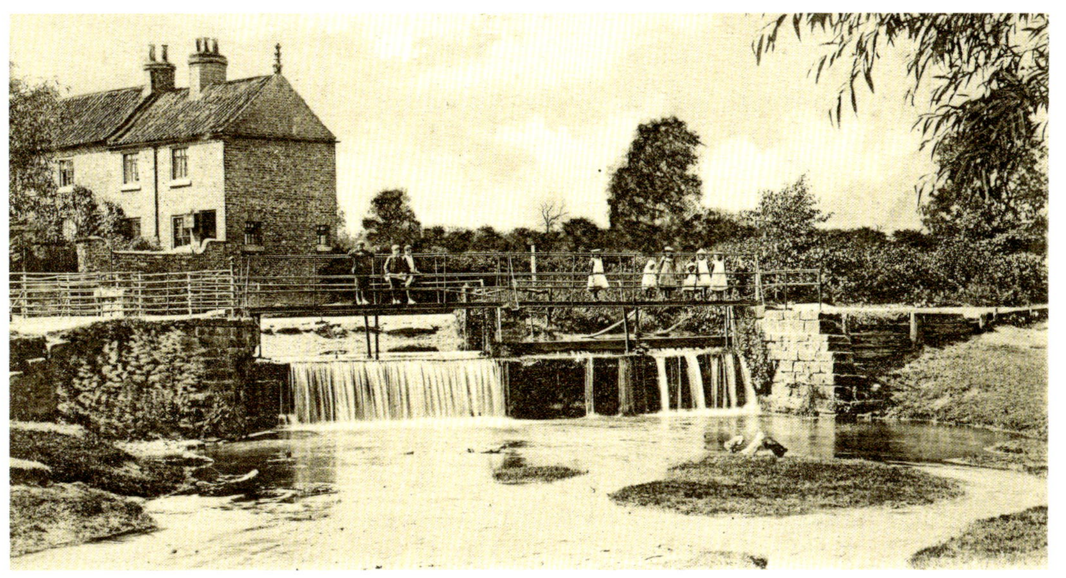

The Bridge over Norby Weir

The footbridge across Norby weir has always attracted children as a good point from which to watch the water tumbling over the stones, especially at times when the beck is running high. The old sluice gate is still *in situ* and is preserved as a local curiosity, though the mill leat was filled in fifty years ago. The cottages in Sunny Terrace, seen in the picture below, have now been replaced by modern housing.

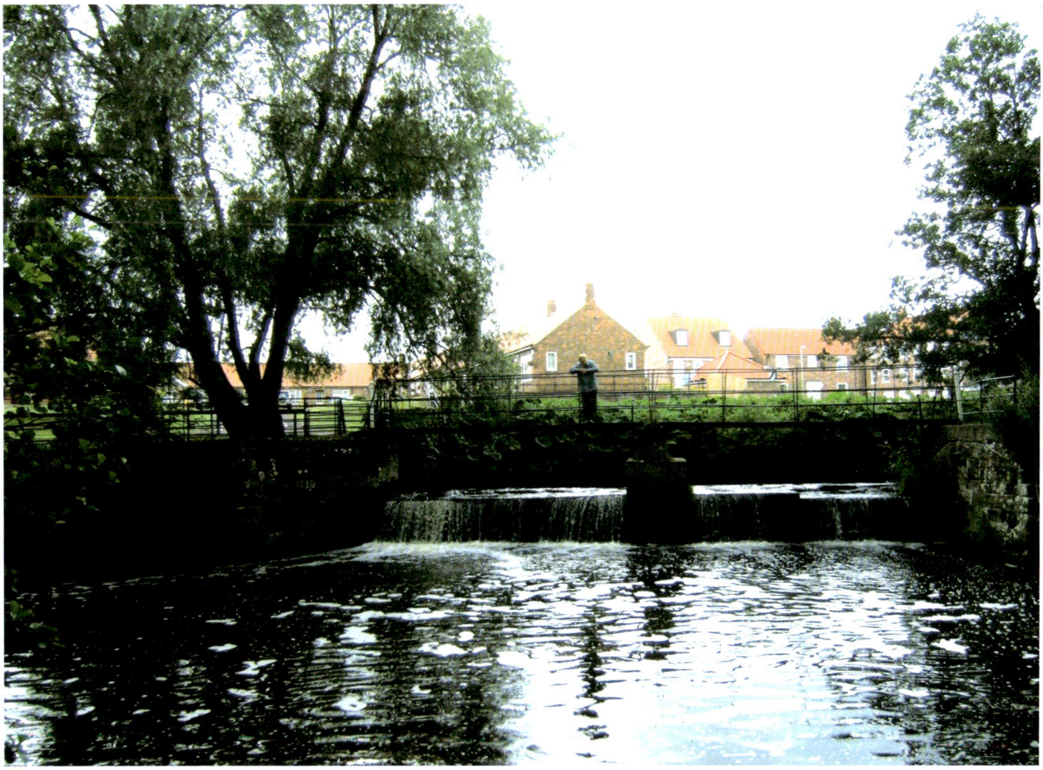

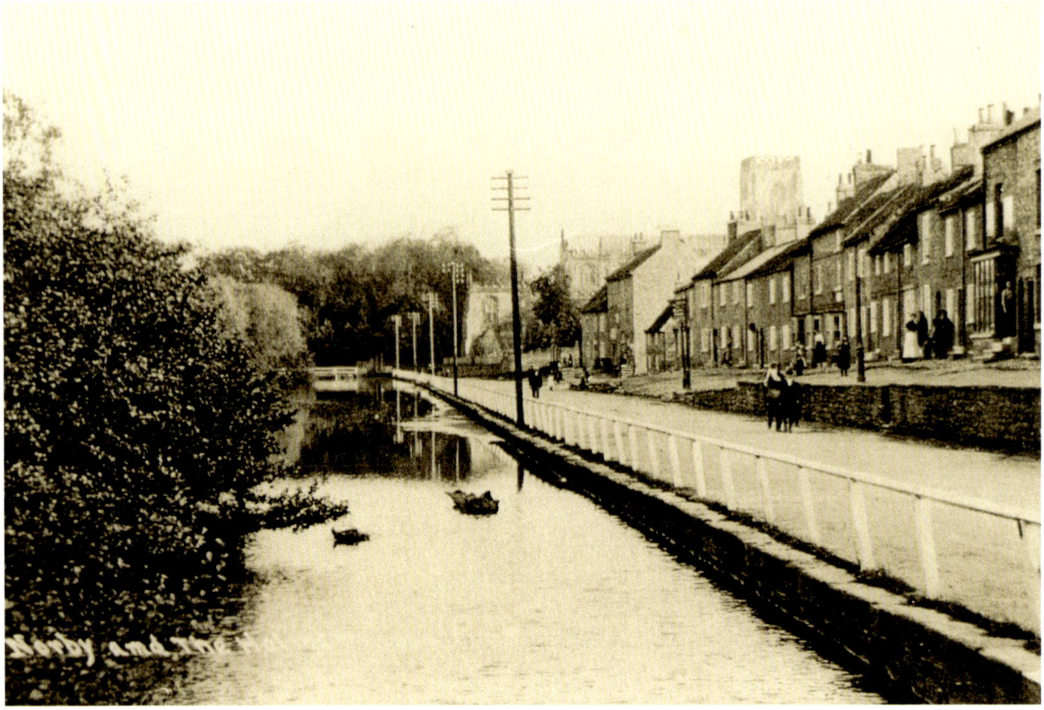

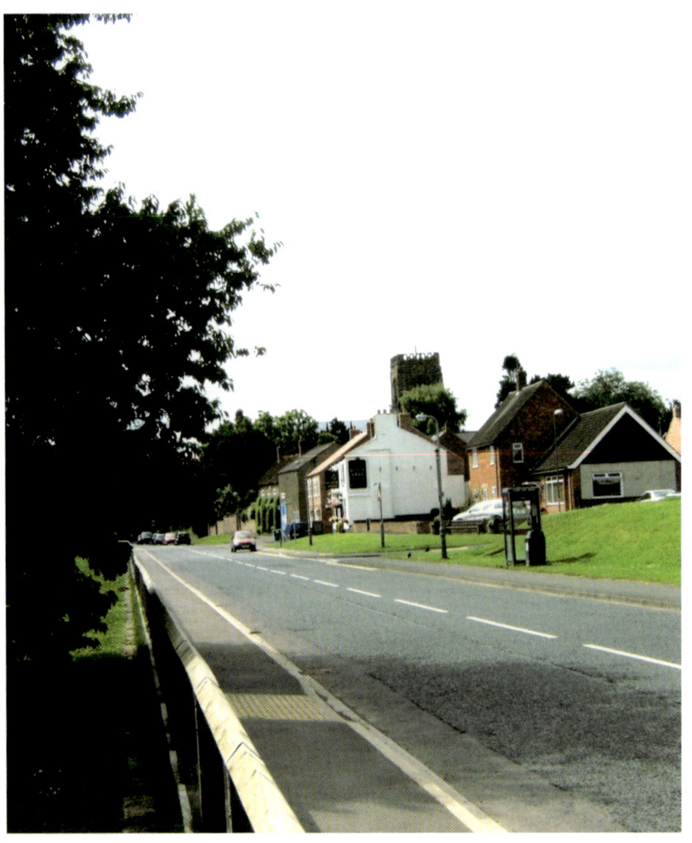

Old Norby and the New

The little district of Norby was picturesque where a row of old-fashioned cottages looked out across the mill dam to the leafy walk through the Holms. Norby, though, was one of the poorest parts of the town; the houses were often overcrowded and sanitation was non-existent. The whole area was demolished in the 1950s to make way for modern council housing and the redundant mill leat was filled in and grassed over.

The Holms Past and Present

The Holms is the name of an open piece of land in Norby planted with willow trees and lying originally between the mill stream and the main channel of the Cod Beck. This has always been a place for recreation. The footpath along the mill stream was a favourite promenade and the beck itself a place for children to paddle or fish. The footpath still follows the line of the vanished mill stream; the trees add to the attraction of the spot and there are information boards to record the history of the site.

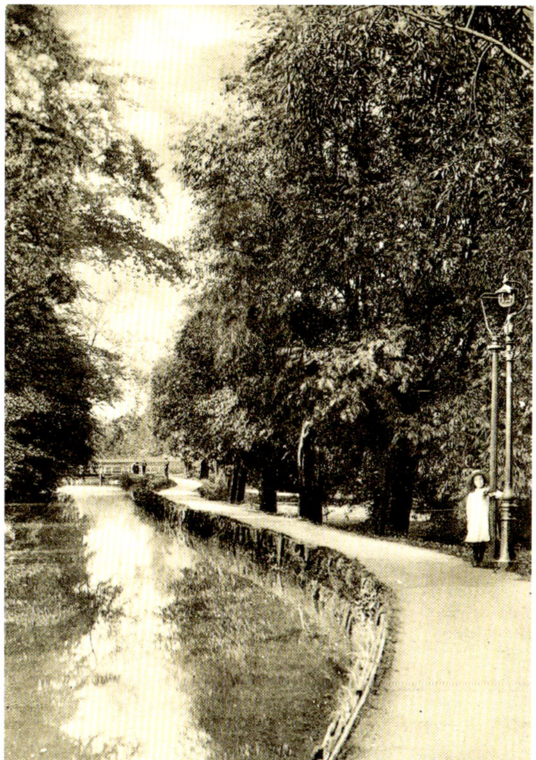

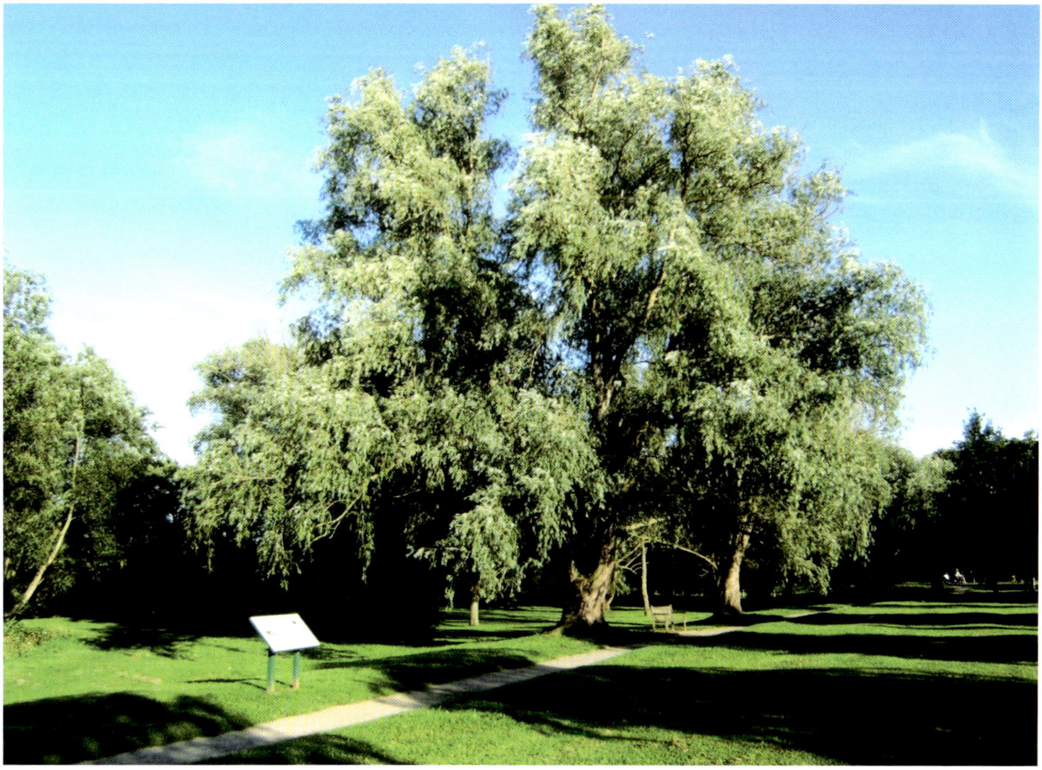

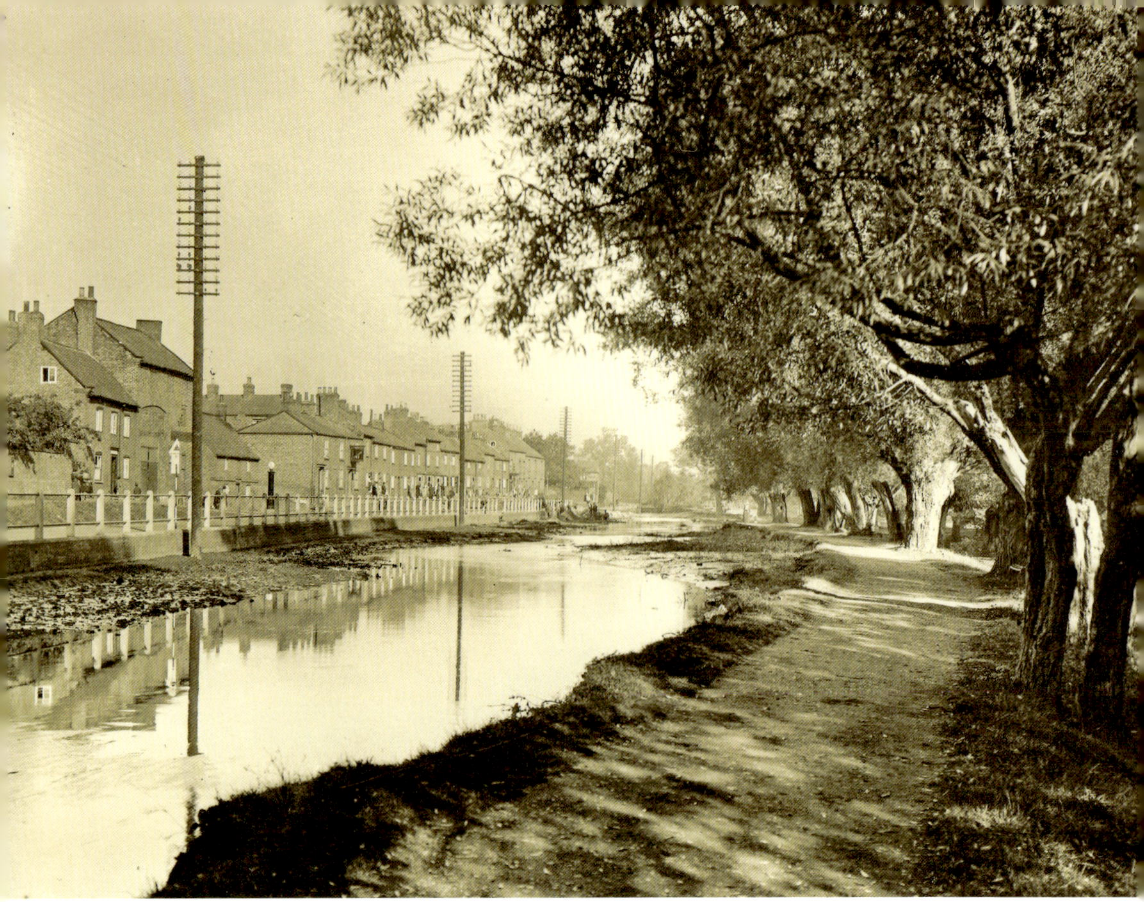

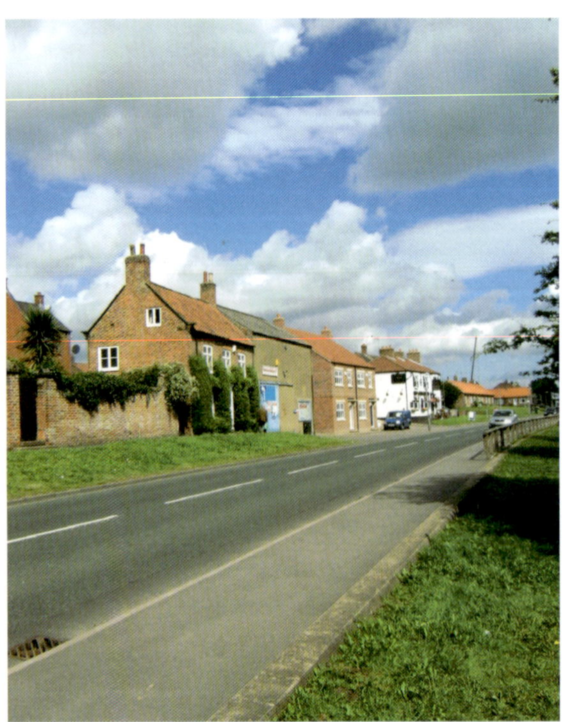

Norby from the South

The first picture shows Norby from the south, with the course of the mill dam railed off from the road. The tallest of the buildings behind the first telegraph pole was an iron foundry. That building survives in the modern view, with a distinctive blue door, though reduced in height. Serving latterly as a tyre depot, it is now closed and most likely due to make way for housing.

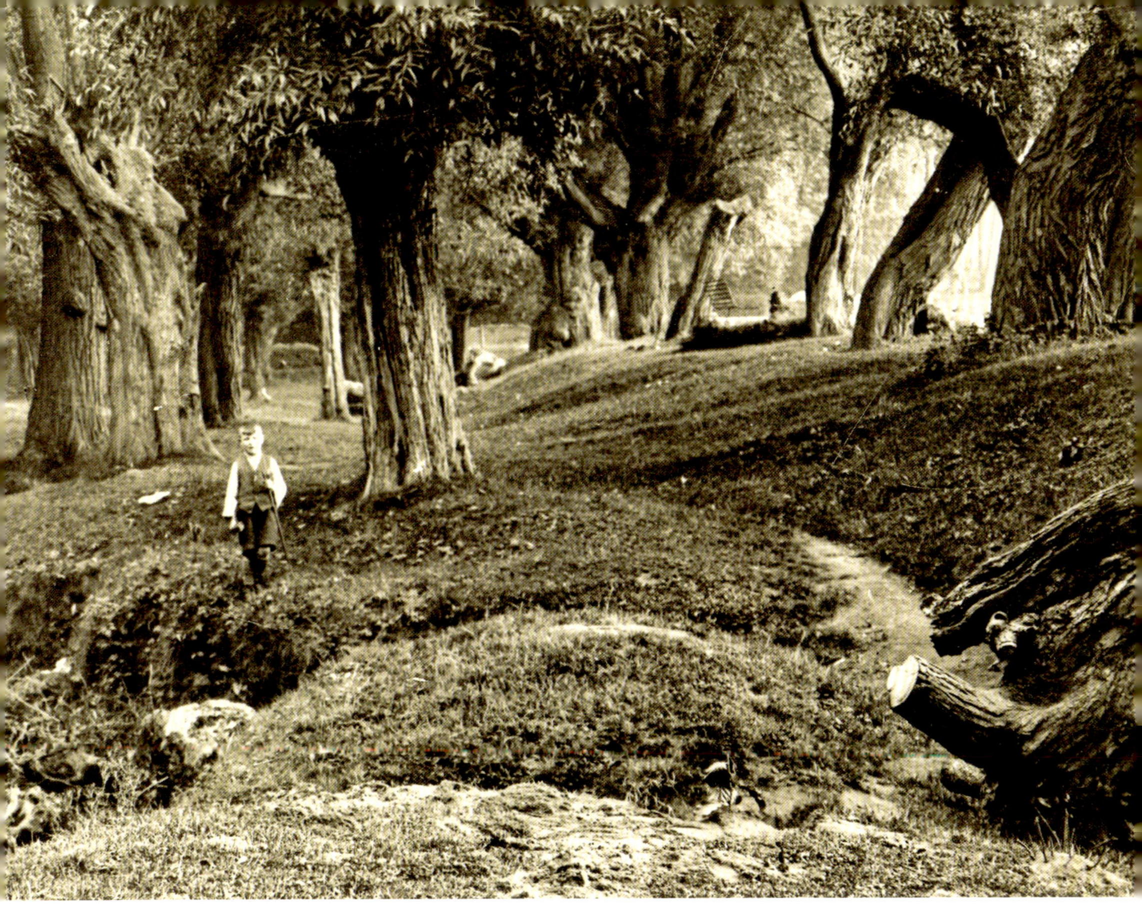

Among the Willows

The first of these photographs was taken in the early 1900s amid trees that had been planted a good century before that. The willows were pollarded regularly; this process of cutting back produced numbers of long, pliable shoots, which were then gathered for plaiting into baskets. The trees are still cut back today but only for safety reasons. The example seen in the recent picture has suffered unusually harsh treatment!

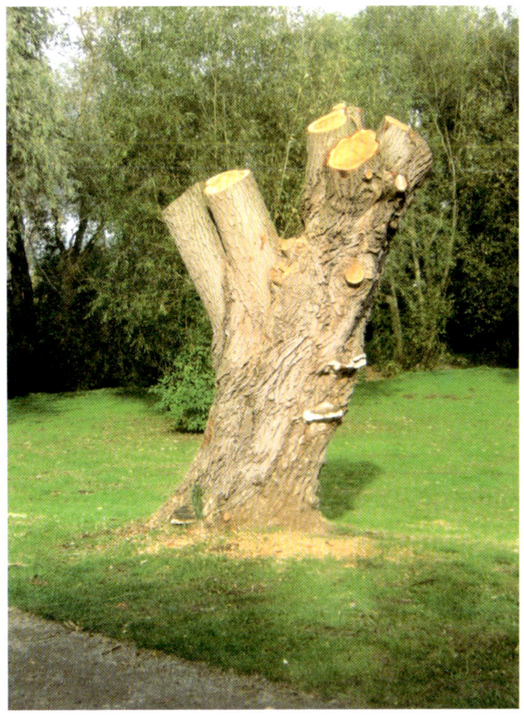

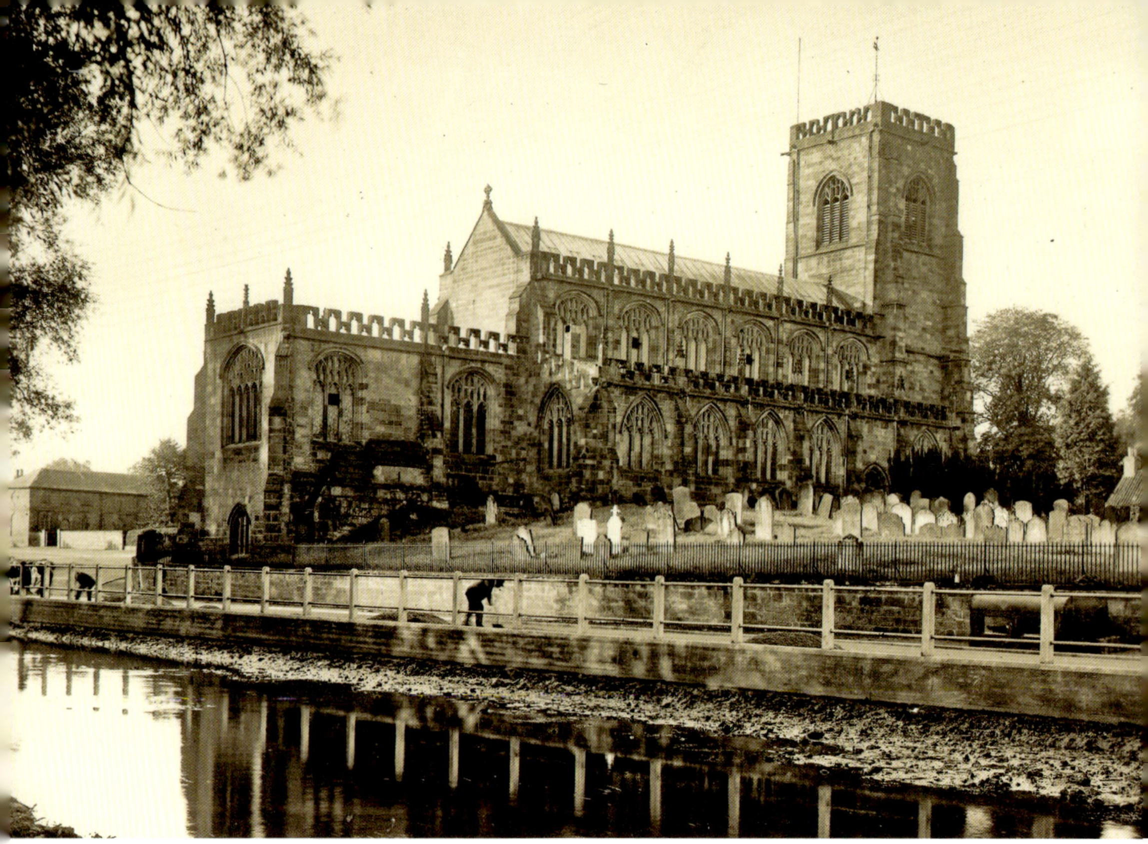

St Mary's Church, North Side

Thirsk parish church has been called the 'Cathedral of the North Riding', and the view in the top picture shows the fifteenth-century architecture of St Mary's in its full splendour. Only a glimpse can be had from the same spot today, between the trees planted in the 1950s along the line of the former mill stream.

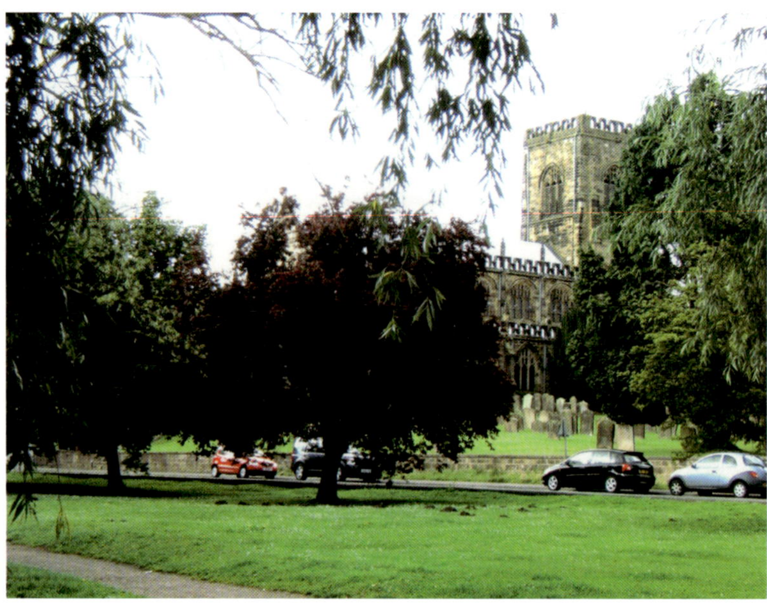

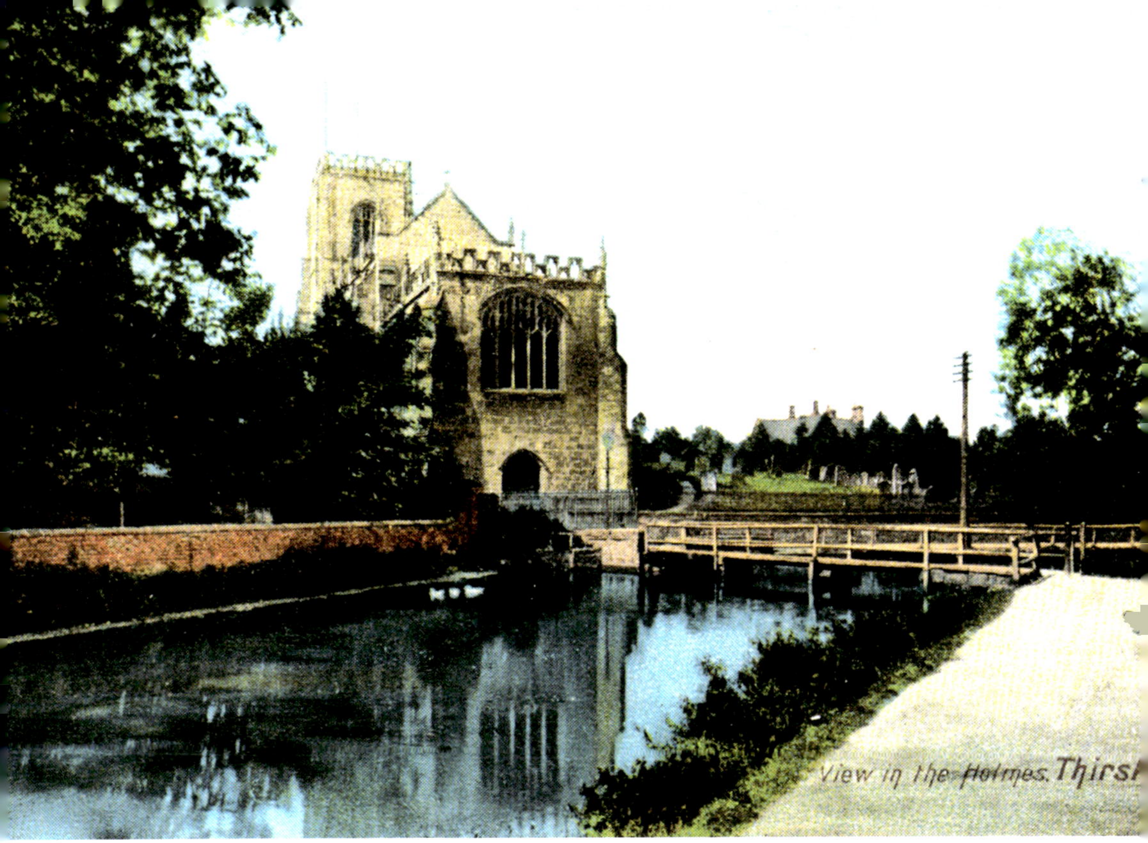

The Church Bridge

The early coloured postcard shows how the mill stream turned left by the church, while the road for vehicles bound for the Market Place continued down Kirkgate. A wooden footbridge allowed pedestrians to cross to a path that took them towards the town centre. Marage Road now runs from the corner of Kirkgate towards the car parks, the name taken from a garden and pond that lay behind the wall, which is seen more clearly in the postcard view.

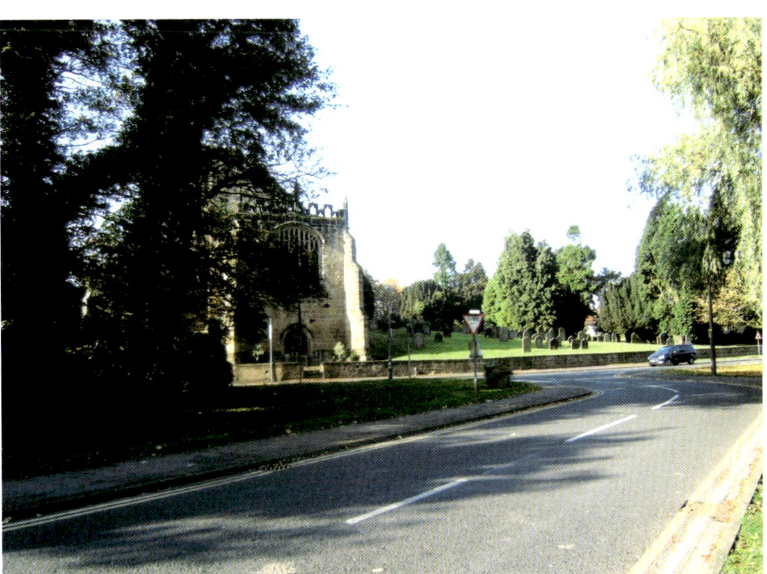

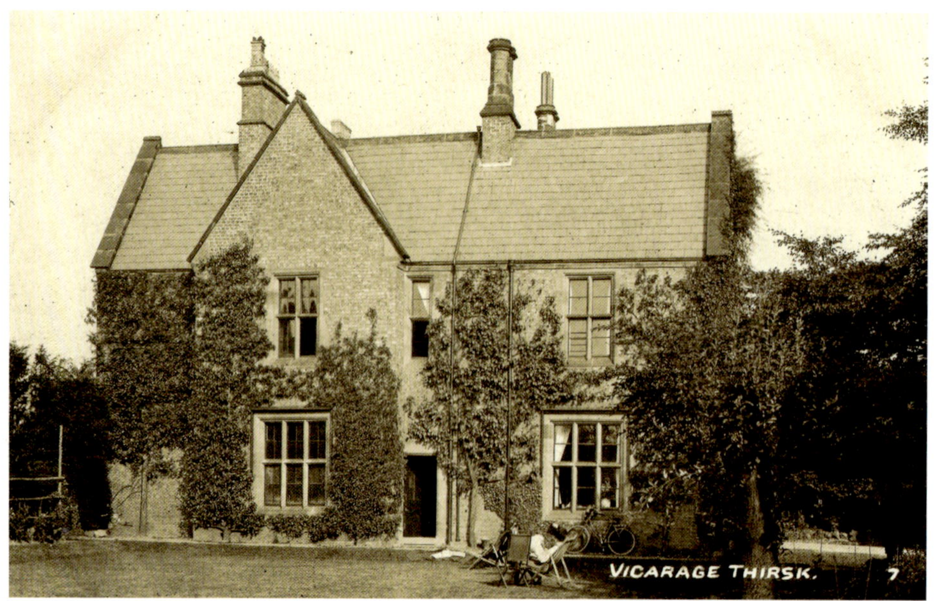

The Vicarage and the Rectory

The original Vicarage, seen in the upper picture, was built in the 1850s and had an extensive garden. In the 1950s this house was no longer suited to the needs of the clergy and was pulled down, leaving only the Victorian stable-block, while a modern house was put up on the site. Part of the large garden was later sold off for building. More recently the 1950s house, too, has been demolished, more of the garden sold and a third clergy house provided as shown below. A merger of parishes means that this house becomes the Rectory.

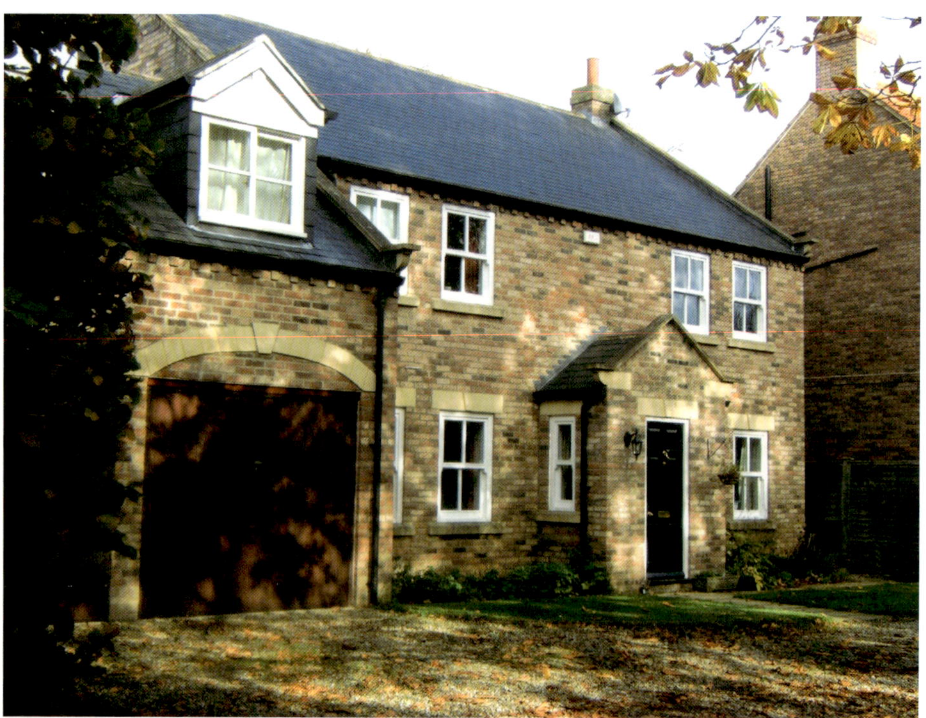

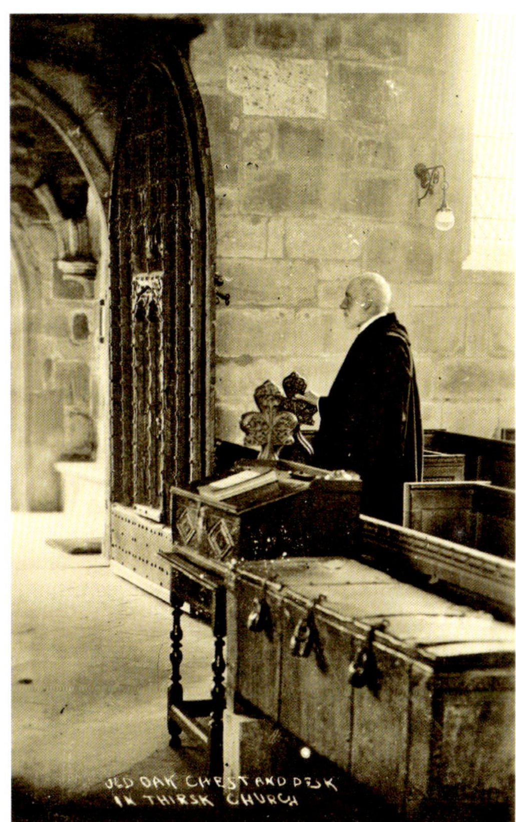

St Mary's Vergers

William Dale Bateman, mentioned on page 19, was made verger at St Mary's church in 1869 and served until his retirement in 1916. His venerable figure appears in the photographs of many church occasions. He stands here near the great West Door, beside the ancient Parish Chest. The post is now held by a habitually cheerful retired postman, John Lazenby, who can be seen in the lower picture by the same West Door.

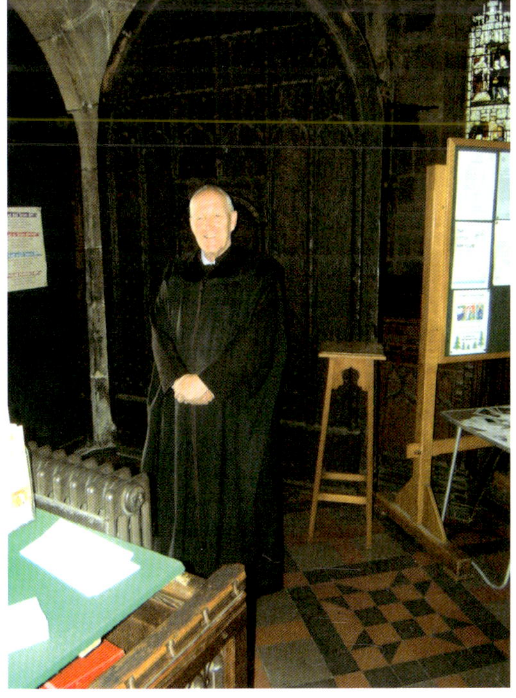

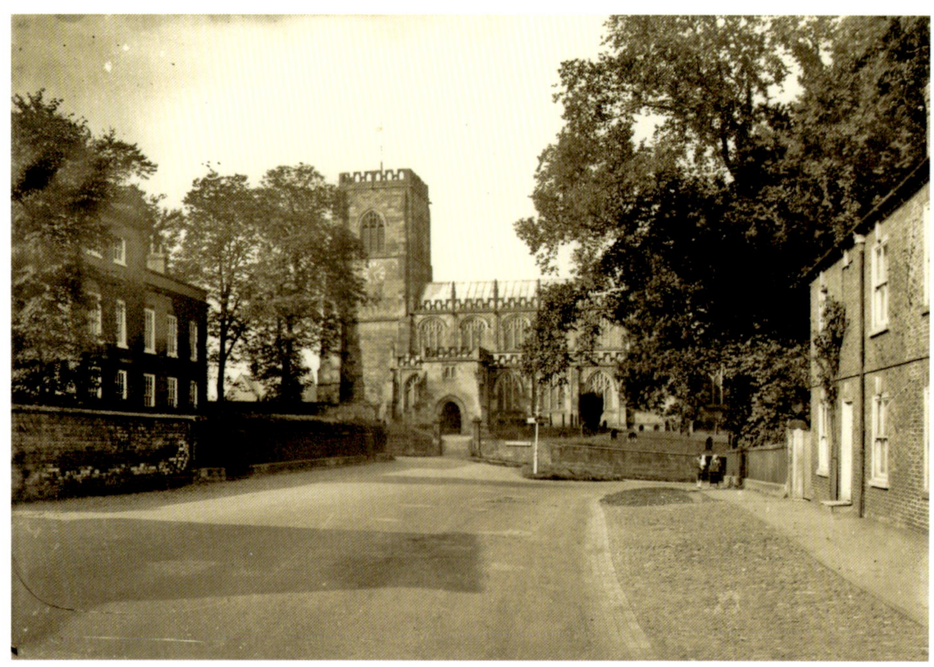

St Mary's and Thirsk Hall

Thirsk Hall, home of the Bell family, lords of the manor since 1723, stands in the traditional position next to the parish church, where during services the squire and household used to occupy the chapel in the south aisle. The Hall was extended by York architect John Carr in 1773 and has noted Georgian interiors. The trees which partly obscure the view in the early picture have now been removed to give a more open prospect.

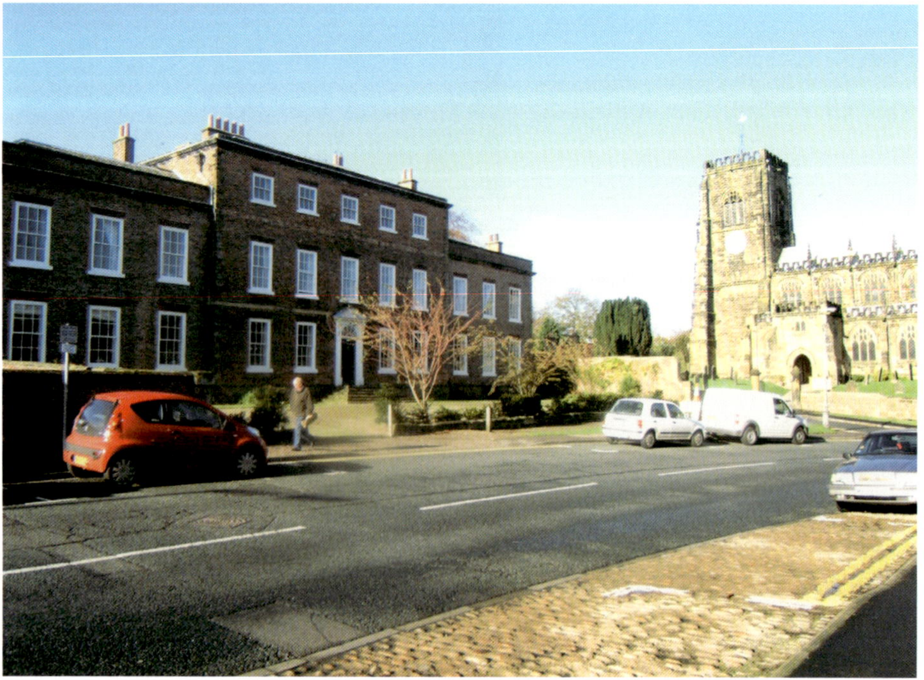

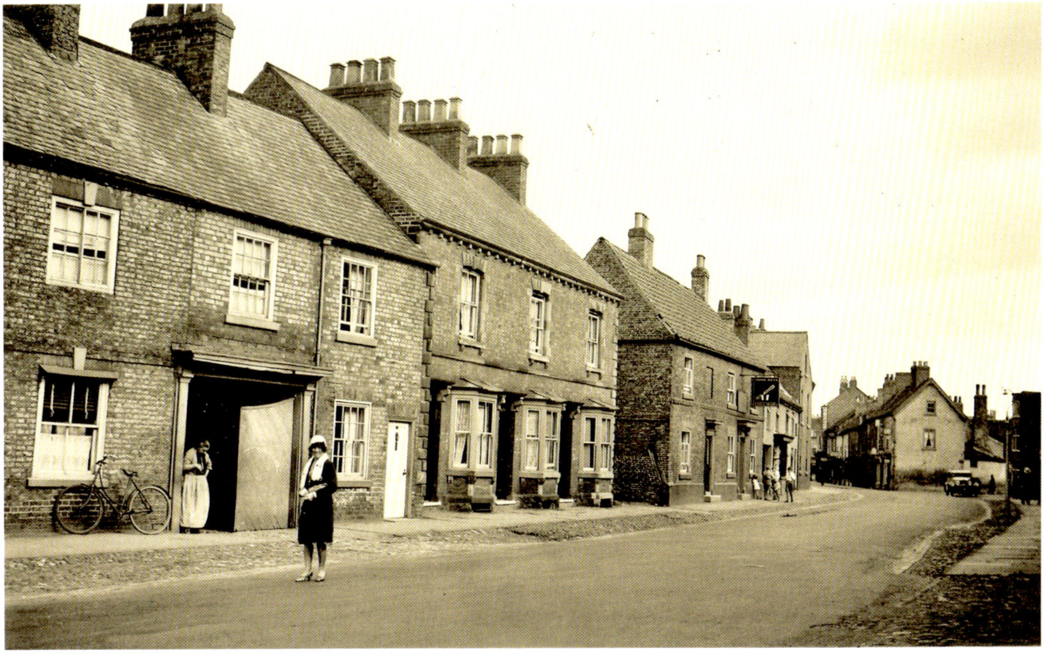

Barley's Yard

The upper picture offers a 1930's view down Kirkgate. The person standing by the gateway was Mrs Barley, whose family had farm buildings in the yard behind. When this area was being cleared in the 1990s to lay out the housing complex now called Barley's Yard, some timbers and iron columns were revealed as remnants of Meek's brewery that stood here in the early 1800s.

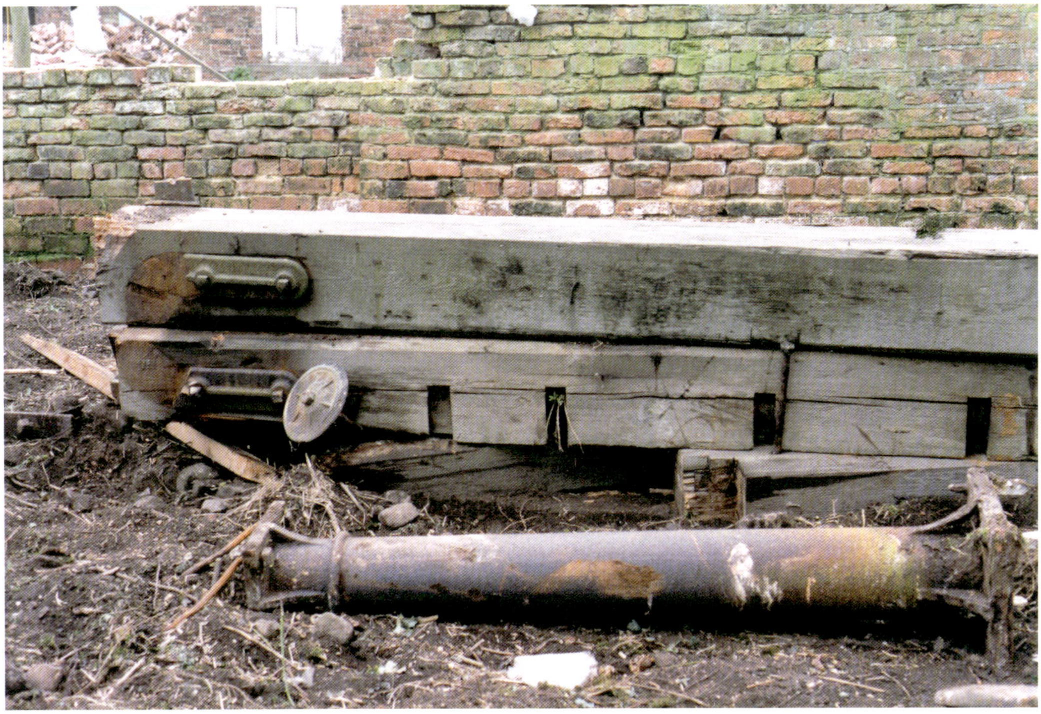

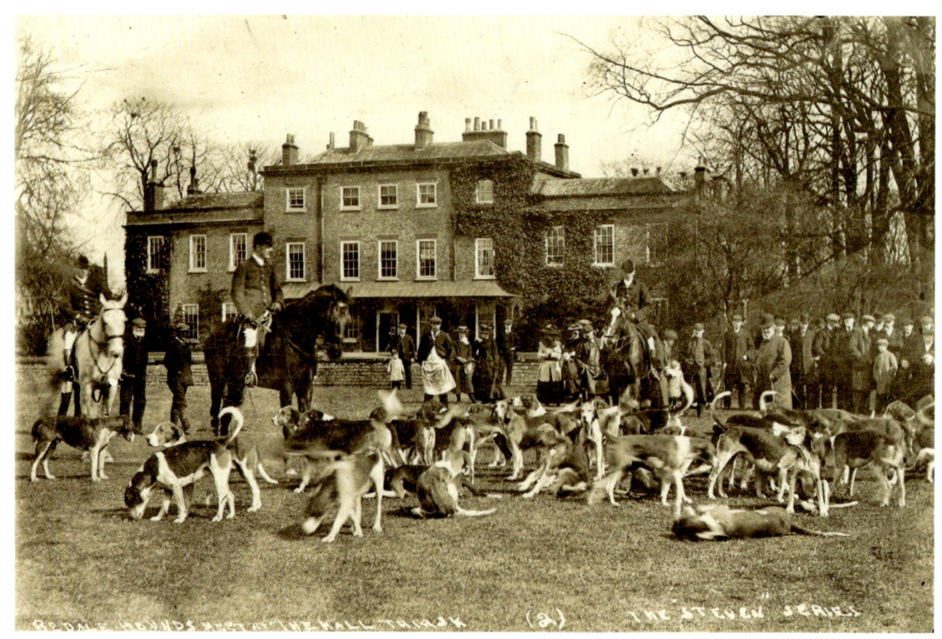

Hounds at the Hall

The extensive grounds of Thirsk Hall have often been the venue for shows and celebrations. The postcard above shows a meet of the Bedale hounds in the early 1900s. A different gathering is pictured in this 2009 shot of a Parish Barbecue.

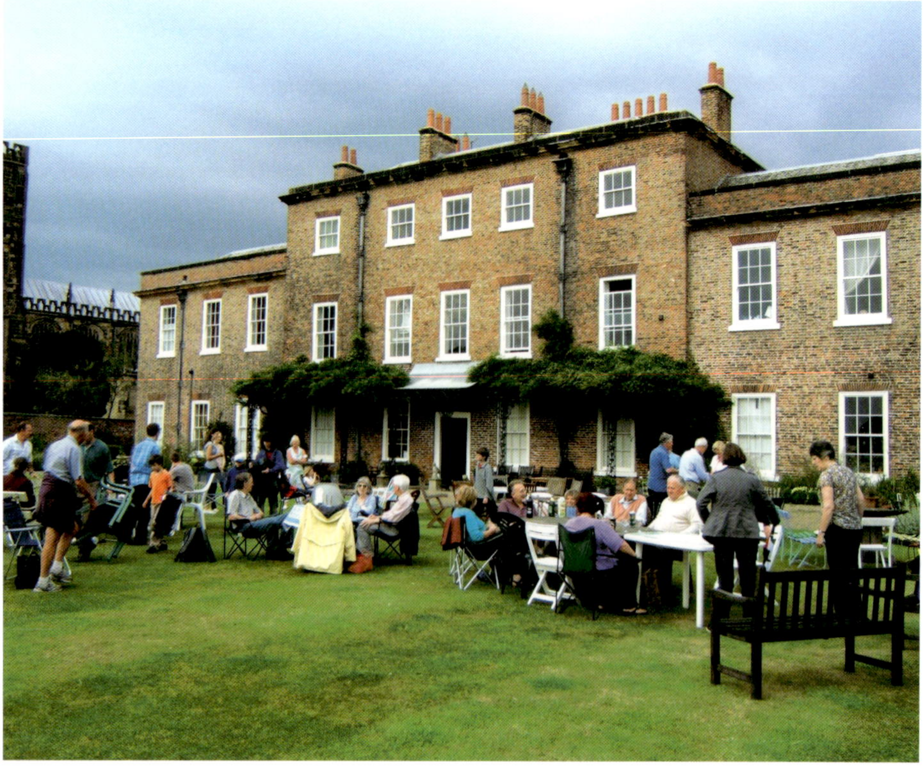

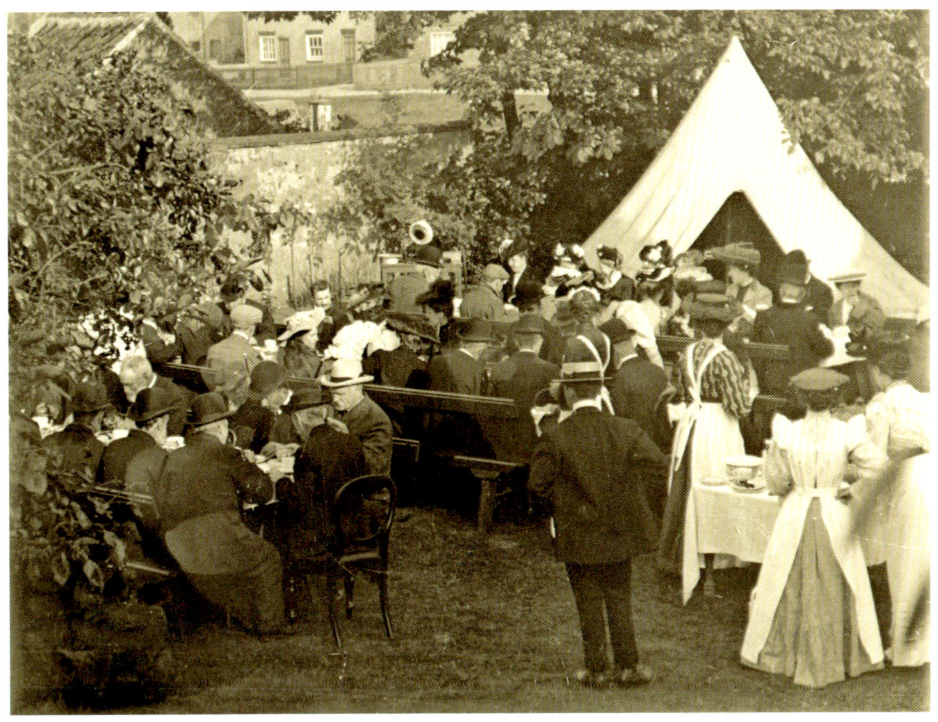

More Feasting!

The coronation celebrations of 1911 in Sowerby included a Parish Tea, being served here in the grounds of Manor Farm. It is interesting to see that it was an occasion when hats, especially bowlers and bonnets, were *de rigueur*! The other picture is a Thirsk Parish Lunch served in the primary school hall, a much less formal occasion.

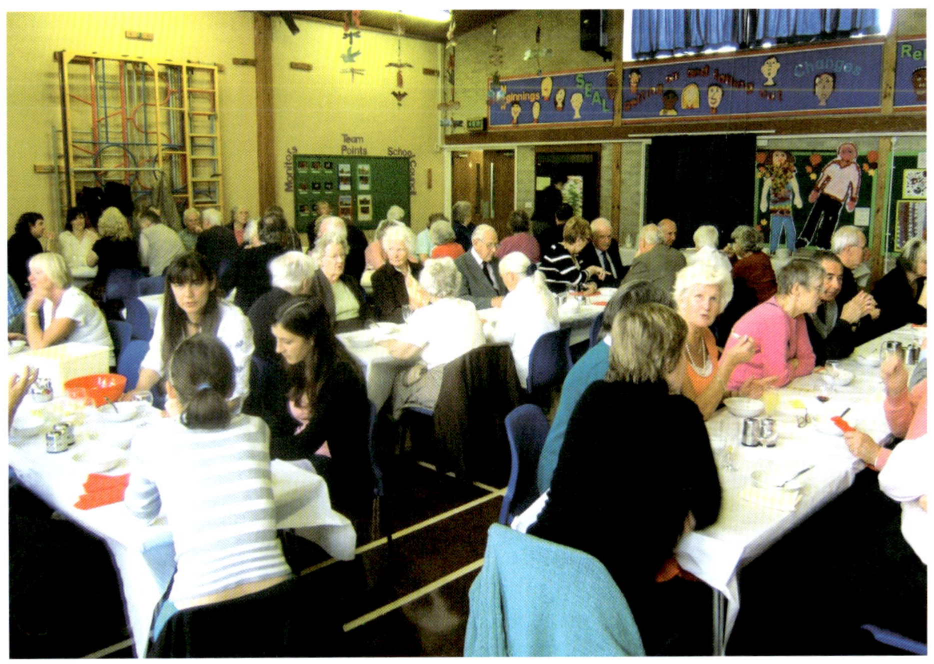

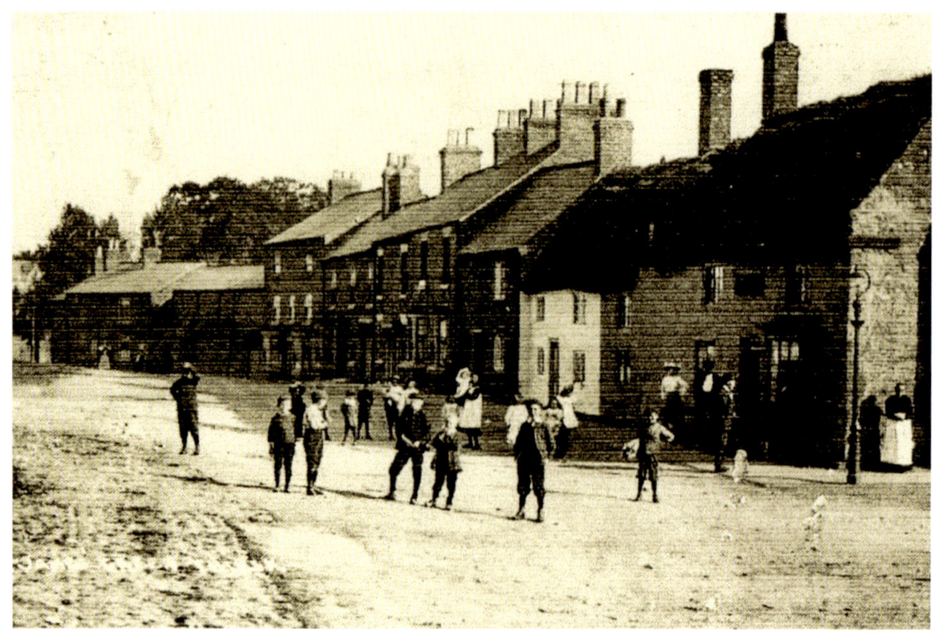

St James' Little Green

The postcard is difficult to date but was probably taken in the 1890s. It shows the Dolphin and Anchor public house with a thatched roof — by then a rare survival in the town. The recent view of this corner shows the brick cottages that were built after the pub was pulled down.

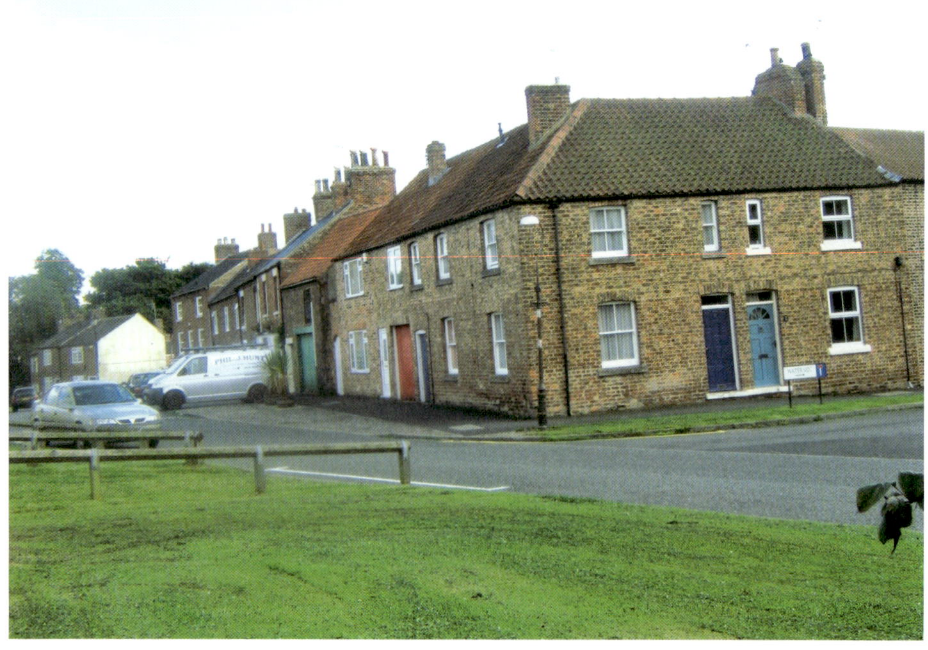

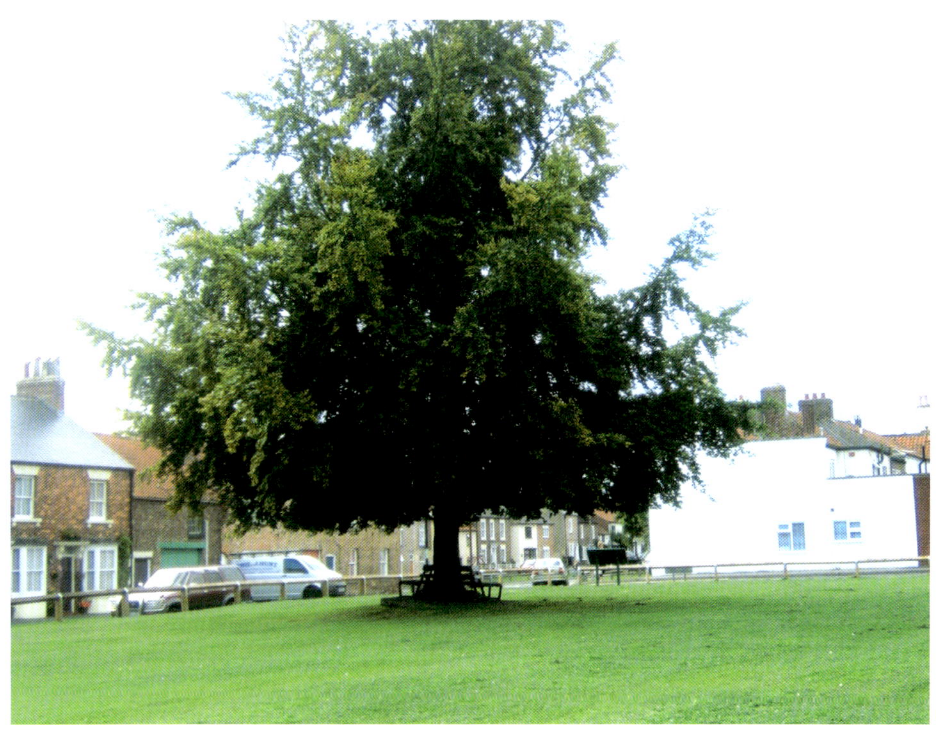

The Tree on Little Green

The history book tells us that here stood an ancient elm beneath which the hustings stood in the days before Reform. It was burnt down one Guy Fawkes Night in the early 1800s. When Little Green was restored in the late 1960s, a beech tree was planted in memory of ancient times. As the recent photo shows, it has grown almost out of recognition!

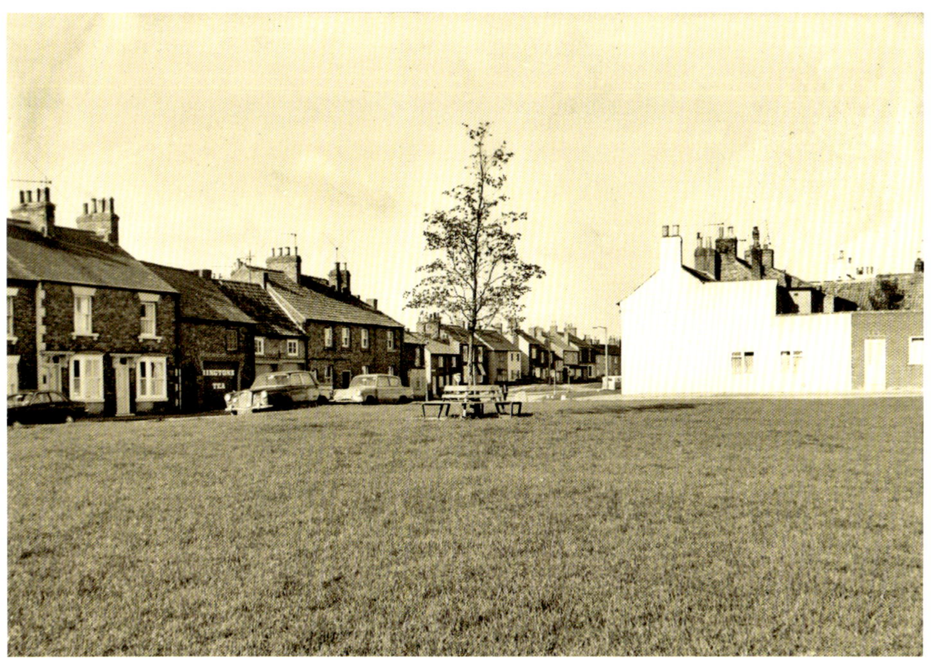

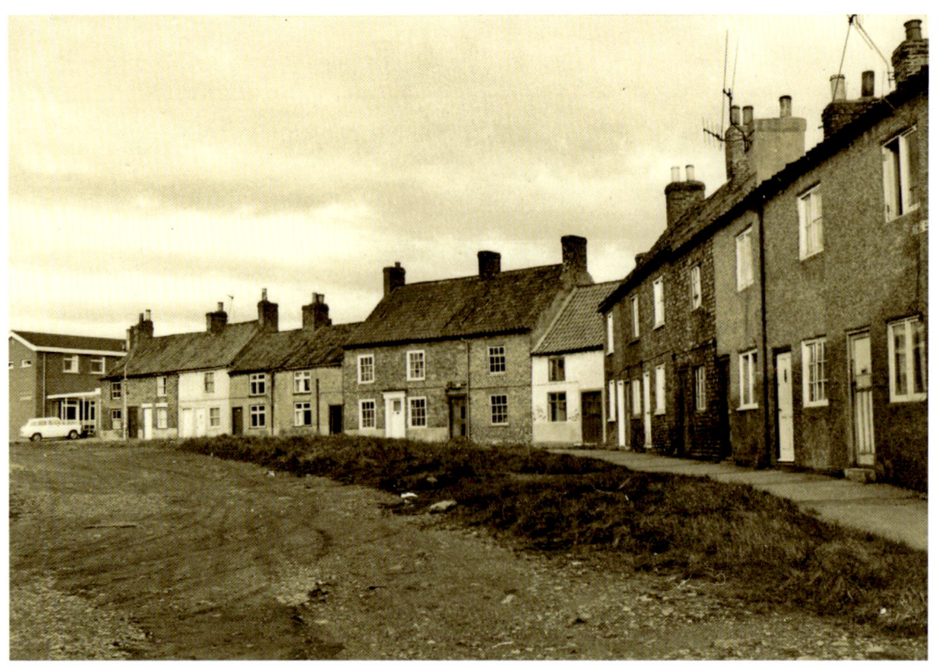

Old Cottages on the Green

A row of old cottages stood at the far end of Little Green. They were demolished as part of a re-housing programme. A short terrace of modern dwellings replaced them on the east side but, as the recent view shows, only some undulations in the turf bear evidence of the older houses.

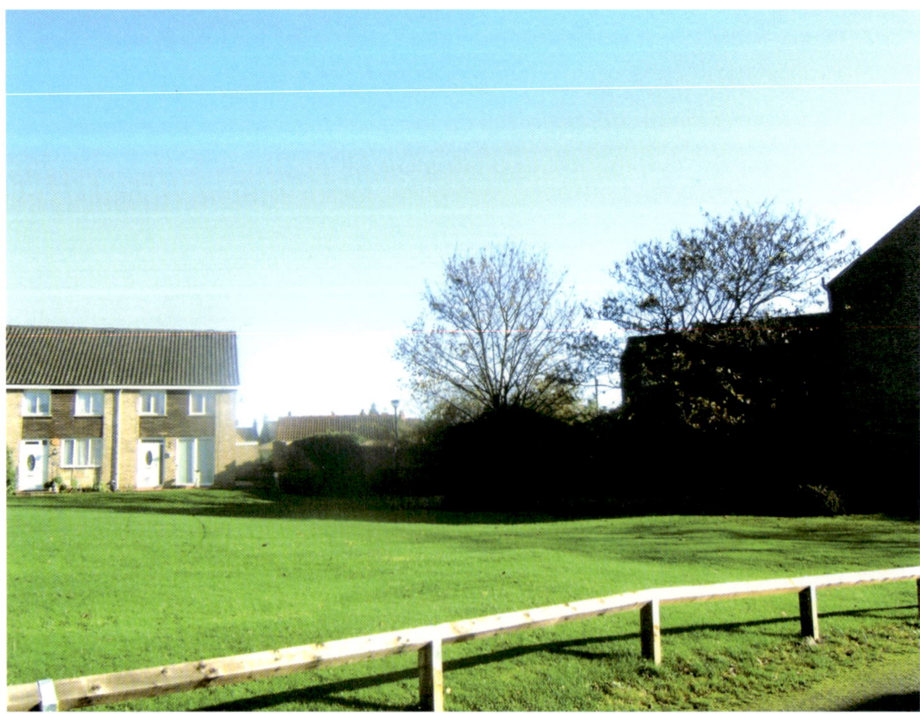

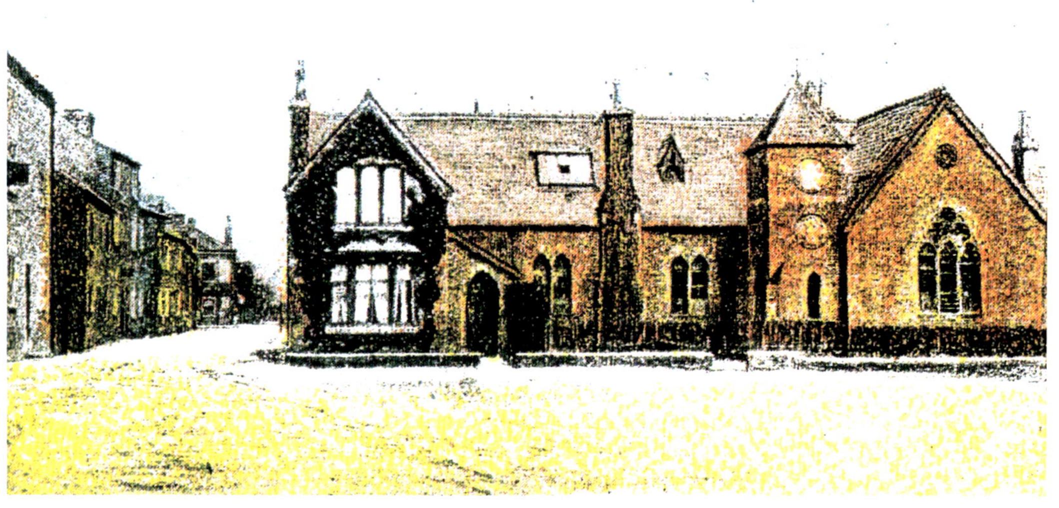

The National School

National Schools were the Church of England primary schools. This school for boys and girls was built on Little Green about 1865. The picture above is the only one we have; it seems to be a drawing from a photograph. The present C.P. school is a modern establishment in East Thirsk. For some years, there was a little private school on the Green, but the site has now been cleared for further development.

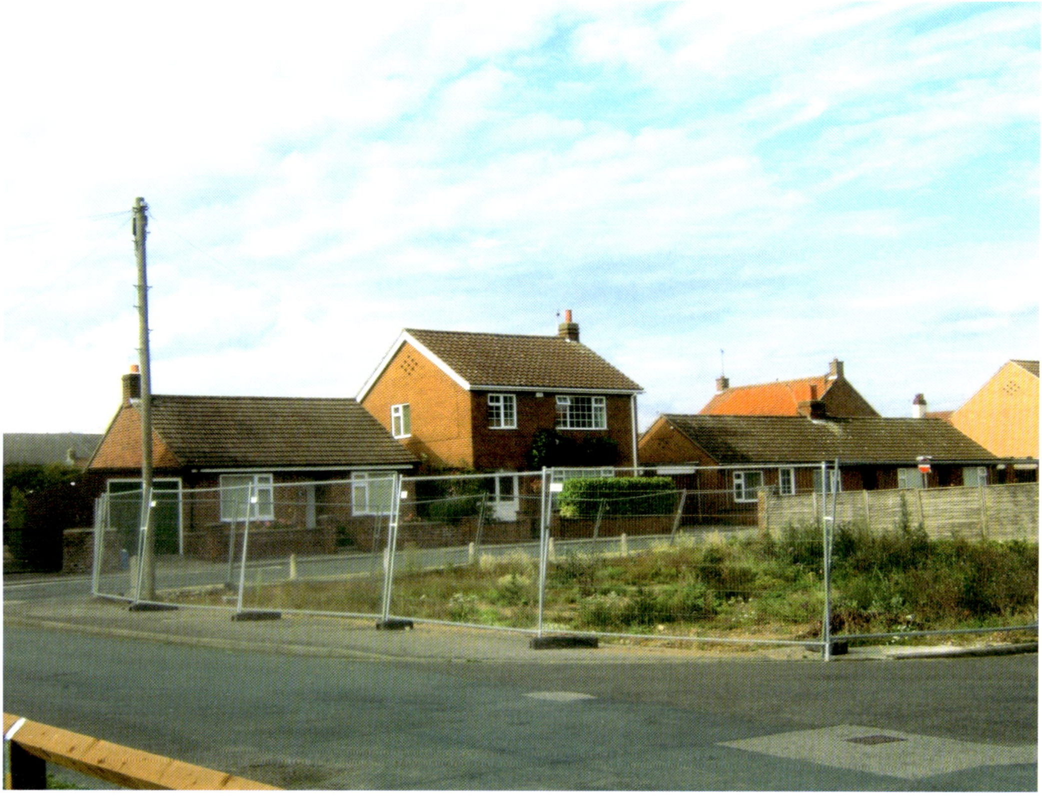

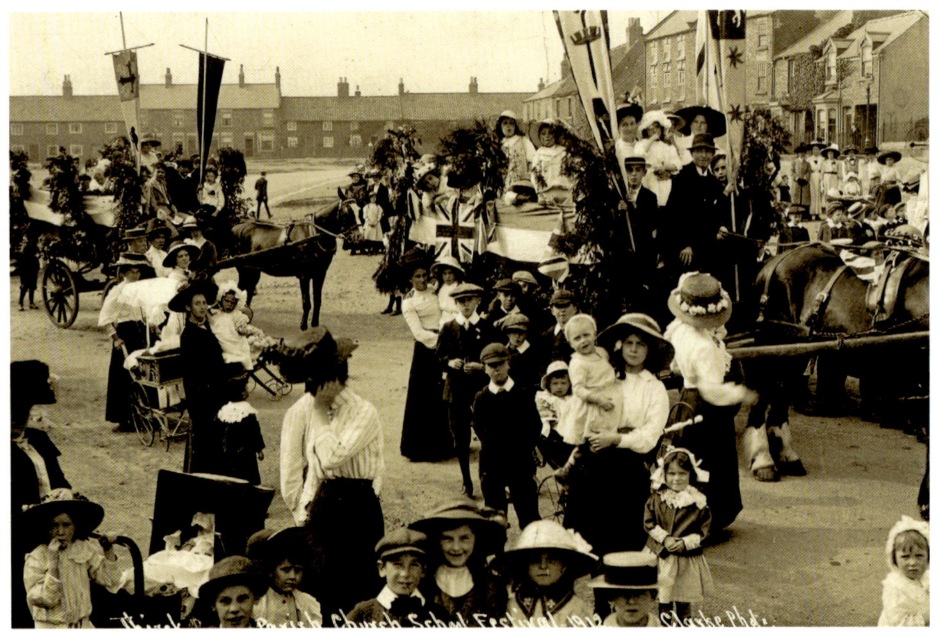

Festival Preparations 1912

The great empty space of St James' Green was not very attractive in the days when this community was a working one, but, as this 1912 postcard shows, it was a good place for assembling the carts and decorated floats for the schools' festival procession and feast which took place each summer. Much has been done in the last twenty years to improve its character; the Green has been grassed and fenced and trees planted. The contrast between the two views is clear to see.

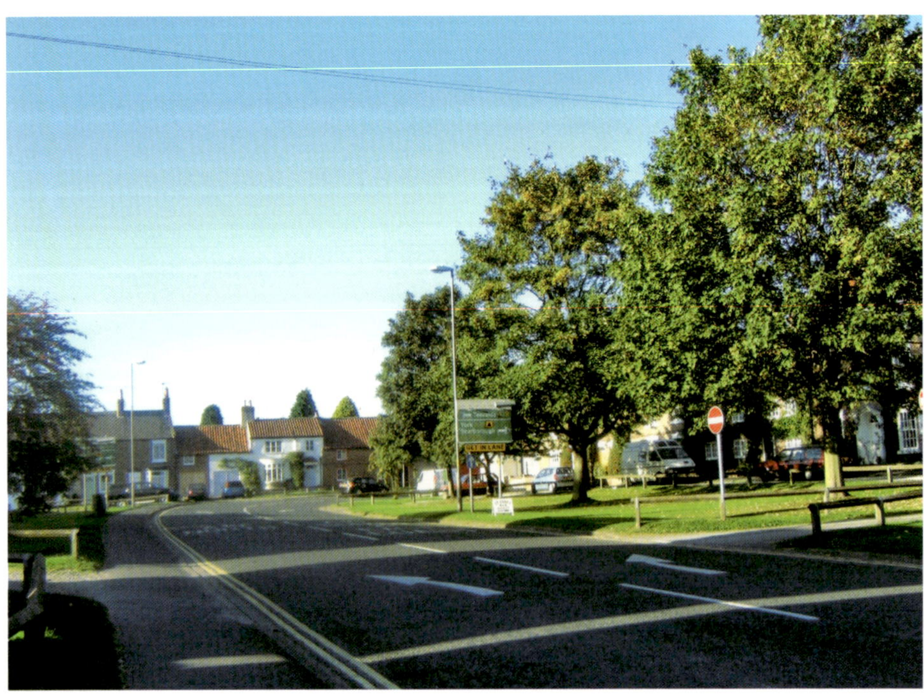

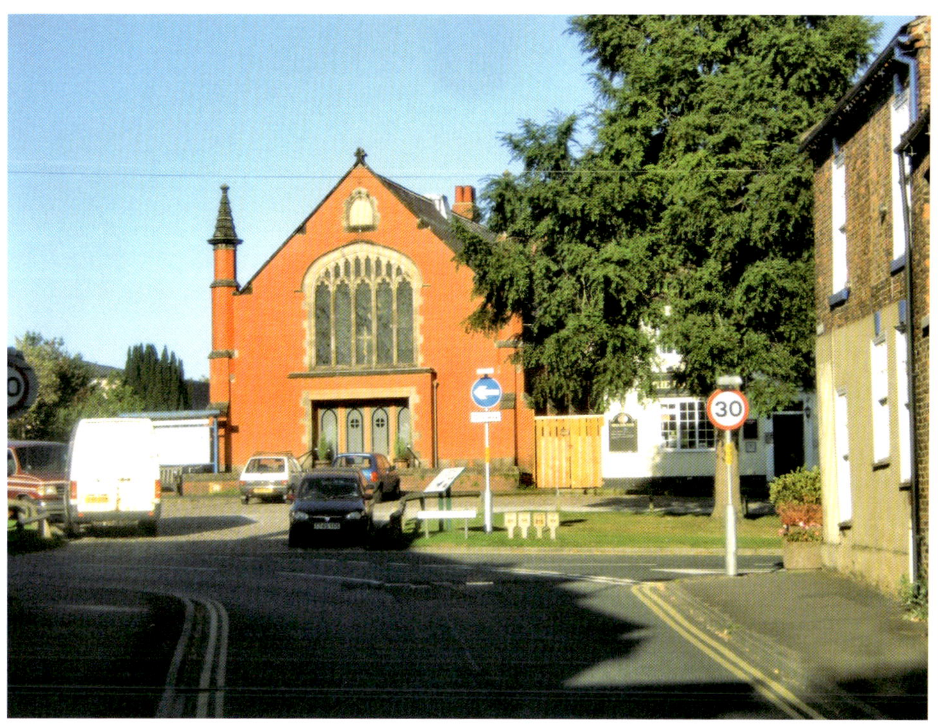

The Wesleyan Methodist Church

John Wesley preached in Thirsk in 1747, and the first Methodist chapel was built on St James Green in the 1760s, with a larger one on the same site following in 1816. Nearly a century later, a Sunday School building was added. The 1908 photograph shows the laying of the foundation stones. The main chapel was demolished in 1960 and services transferred to the school. The centenary was celebrated here this summer in the chapel seen in the picture above.

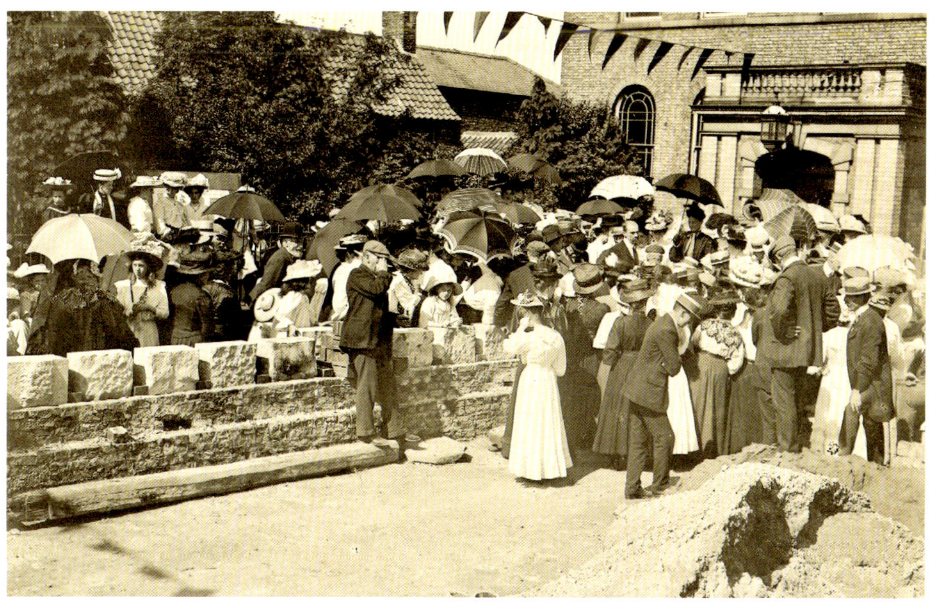

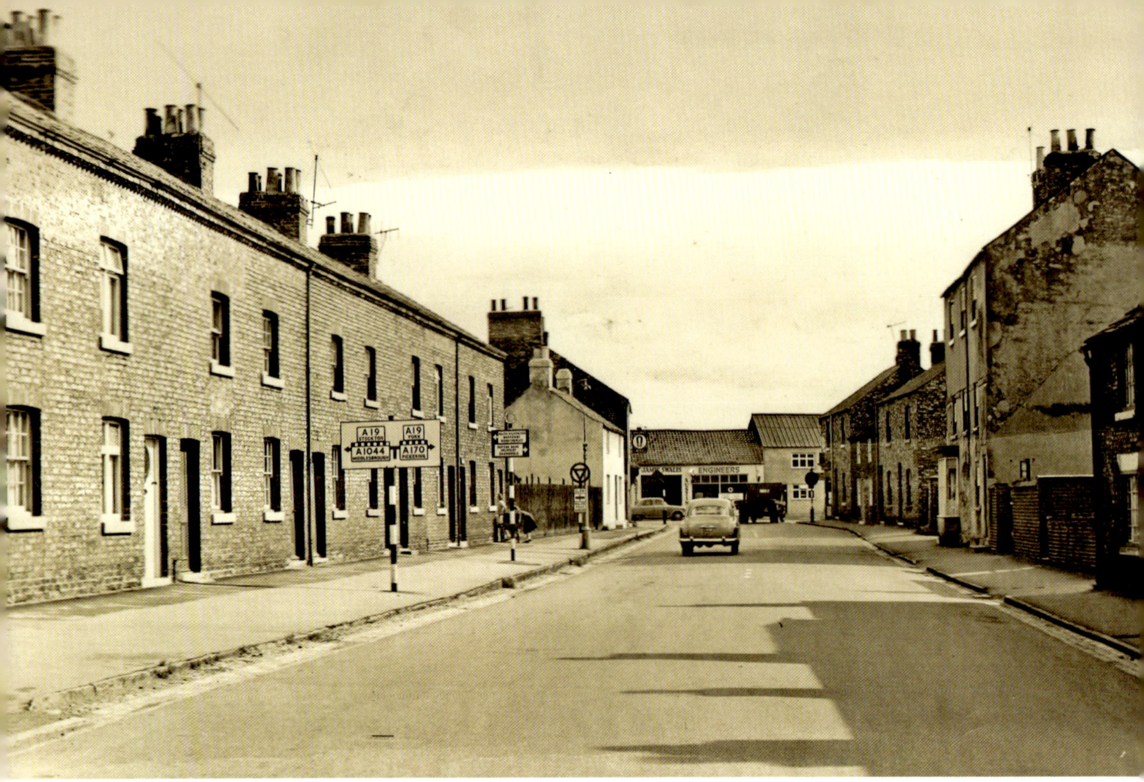

Stammergate

The unusual name of this short street is probably a corruption of 'stony moor' from the days of the open town fields east of the main highway. The White Horse pub stood at the left-hand corner with Long Street, but by the 1960s this was already part of the one-way traffic system, marked out much more clearly in the modern photo.

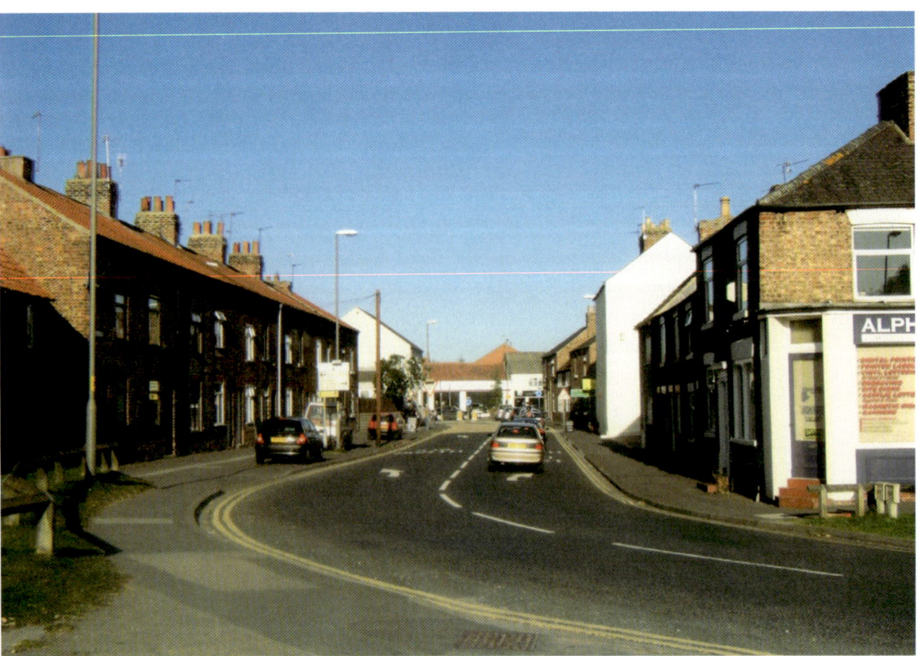

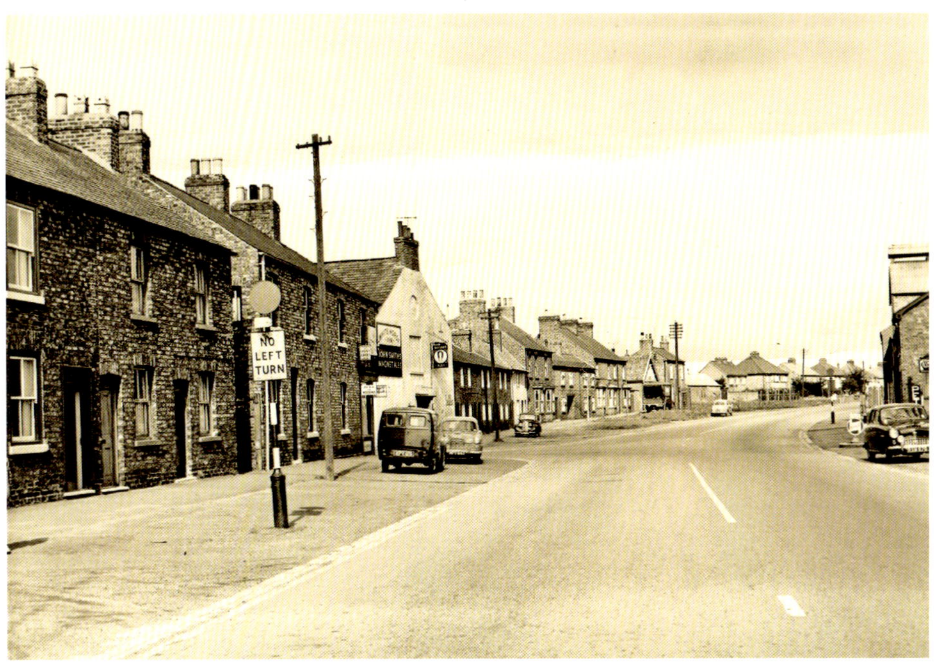

The White Horse Inn

The White Horse Inn is seen more clearly from Long Street in the first picture. The view north is hardly recognisable today as one taken from the same spot. A Texaco garage and filling station has replaced the pub, the road junction is now marked out with all the trappings of posts and signs, while trees conceal the distant houses on Stockton Road.

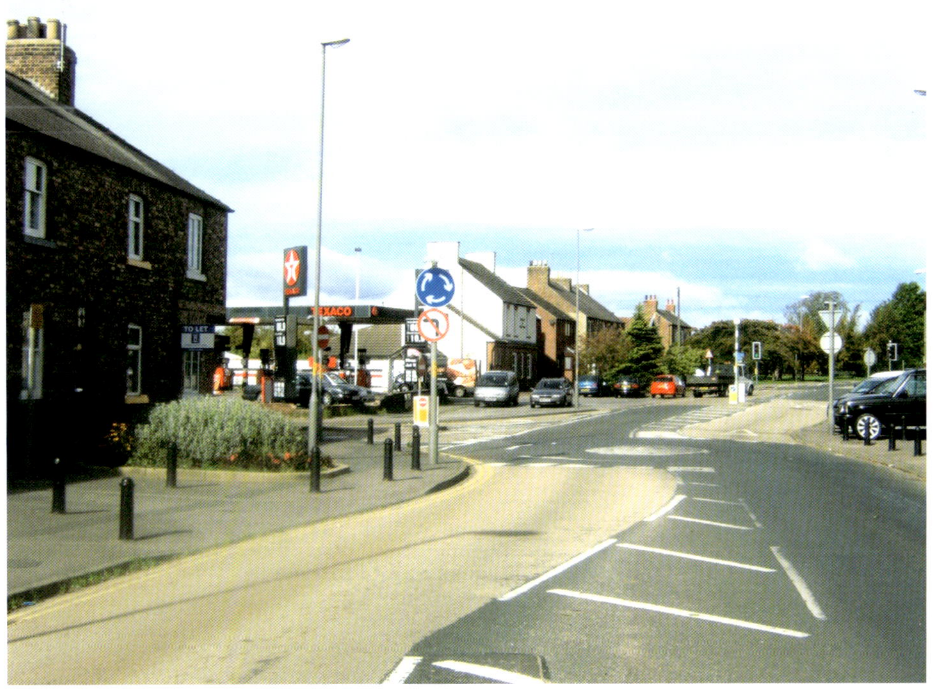

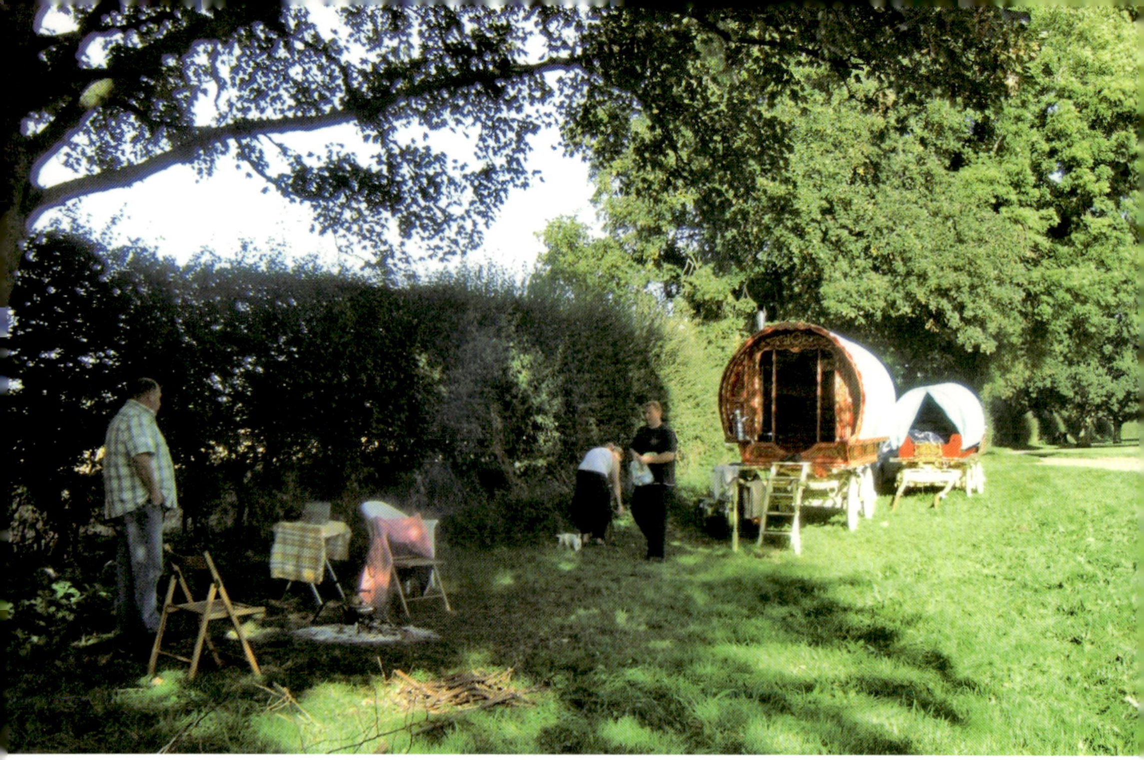

Painted Wagons

Thirsk has long been a halt for gypsy and traveller families, since the wide roadside verges offer free grazing for horses and ponies on the way to meetings like the annual fair at Appleby. There was a fair at Topcliffe until 1969. The upper picture shows two bow-top wagons on Stockton Road. The larger of the two was built in Bradford about a hundred years ago and both it and the smaller dray are splendidly decorated in traditional style.

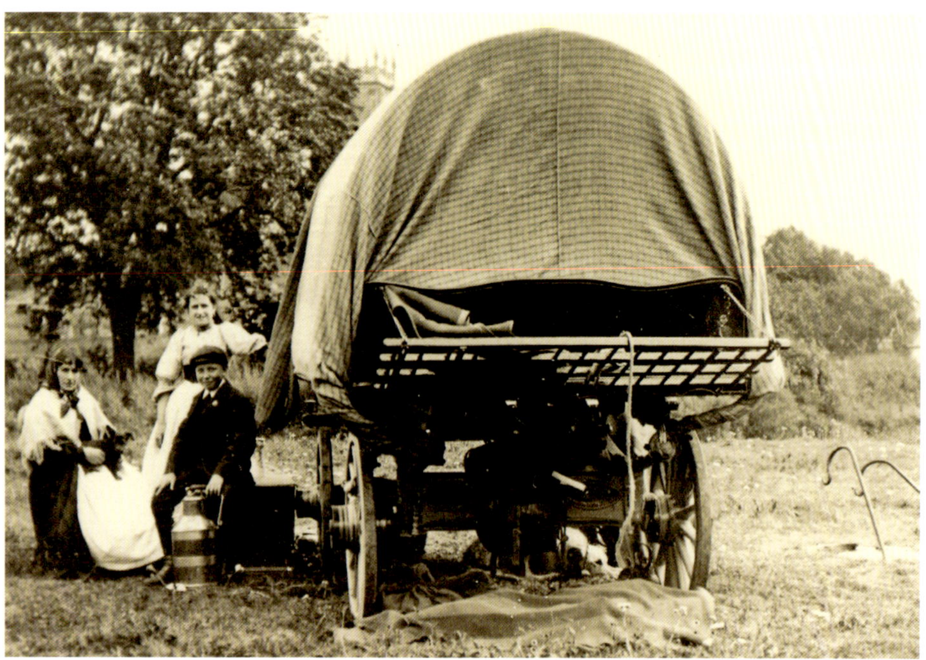

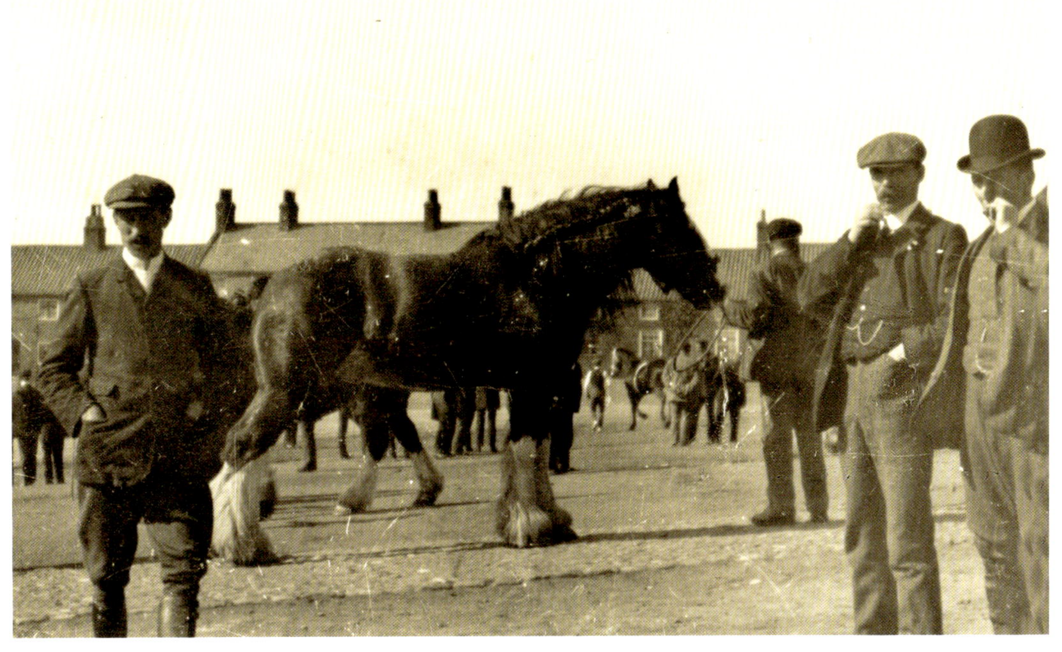

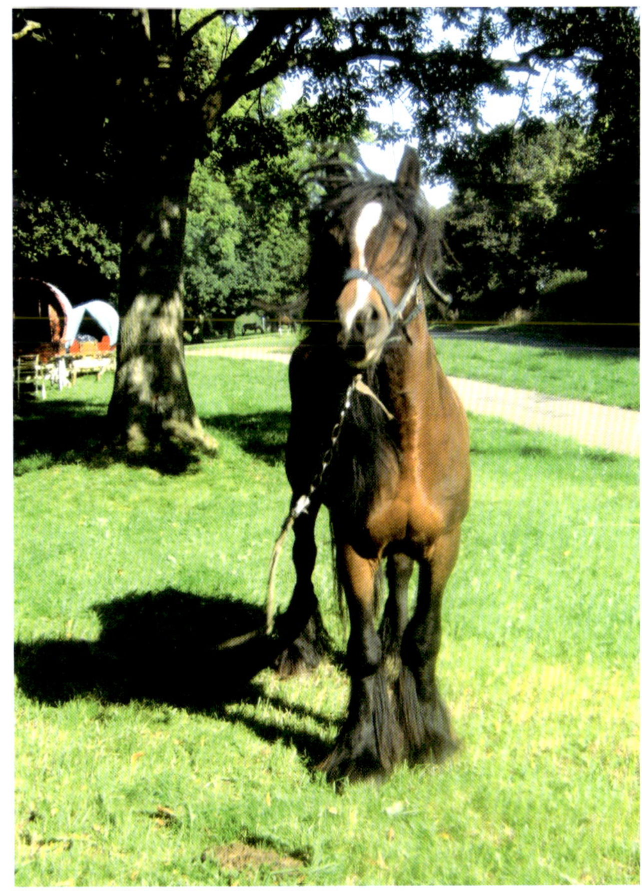

Horses for Sale

Thirsk had several cattle fairs held on traditional dates. Until a covered shed was built at Town End near the goods yard, these sales were held on St James Green, the 'Beast Market' in an eighteenth-century deed. Horses were still offered for sale here into the early 1900s, as seen in the first photograph. The gypsy dealer seen on the opposite page had a string of ponies for sale. One was especially curious!

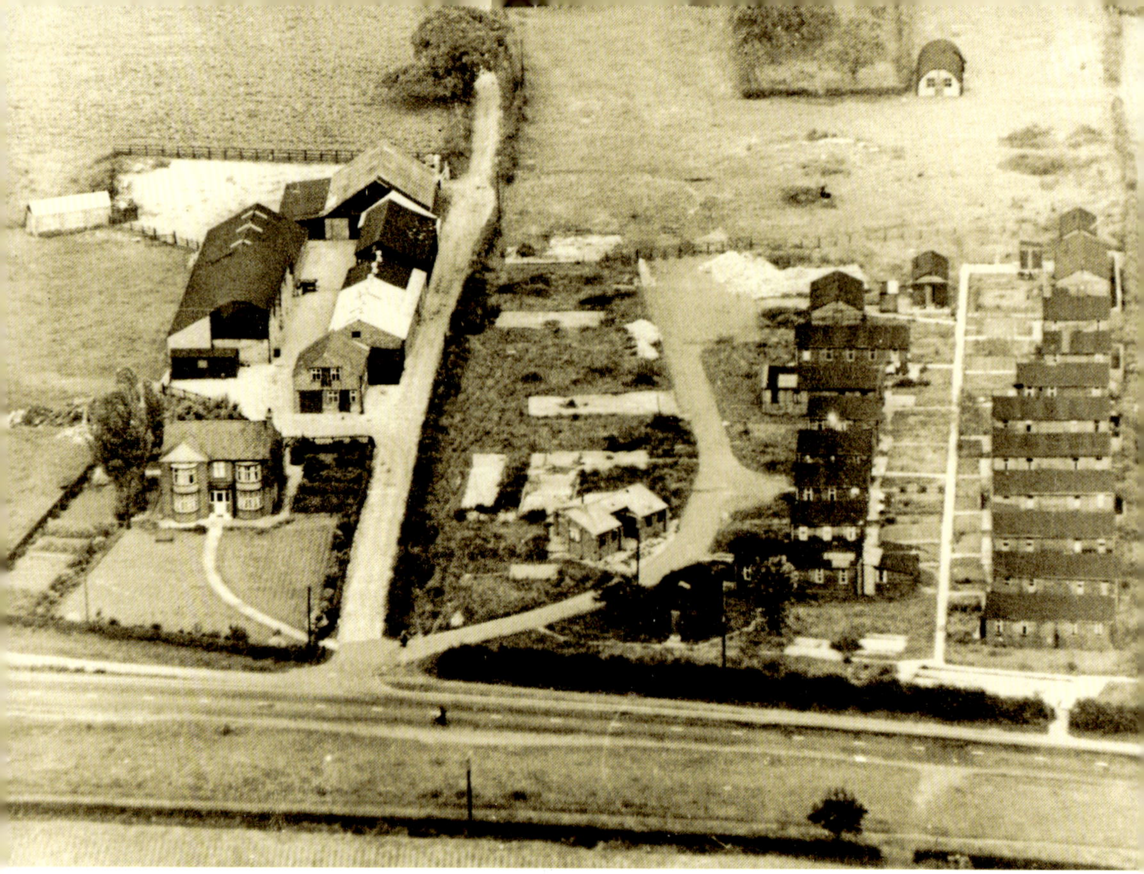

Housing Then and Now

In the years following the Second World War, there was an acute shortage of houses. This wartime army camp on Stockton Road, seen here from the air, was converted into emergency accommodation for local families. By contrast, a Volvo truck repair depot is now the site of a block of quality retirement homes in a garden setting.

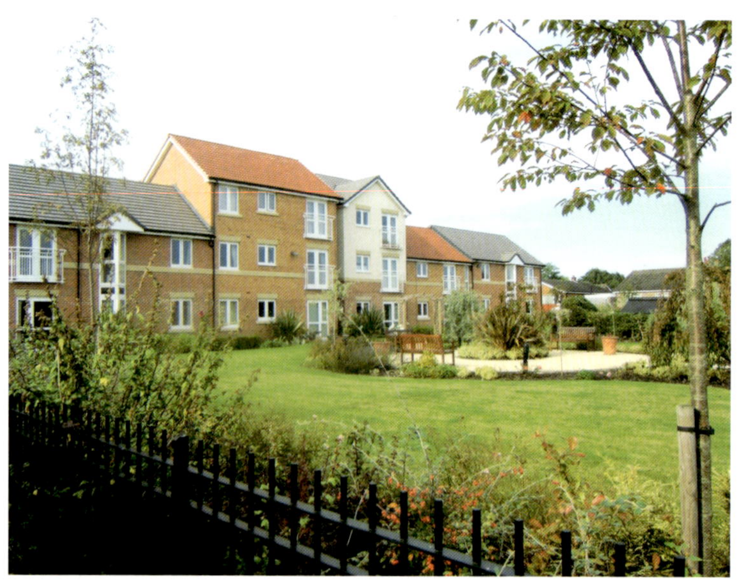

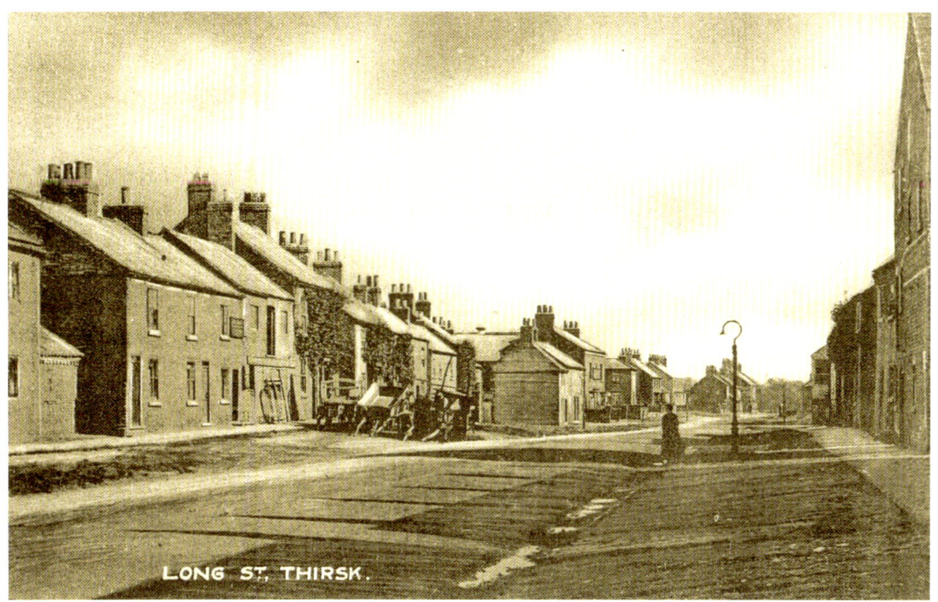

Long Street

Until by-passed in 1972, Long Street carried the main route north from York to the Tees. It has more than a fair share of garages, car sales and repair shops. The first photograph gives it a particularly grim aspect. The carts are stacked outside Harker's the wheelwright. The gabled building on the extreme right was Tweedy's brewery. The automobile predominates in the modern picture. The brewery building is now a motorcycle showroom, as is the block across the road.

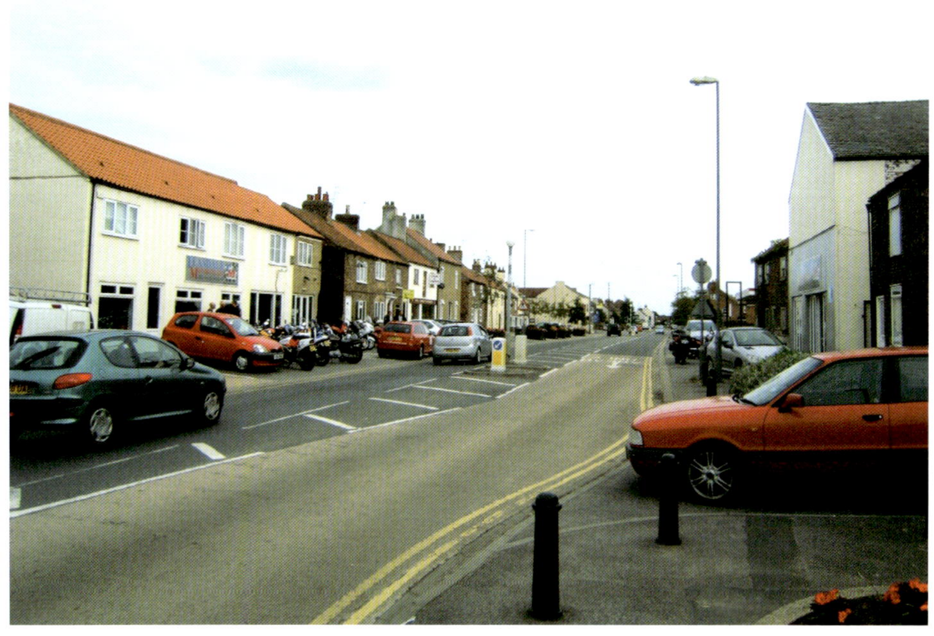

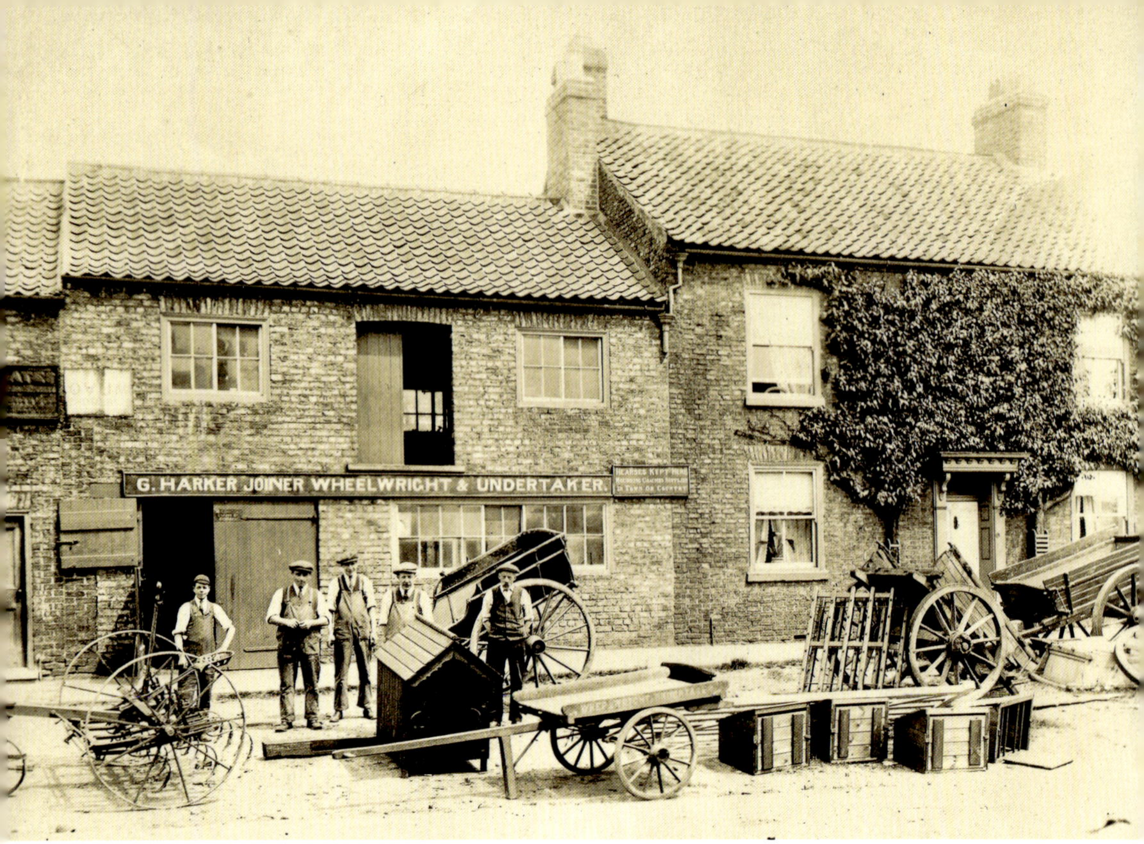

Cartwheels or Fish and Chips?

A fine picture, taken in the 1920s, of George Harker, joiner, wheelwright and undertaker, with his workmen. Samples of his craft are on display, apart from coffins, that is! Note the loading door open on the first floor, a regular feature of a joiner or carpenter's shop. This has served to carry the signboard for the Long Street Fisheries that now occupy the premises.

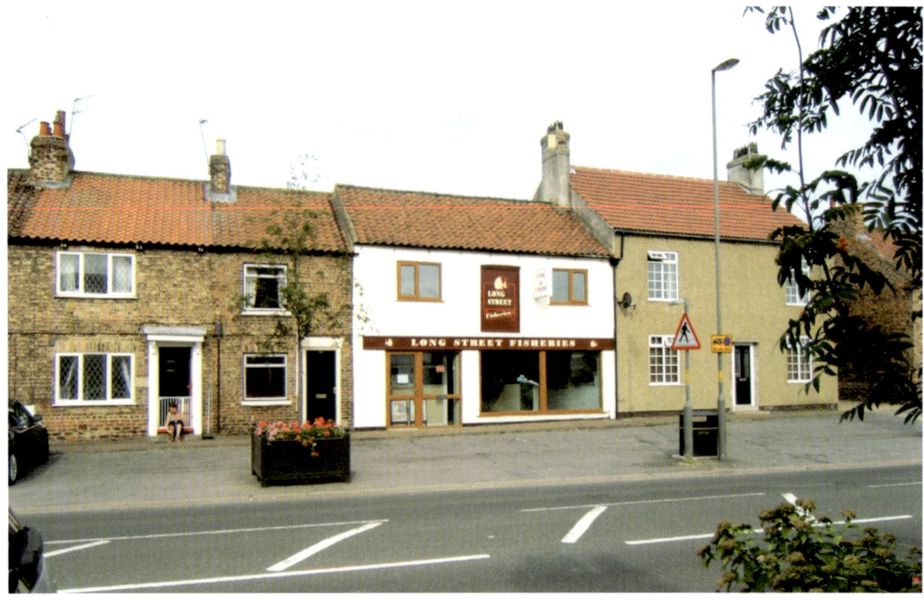

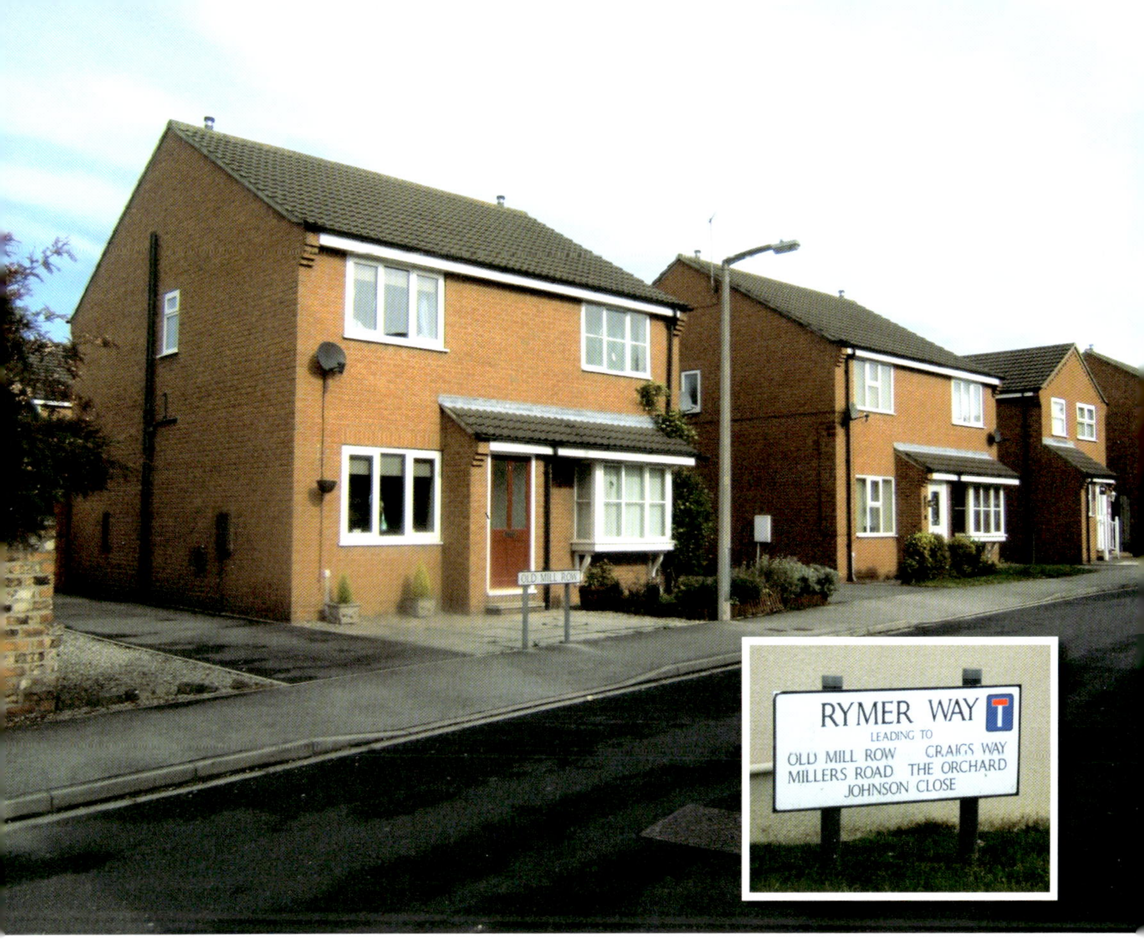

Rymer's Mill

As well as the watermill in the town centre, the Rymer brothers owned this machine-driven mill off Long Street. It displays their name three times, though it was animal feeds for Spillers that they milled; houses stand there today, but the millers are not forgotten.

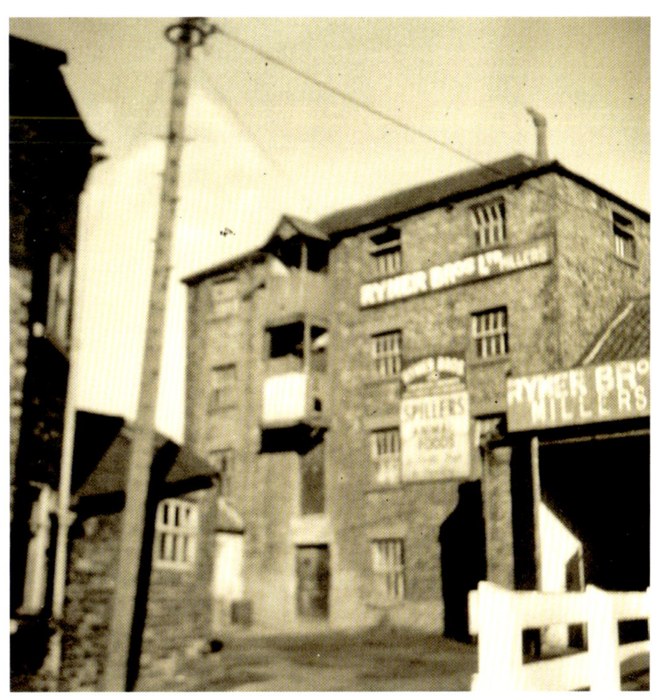

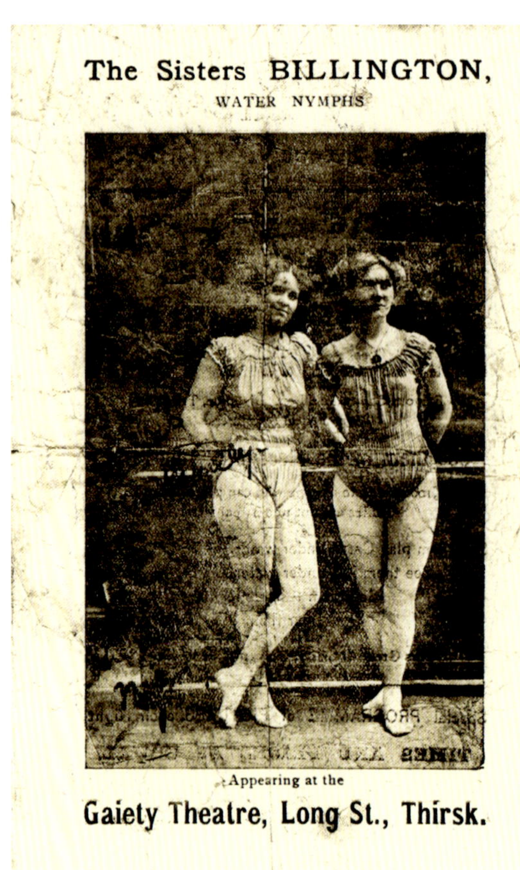
The Sisters BILLINGTON,
WATER NYMPHS
Appearing at the
Gaiety Theatre, Long St., Thirsk.

The Gaiety and the Girls

In the 1900s John Bell had a cycle and garage business here, but in 1912 he built the Gaiety cinema to show the new movies. Variety acts appeared as well as films. This flyer features the Billington sisters — 'Trick and Ornamental Swimmers in the Electric Crystal Tank'. As well as swimming, they ate, sang and knitted under water — it had to be seen to be believed! Sadly, in 1932 the Gaiety met the fate of many early cinemas and burnt down. What remained was rebuilt as a garage and is today an ATS repair depot.

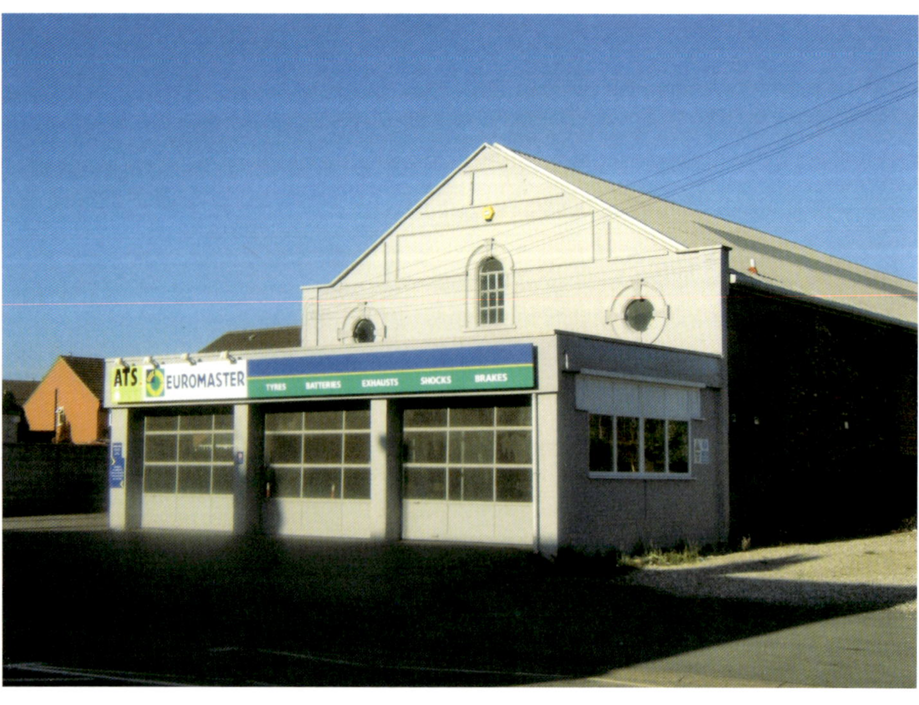

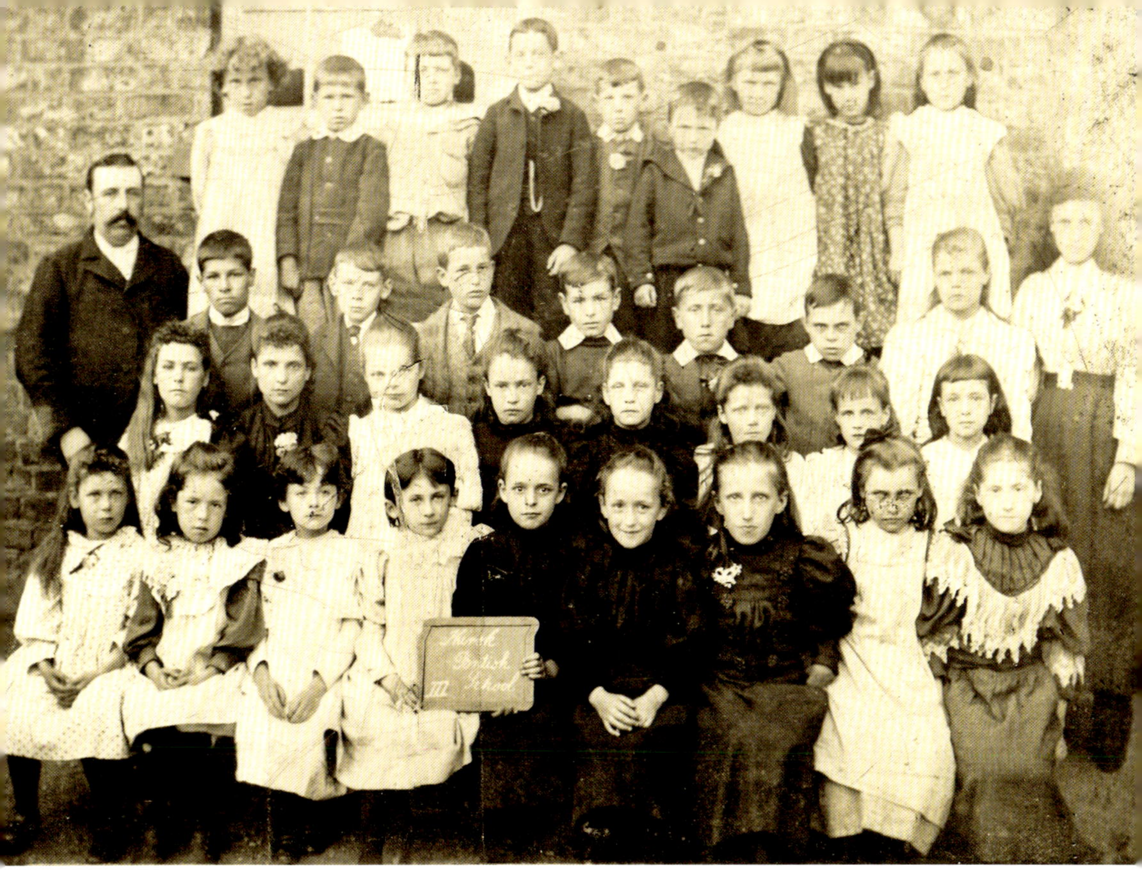

The British & Foreign School

The slate tells us this is Class 3 of Thirsk British School but is not dated. The non-sectarian British and Foreign Schools were established in the early nineteenth century to give working-class boys and girls a basic education. Since Anglicans attended the National schools, the British schools tended to draw their pupils from the non-conformist congregations. The school in Long Street was built in 1841, teaching generations of local children till merged with the new C.P. school in East Thirsk. The building now houses a glazing firm.

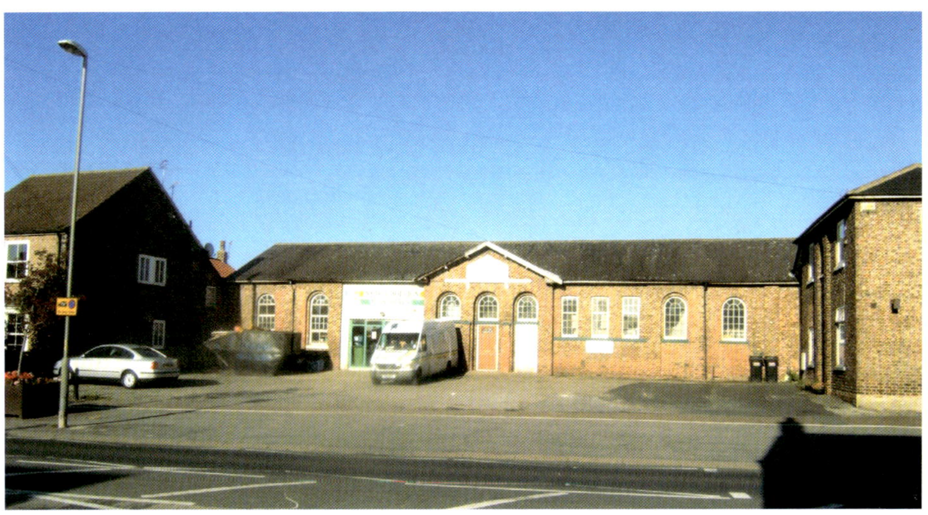

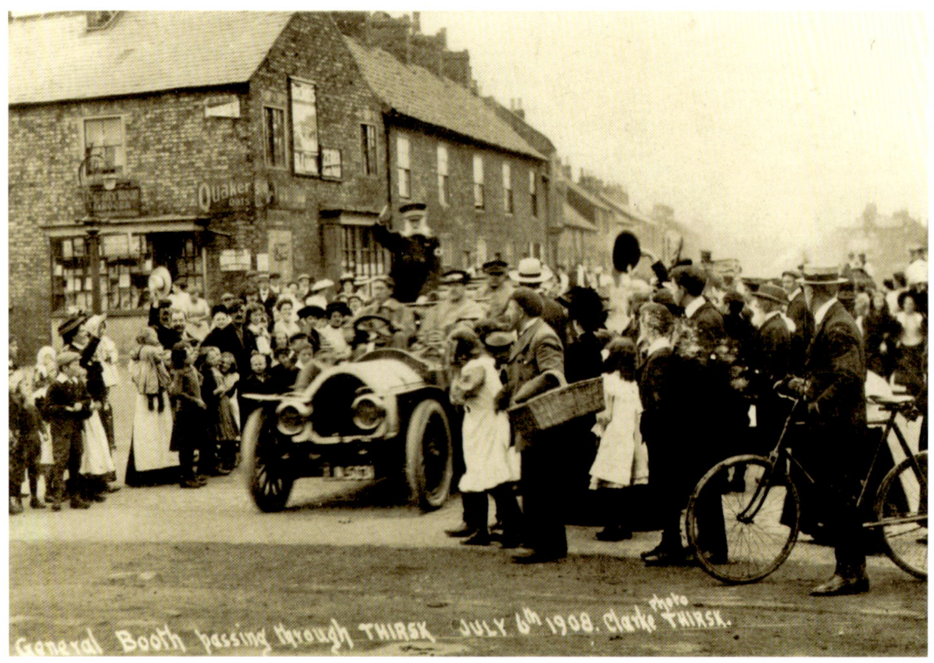

General Booth 1908

General William Booth, founder of the Salvation Army, is seen here making a triumphal progress down Long Street on his way from Northallerton to York. He is acknowledging the crowd as he passes the corner of Ingramgate. Traffic past the roundabout on this spot today would make it a dangerous place to stand in the road!

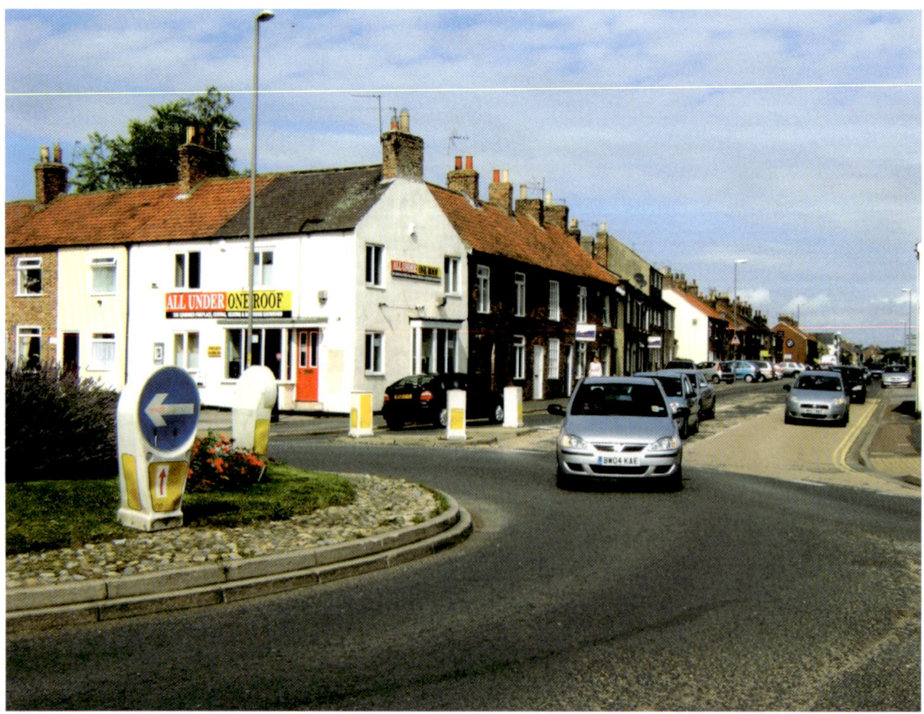

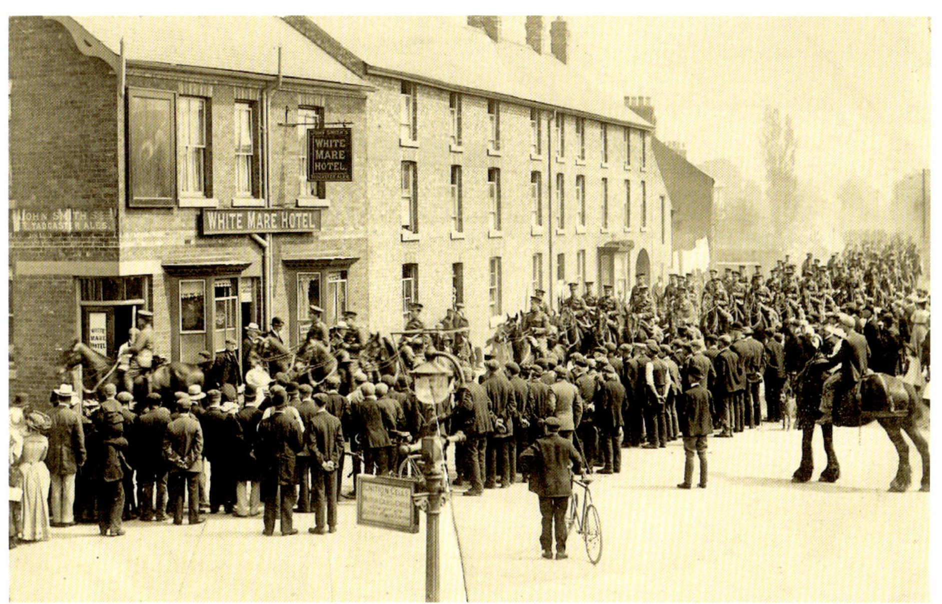

The 18th Hussars Arrive in Thirsk

A crowd has turned out to watch these mounted troops arriving in Thirsk in June 1906 for the annual summer camp. The men of the 18th Hussars are passing the White Mare Hotel at the junction with Sutton Road. The pub was demolished in the 1930s to make room for the roundabout there today. The building that remains in the recent view was the Model Lodging House. The sign on the lamppost in the first picture tells motorists that batteries can be charged at the 'Electric Power Station'.

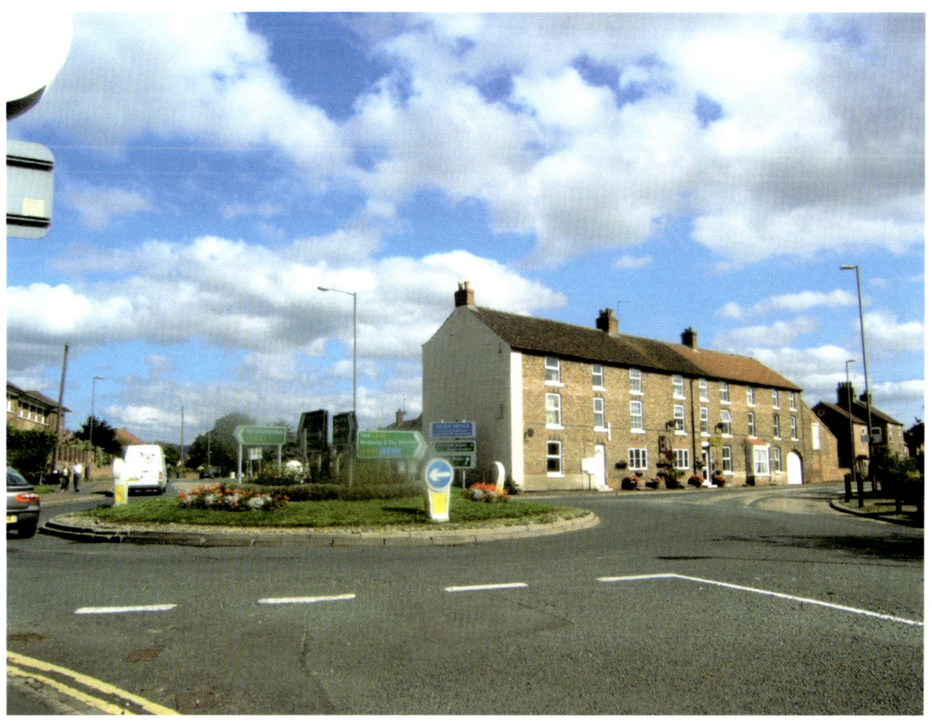

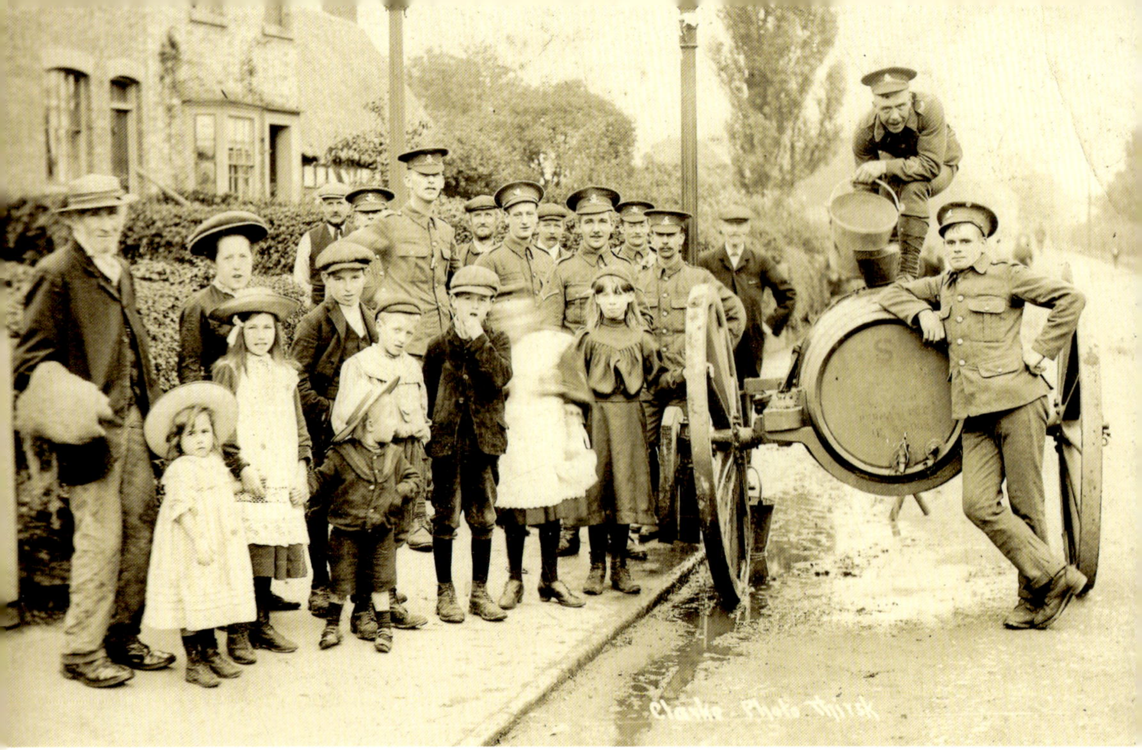

A Watering Party

This squad of soldiers is busy drawing water from a stand-pipe halfway down Barbeck. Like the cavalry on page 63, they are probably at an annual camp here. They have attracted a small crowd of passers-by, making an interesting group for the photographer. The thatched cottage visible in the background used to stand where the new terrace of houses can be seen in a present-day view of the same part of the street.

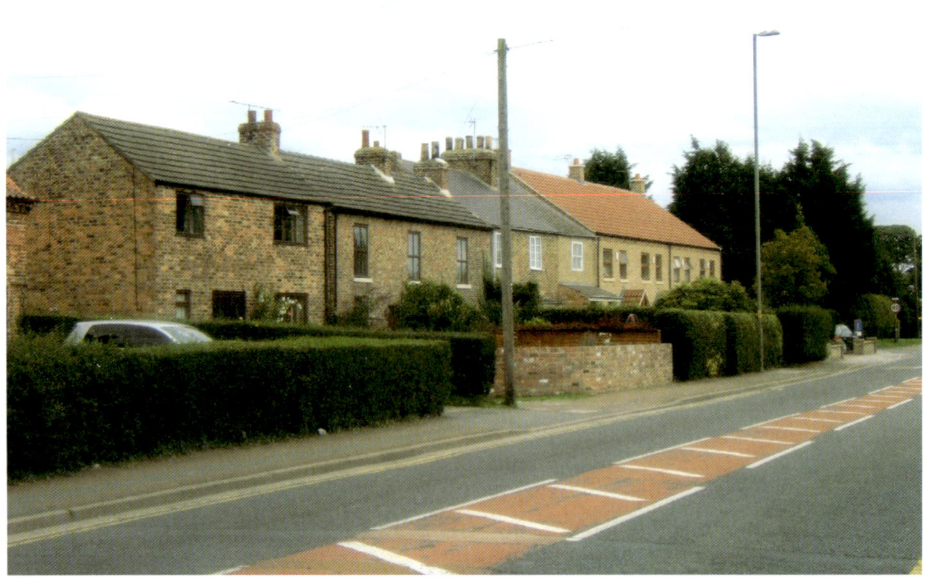

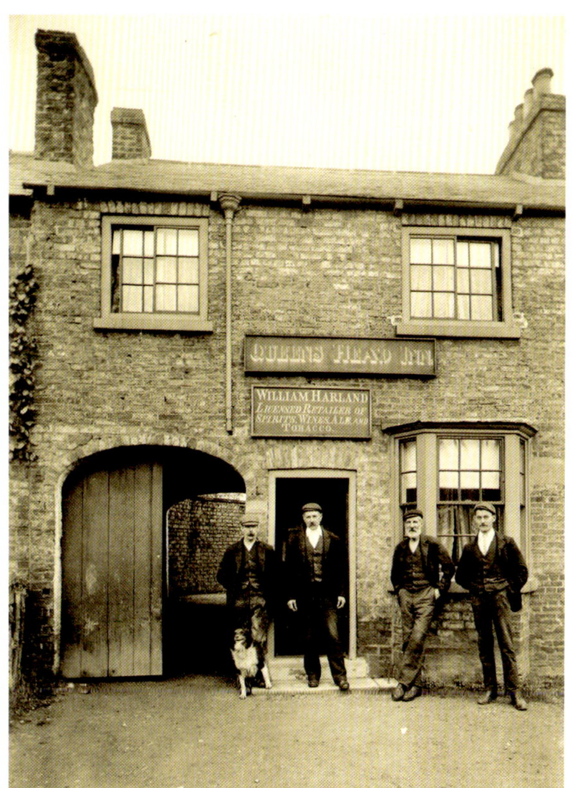

The Queen's Head Inn
William Harland stands in the doorway of the little public house of which he is the licensee and which is rather grandly styled the Queen's Head Inn. Really not much more than a one-room beer shop, it had earlier been known as the Jolly Sailor, though with no known nautical connection! It stood halfway along the east side of Barbeck. The house is still there, though with front bay removed and the archway converted into a porch.

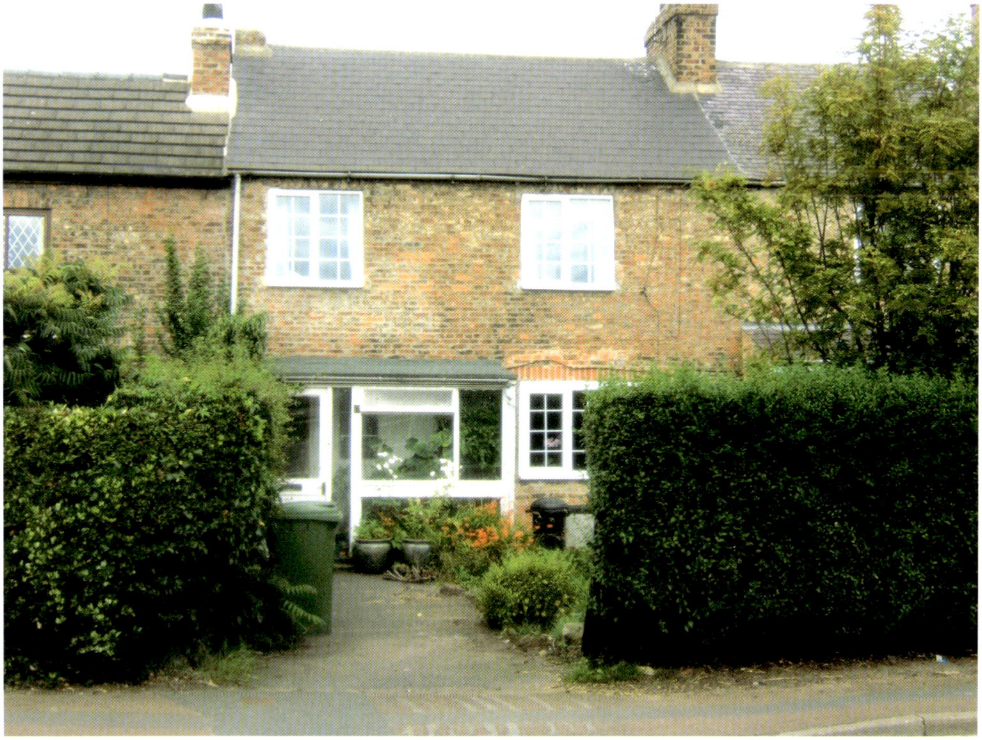

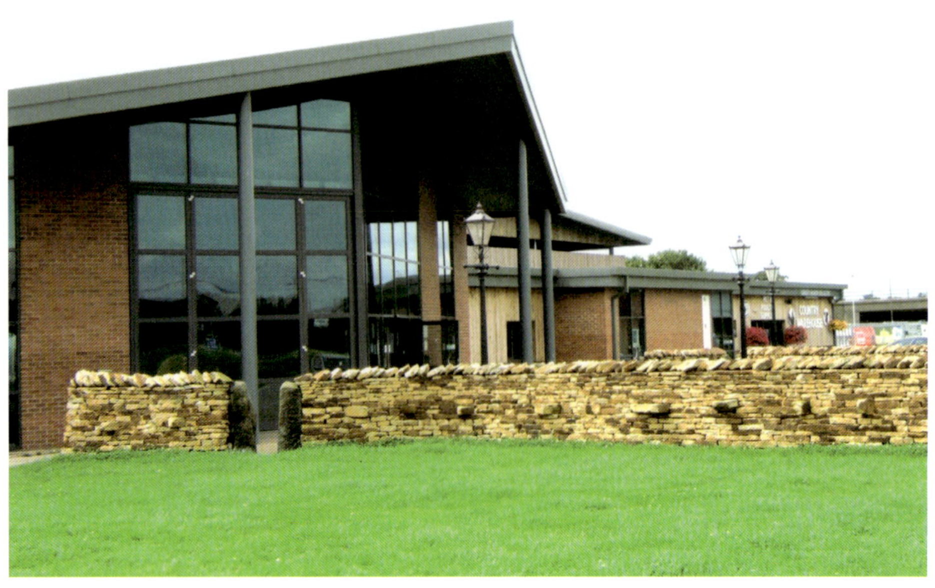

The New Auction Mart

The cattle trade has always been important to Thirsk. The fine new complex seen here has been opened off the York road, centred on a Cattle Auction Mart, with a range of associated facilities. The photograph below shows possibly the last open-air cattle sale on St James' Green in the early 1900s. The snow suggests that this was the final fair of the year, which fell in mid-December.

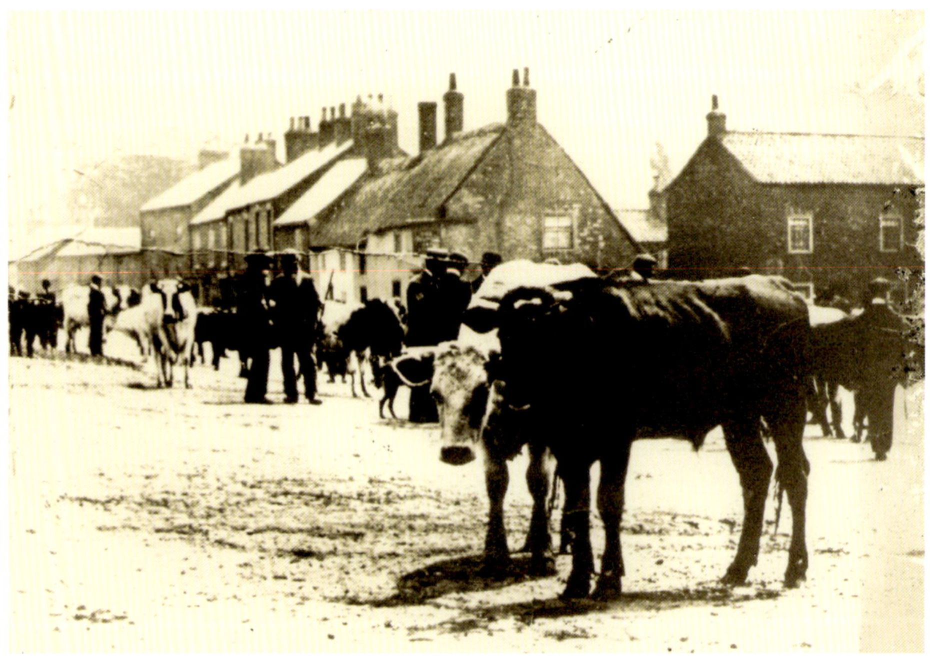

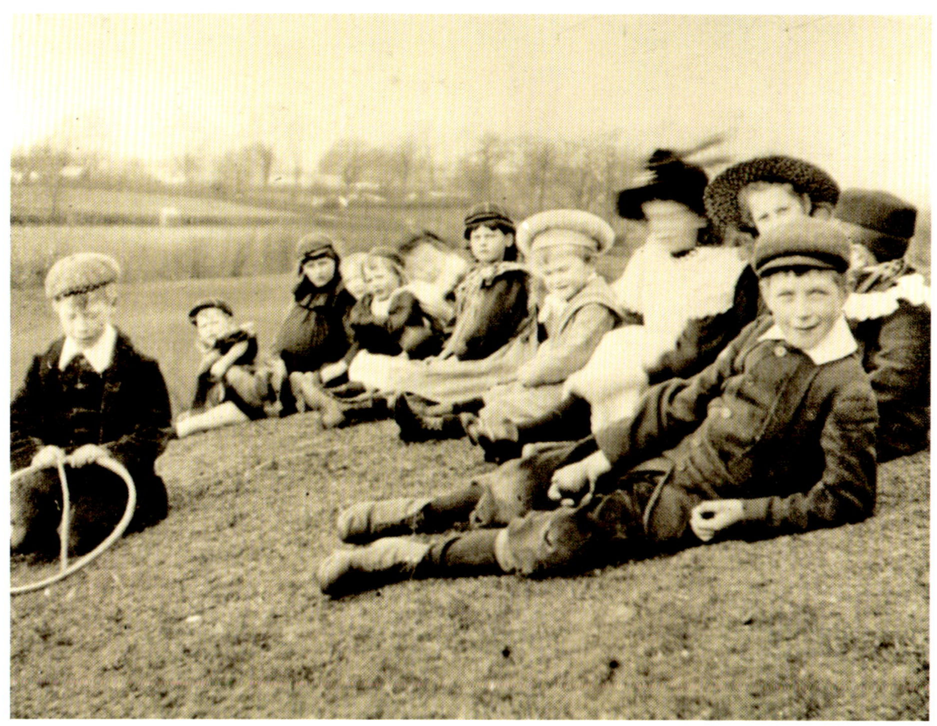

Pudding Pie Hill

These children are sitting on top of Pudding Pie Hill, an ancient burial mound in a field south of Sowerby. It is a grand spot for tobogganing in winter or egg-rolling at Easter. There is also a story that if, after a ritual seven-lap run round the hill, a knife is stuck in the top of the mound, one can hear the fairies! The mound is still impressive today, though a dual-carriageway now runs on an embankment behind it.

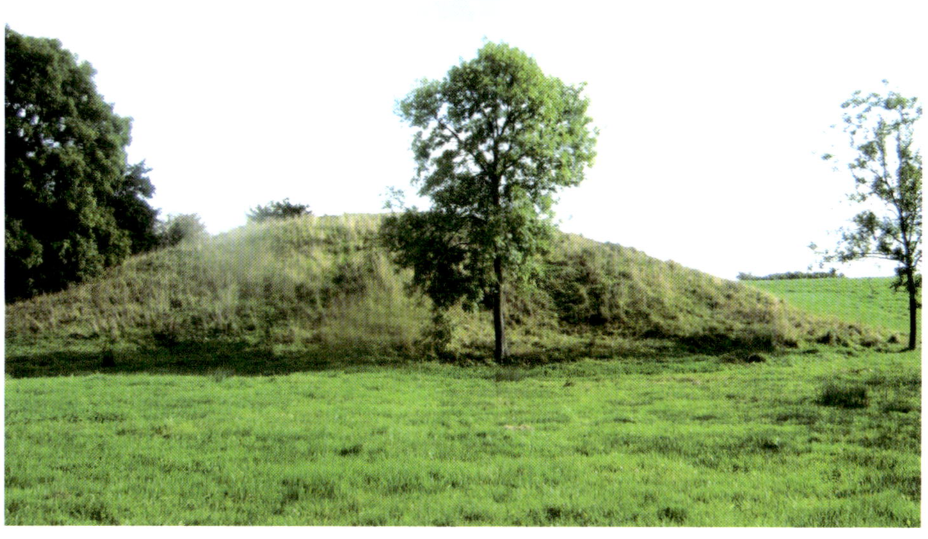

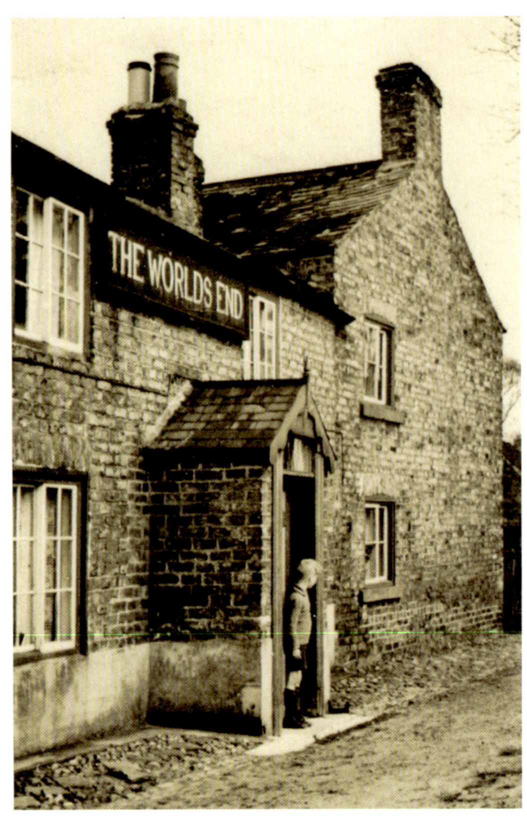

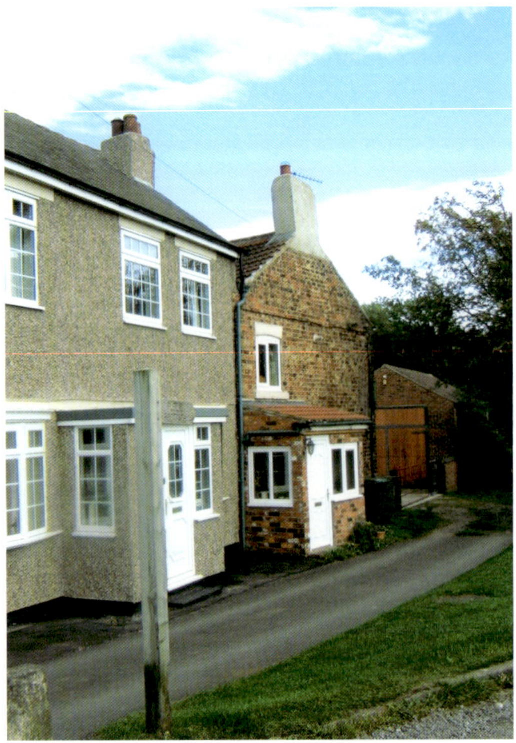

The World's End

This public house stood far down the road through Sowerby on the limits of the parish. So far as the villagers were concerned, their world ended here! The licensee probably drew his custom from waggoners and others halting at the ford which this house overlooked. The pub closed many years ago, but the spot still bears its name.

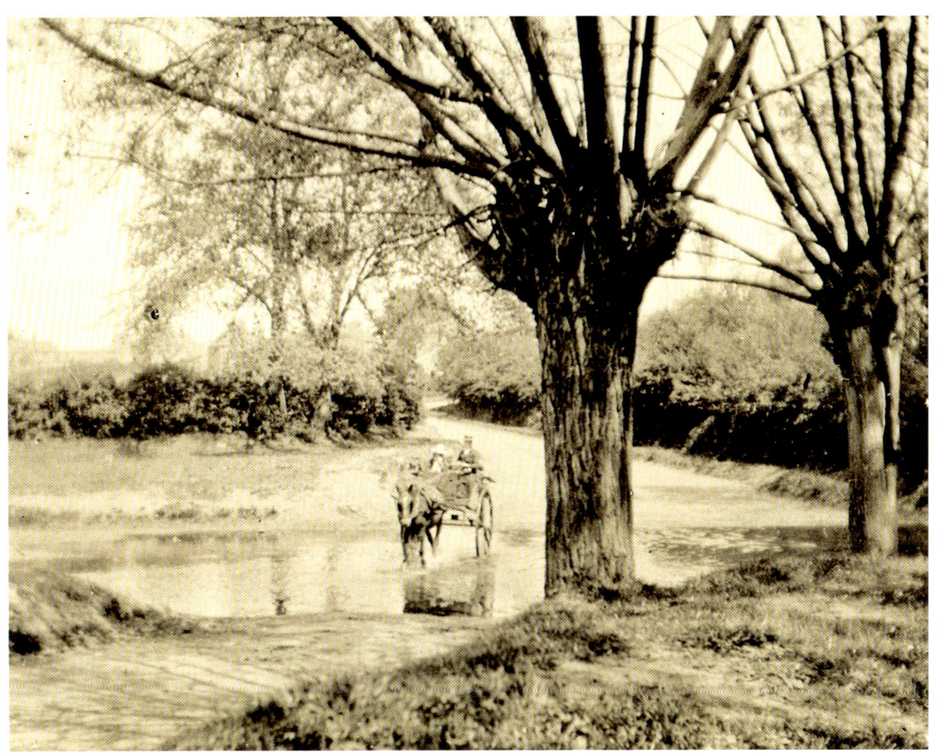

The Ford over the Cod Beck

In the days when transport was horse-drawn, the road south from Sowerby to Dalton did not merit a bridge here. The Cod Beck was crossed by a well-established ford. It was a picturesque spot, often painted or photographed. Modern traffic requires a bridge and the one here was recently rebuilt.

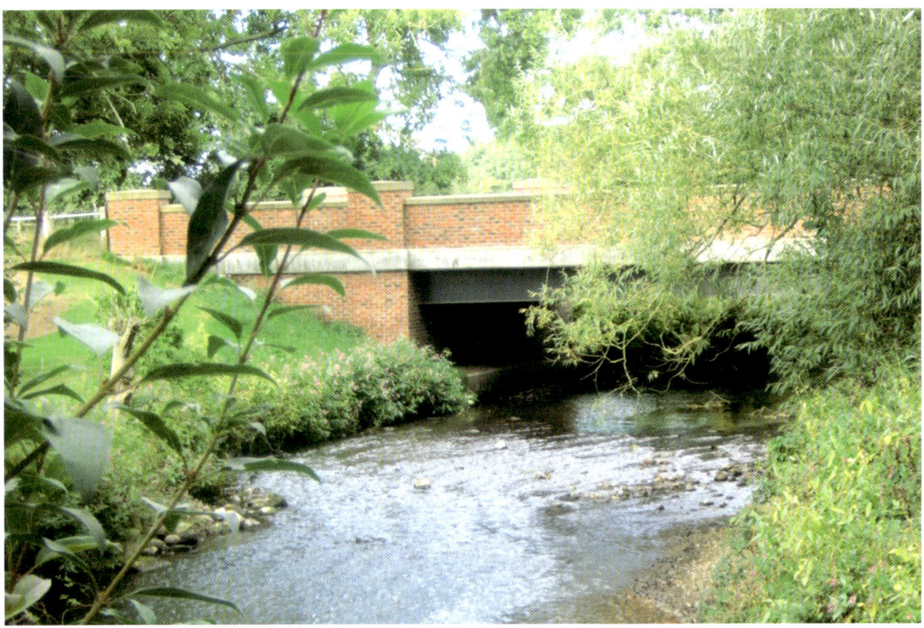

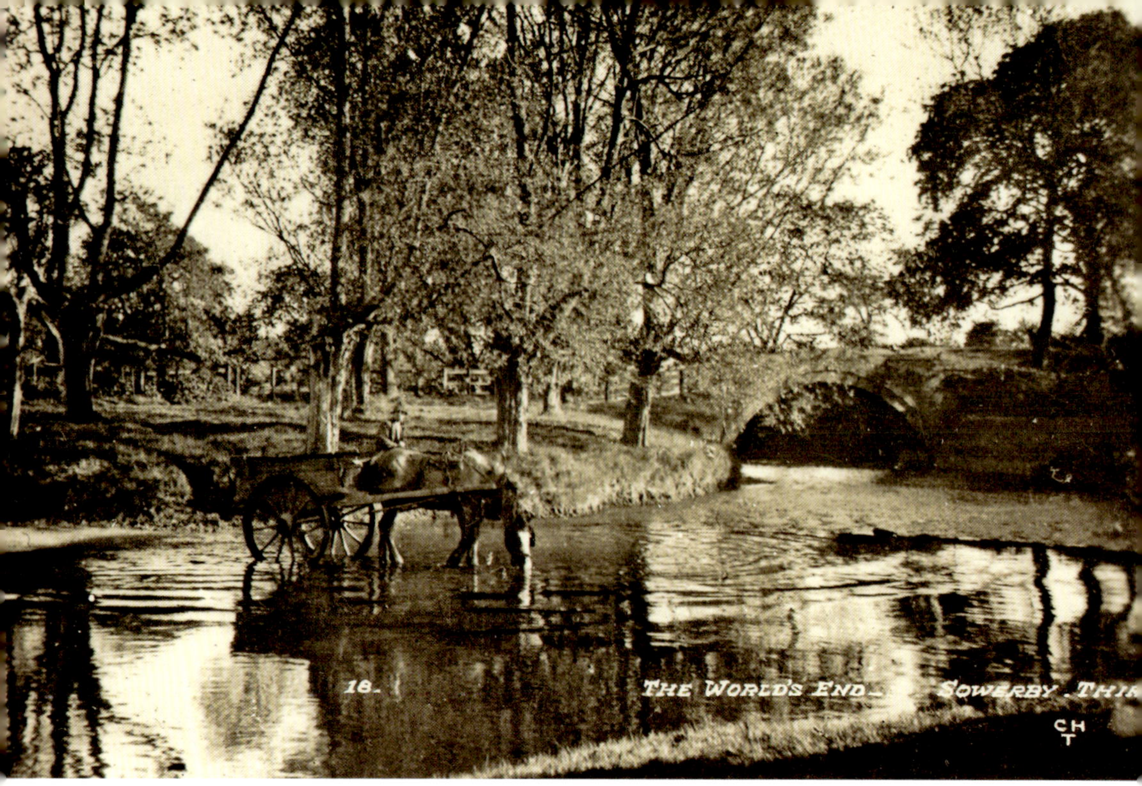

The Pack-Horse Bridge

Just beyond the ford there is an ancient pack-horse bridge. It is narrow to accommodate trains of ponies trotting in single file and the parapets are low so as not to impede the loads carried in packs or panniers slung on either side of the beasts. It, too, is a favourite subject for photographers.

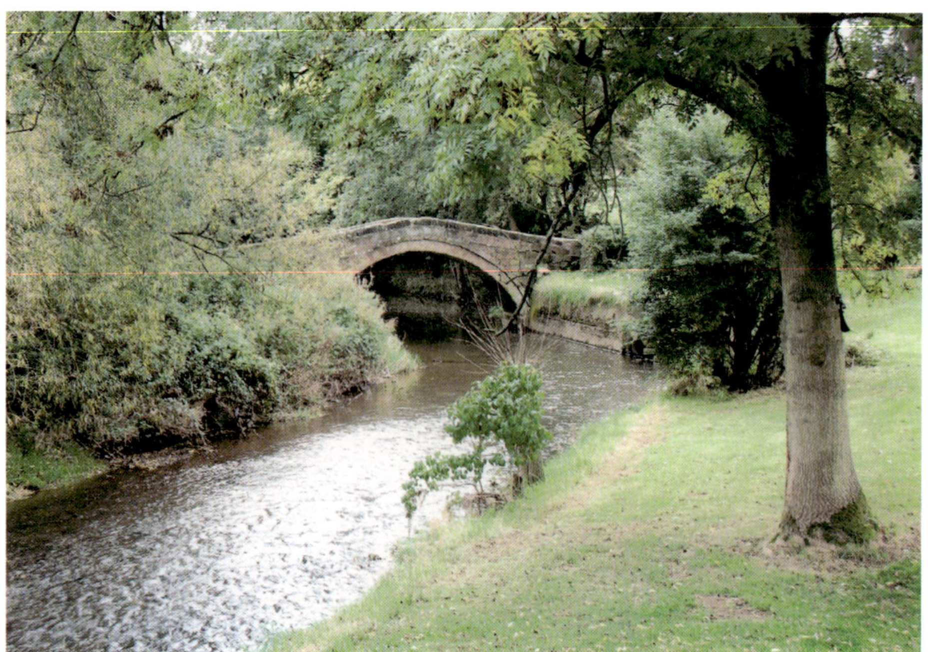

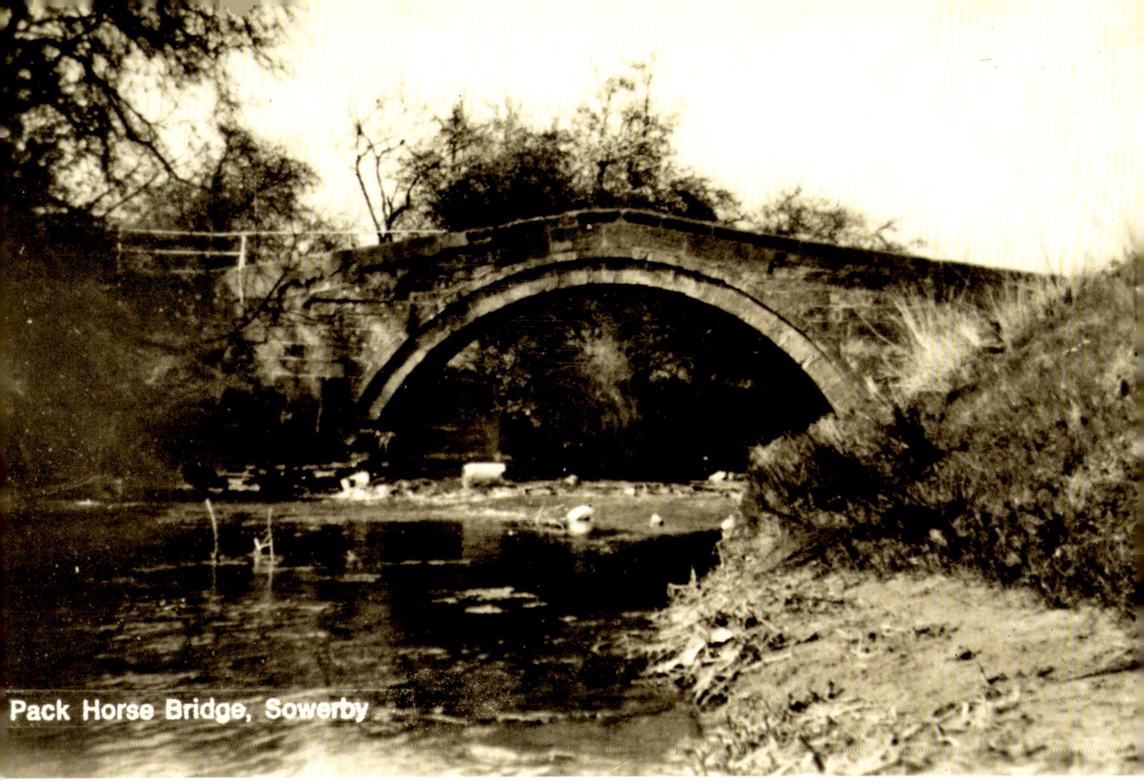

Pack Horse Bridge, Sowerby

The Bridge Under Repair

Another early view of the pack-horse bridge shows it in apparent good condition, but with the passing of the years the stonework has deteriorated. Restoration work has been carried out recently. These new stones will need time to blend in with the old.

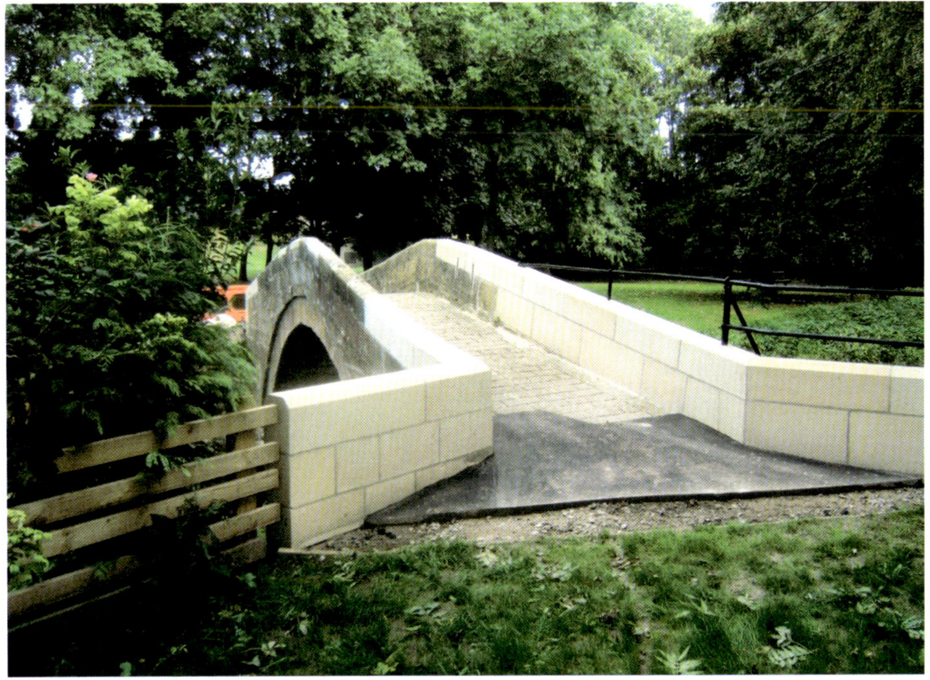

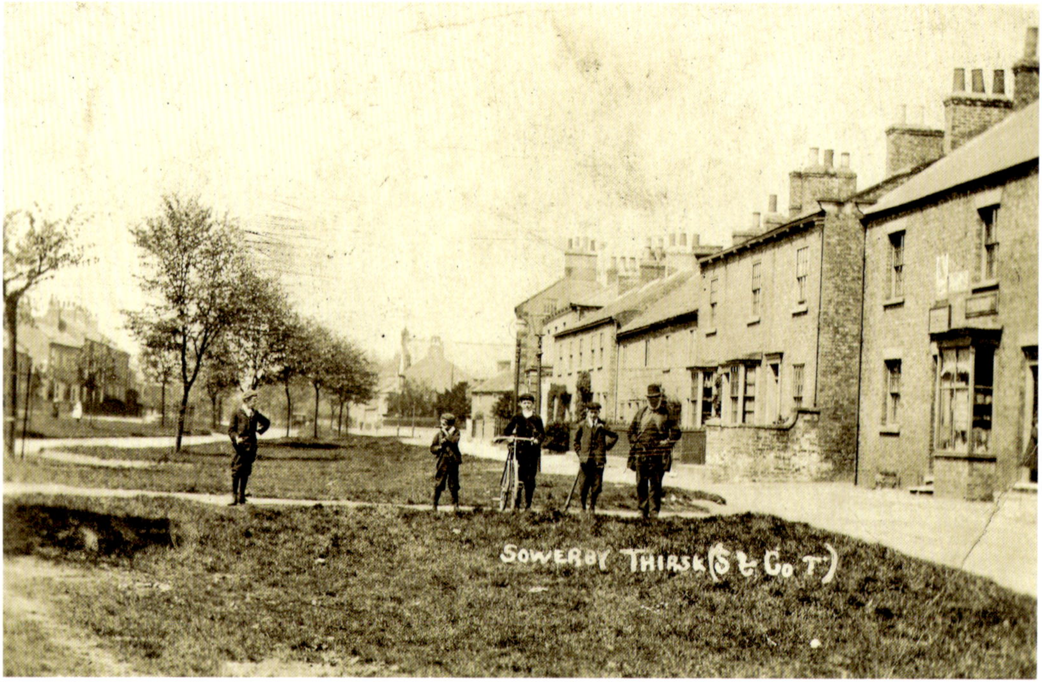

Sowerby from the South

This view of Sowerby must date from the 1890s. The avenue of lime trees, still not much more than saplings, was planted down Front Street in 1887 to commemorate the Golden Jubilee of Queen Victoria. The view then is impossible today, with the limes now in full maturity.

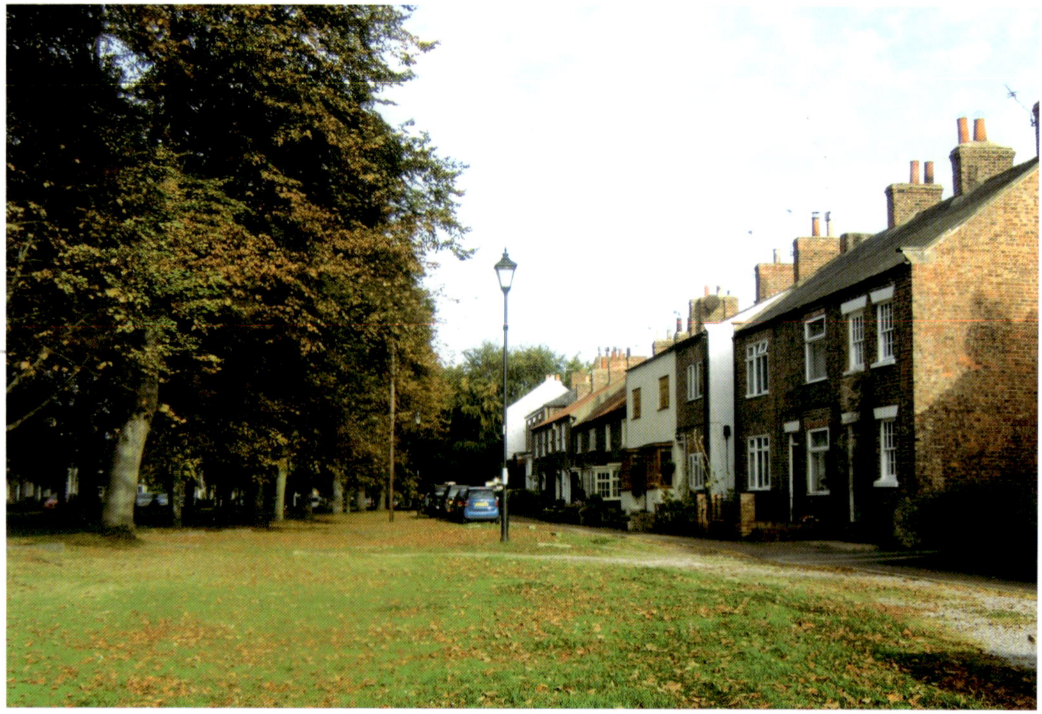

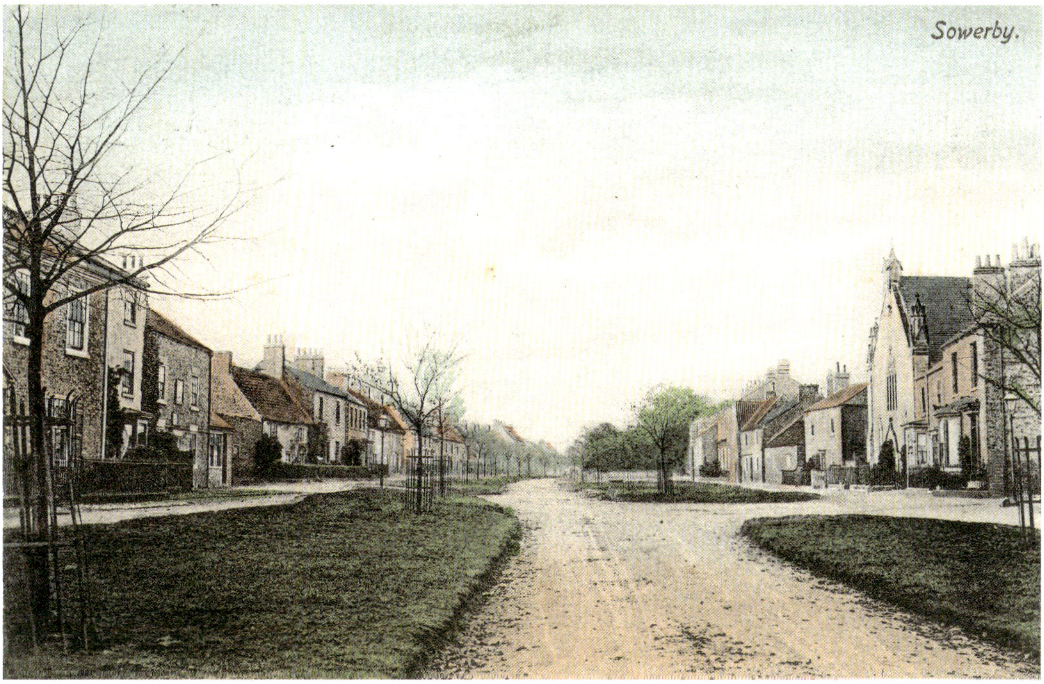

Sowerby.

Sowerby Methodist Chapel

The Wesleyan Methodist Chapel was built here in 1865 and stands just beyond the point where Blakey Lane, on the right, emerges into Front Street. As is the case with pictures on the page opposite, the mature trees now obscure the view north.

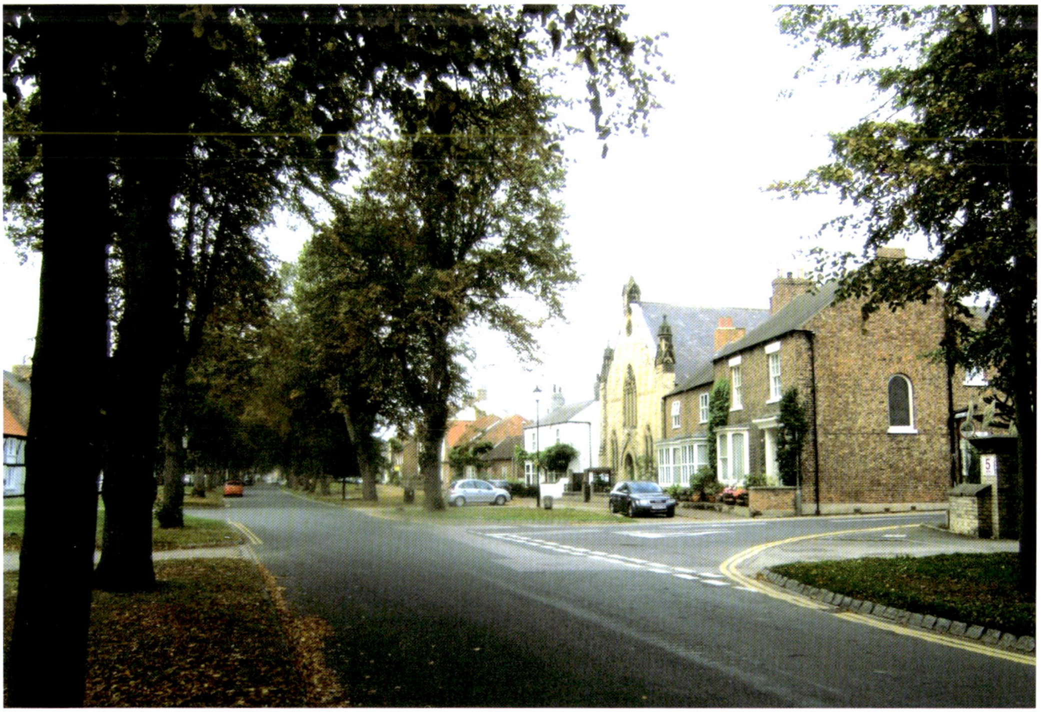

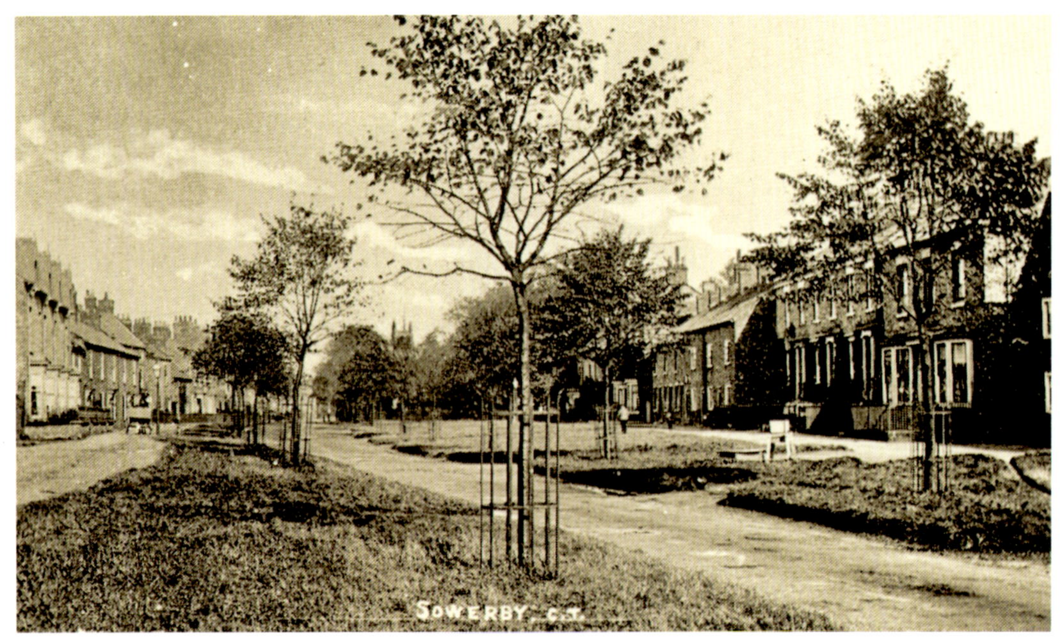

The View North up Front Street

Sowerby Front Street is one long village green; there is no centre as such, with St Oswald's parish church set at the north end, the tower just visible in the postcard view. There has always been a social mix in the houses here, with cottages and workshops interspersed with the neat little villas which nineteenth-century historian William Grainge thought gave the village 'quite an aristocratic air'.

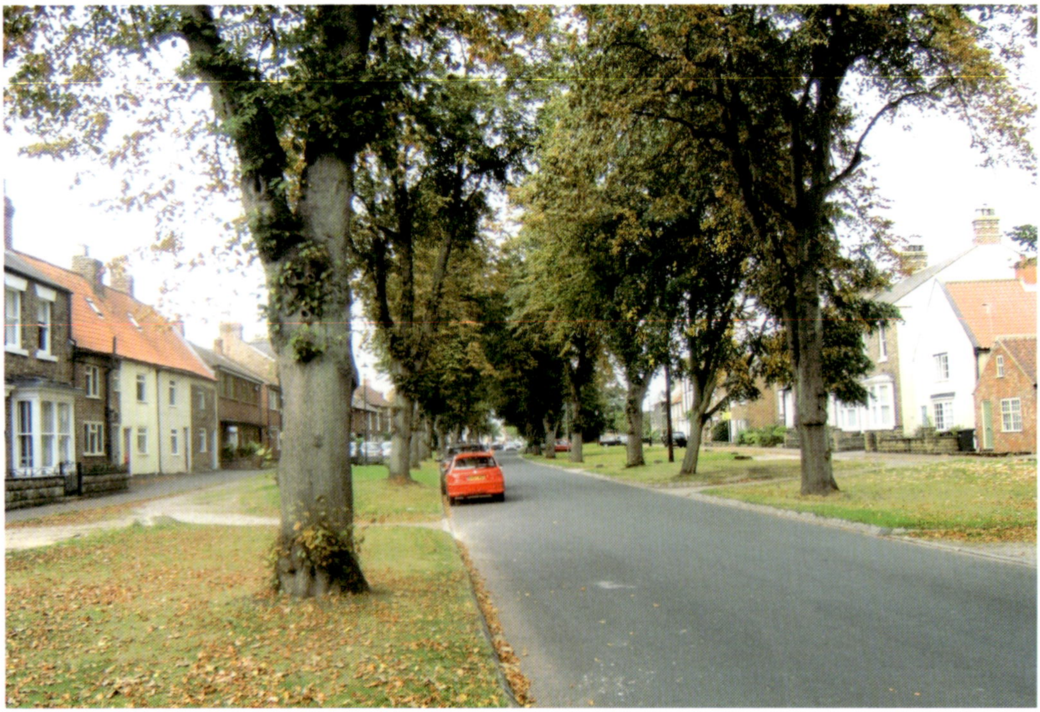

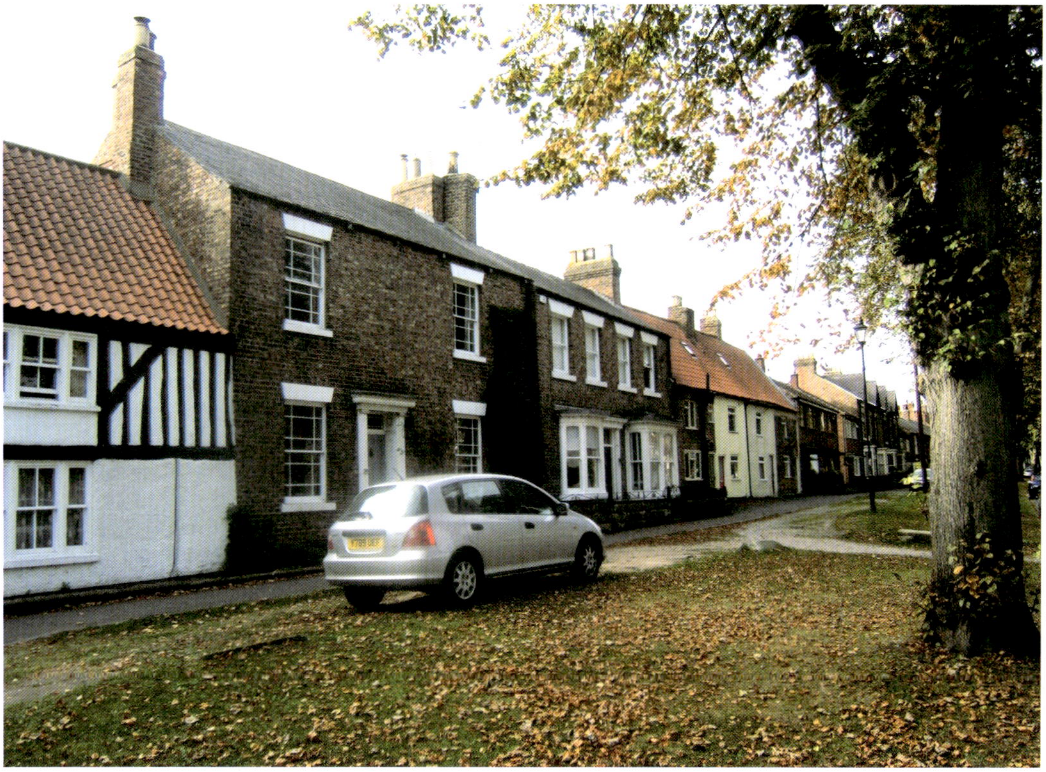

Oxmoor Farm

This house, just visible on the extreme left in the old postcard view, is one of the oldest in the village. It was not until the nineteenth-century render was stripped from the outside that the timber frame was revealed. The pitch of the roof which is now clad in pantiles shows that it was originally thatched. The same is true of the red-roofed house seen a few doors along.

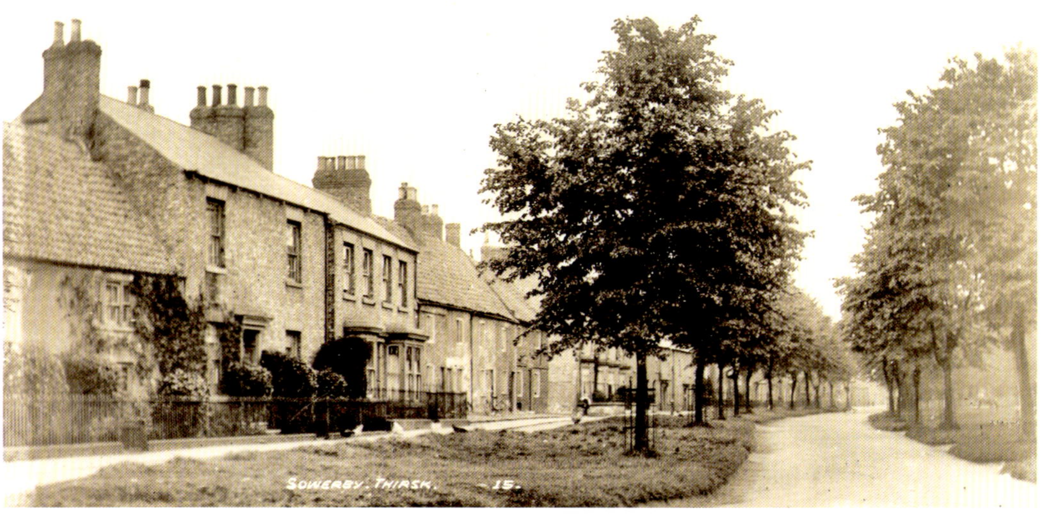

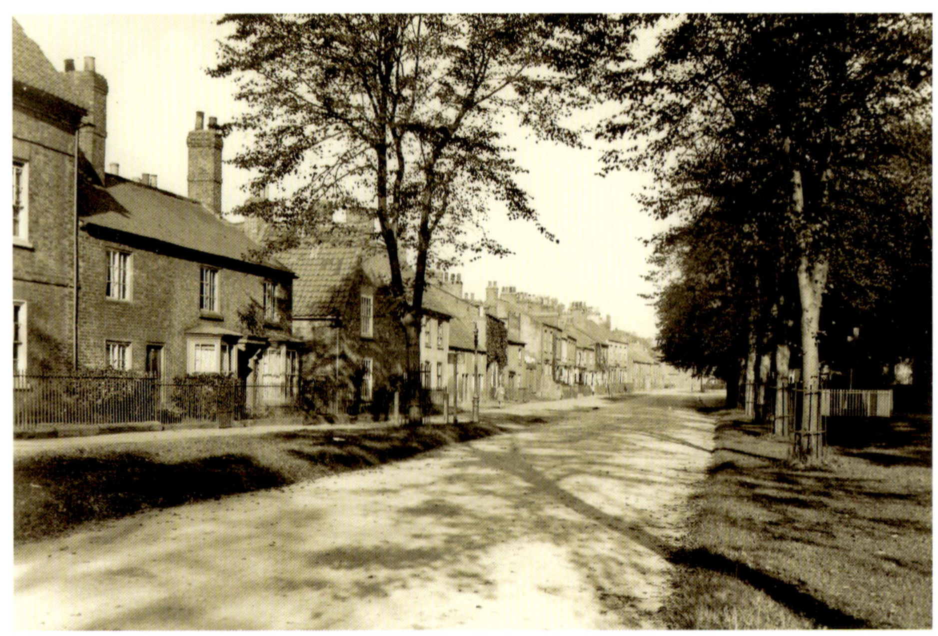

The North End of the Avenue

As one approaches St Oswald's church, the Green and the avenue of lime trees come to an end. The wall of the churchyard is more clearly visible in the colour shot, but apart from the road surface and the vehicles in the distance, the appearance of this part of the village has changed little.

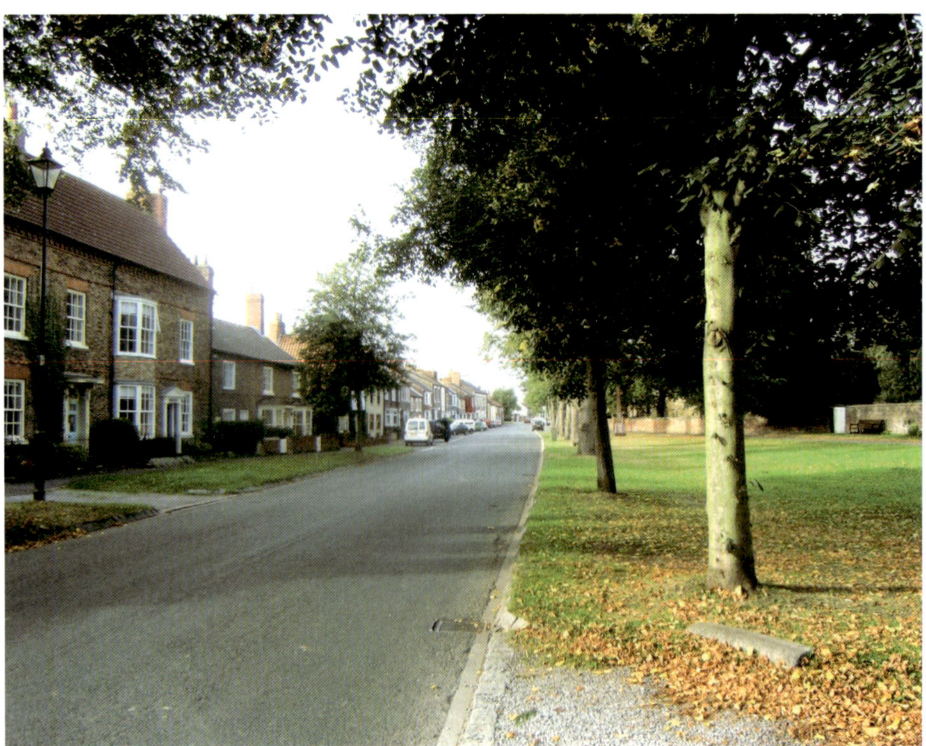

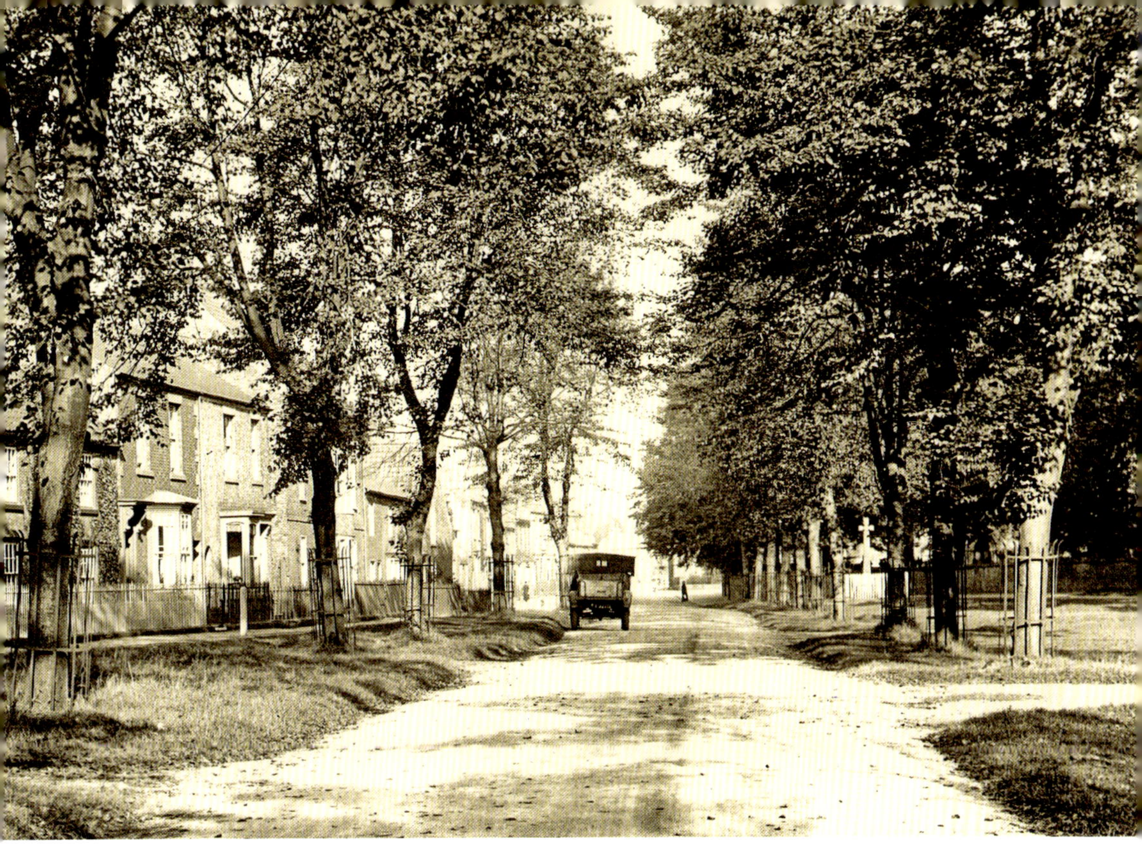

The War Memorial

When the picture above was taken in the 1920s, the village war memorial had not long been erected. Still fenced off, it stands out among the trees at the top of the Green, near the churchyard wall. The picture below shows the memorial in November 2009 after the wreath-laying ceremony. The names of those who died in the Second World War have been added on the column.

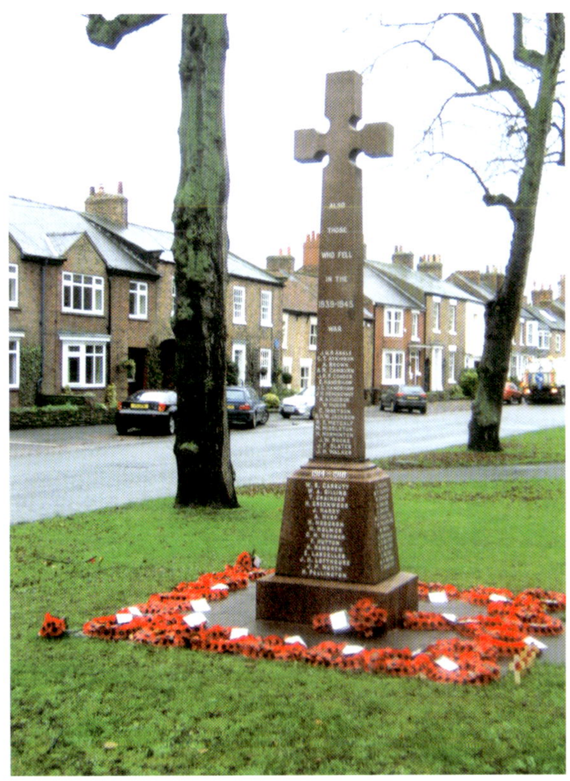

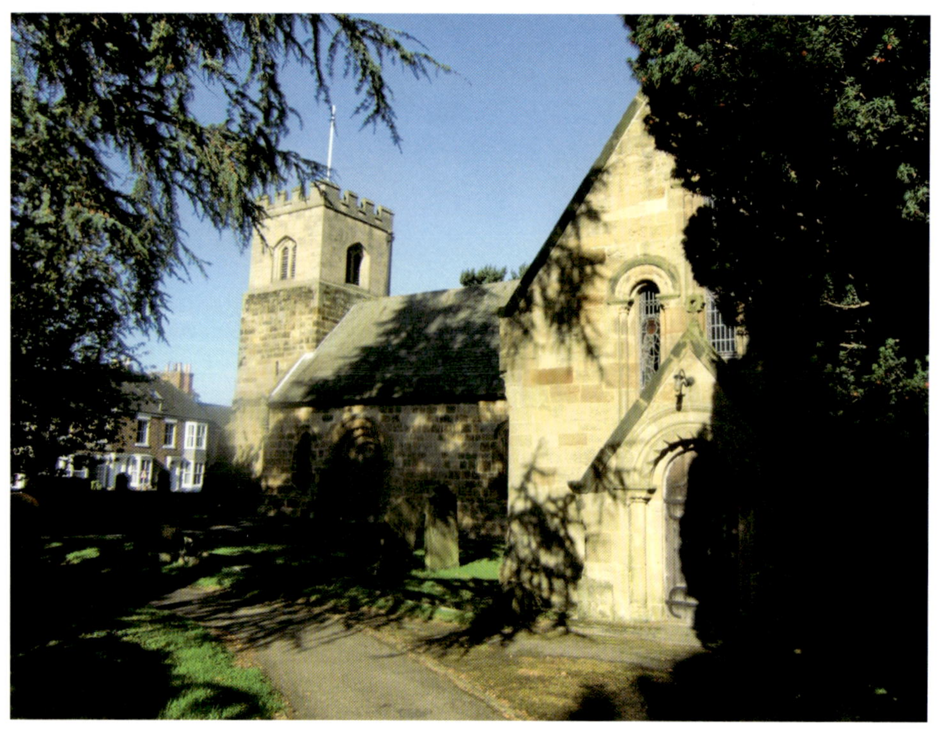

St Oswald's Parish Church

St Oswald's church was heavily restored in the 1840s but retains some fine Norman work, notably the South Porch. The Victorian architect Lamb added a central lantern, which makes the interior surprisingly bright. Comparison between the two photographs shows that the pinnacles on the tower have been removed — for reasons of safety — and that, as elsewhere, the trees have grown to the point where they obscure the view.

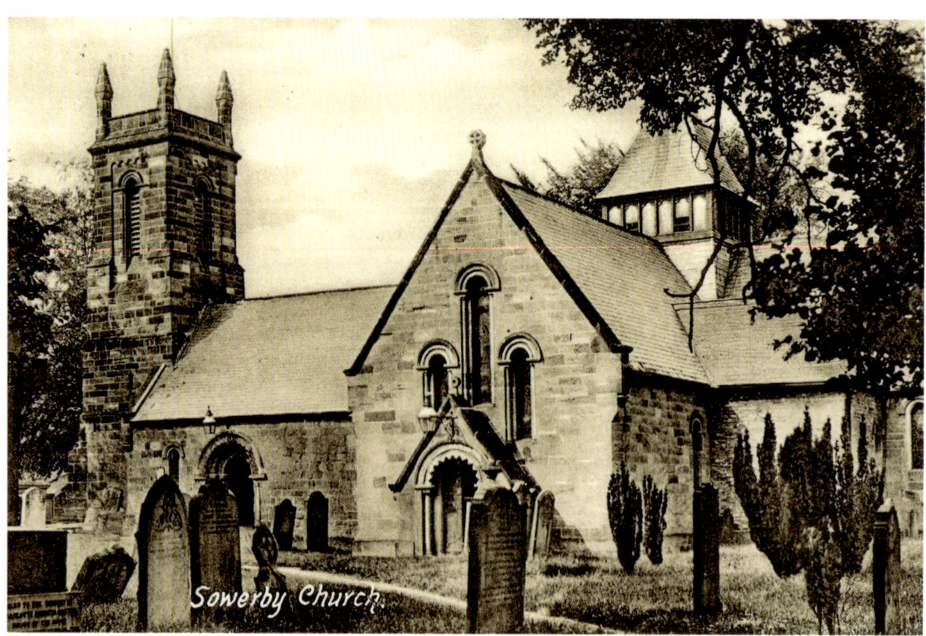

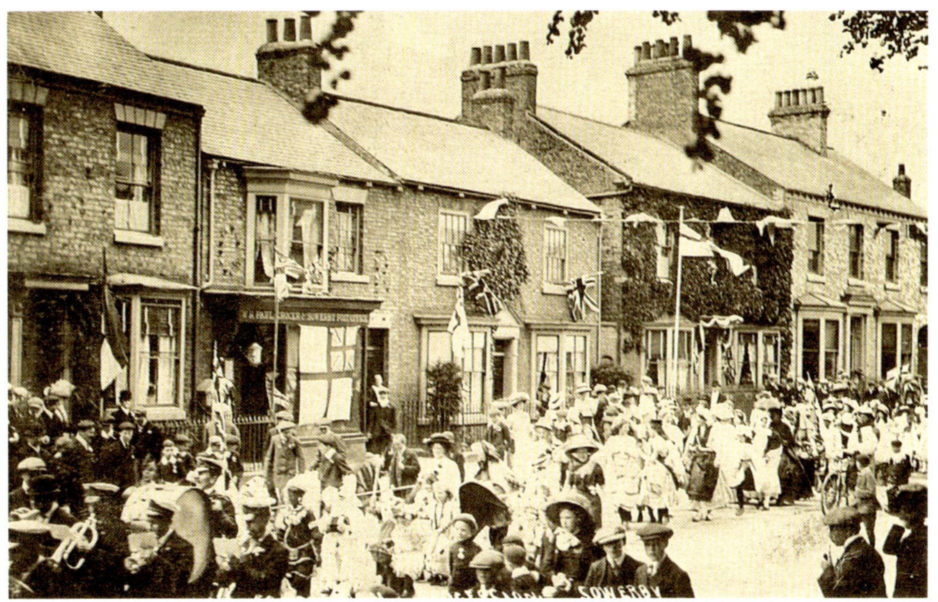

Sowerby Post Office

The postcard is marked 'Coronation Procession'. It is not clear whether this was for Edward VII in 1902 or George V in 1911. In either case, the important detail is the shop the procession is passing. It displays a large White Ensign in the window. It is Sowerby Post Office, a centre of village life, which survived until 2008 when it was closed against the wishes of the whole local population. It is now returned to private residence; only the letterbox survives!

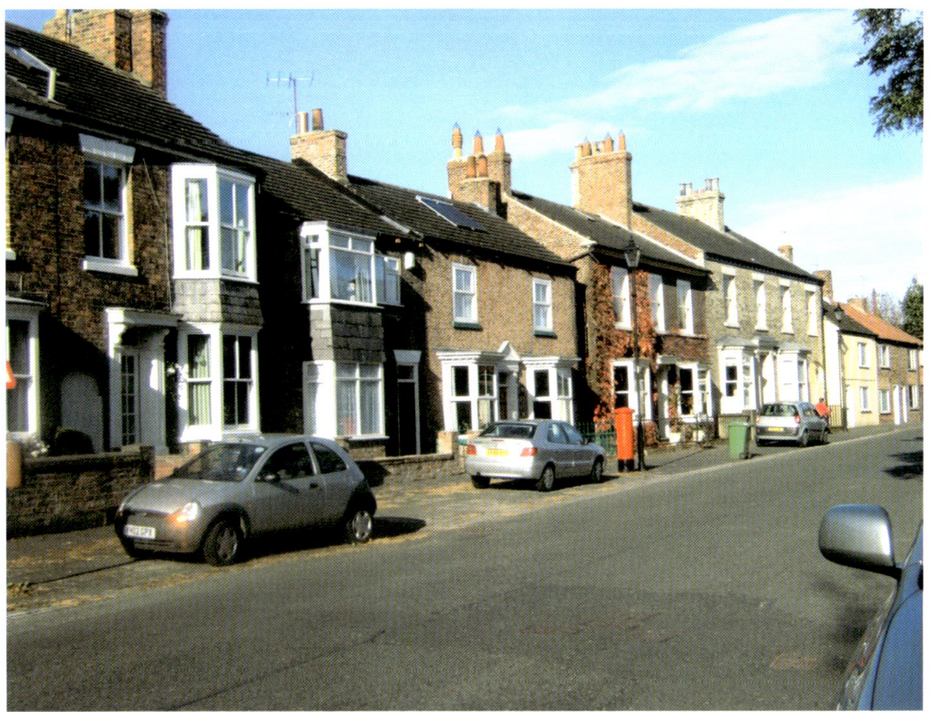

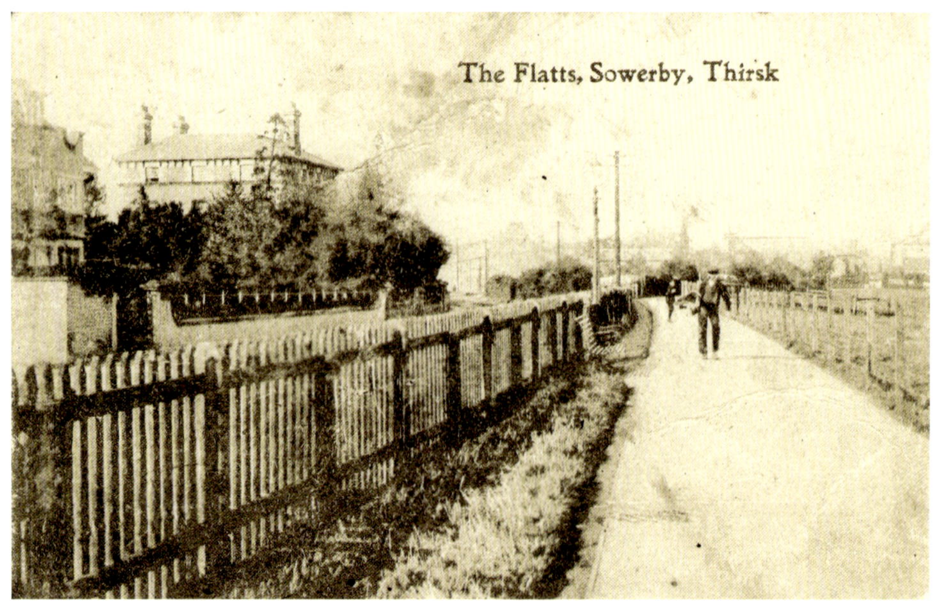

Footpath Past the Flatts

The footpath featured here runs from Sowerby into Thirsk alongside the Flatts, an open space preserved for the benefit of all for pleasure and recreation. The grassland of the Flatts has its origin in medieval plough land that was eventually given over to pasture, thus still displaying the ridge and furrow patterns of earlier cultivation. The footpath itself has not changed in a century, though it is no longer fenced off from the road.

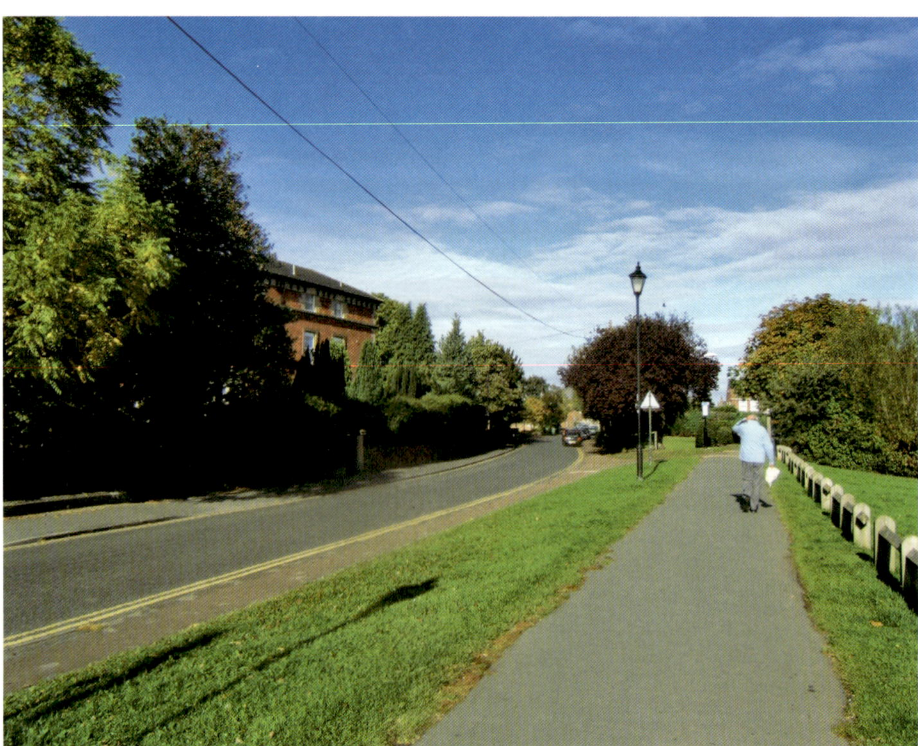

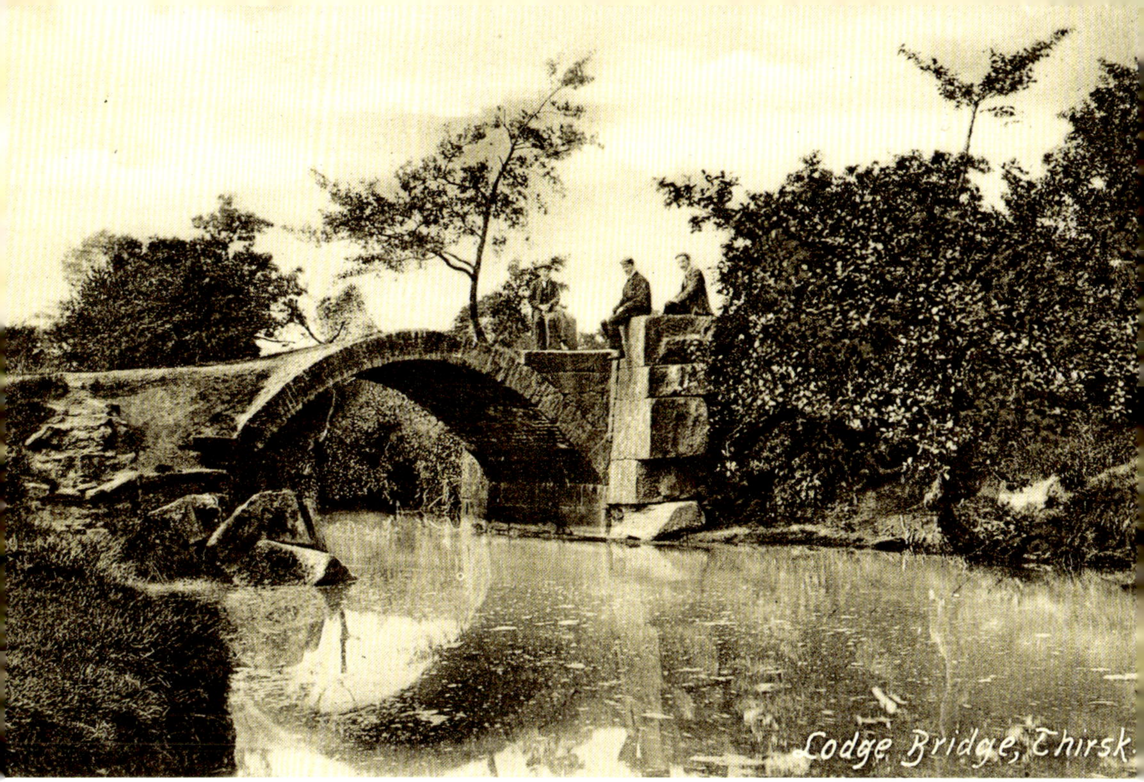

Lodge Bridge, Thirsk

The Lock Bridge

In 1767, a project was launched to make the Cod Beck into a canal that would join the Swale at Topcliffe and hence link Thirsk to the navigable Ouse, the Humber and the sea! Work began with the building of a canal basin and wharf close to the bridge in the town, the straightening of the Cod Beck as far as Sowerby and the construction of the first lock. Funds ran out and the scheme foundered. Some of the stone for the unfinished lock was used to build a bridge over the beck which stands to this day, a picturesque feature and the goal for a walk across the Flatts.

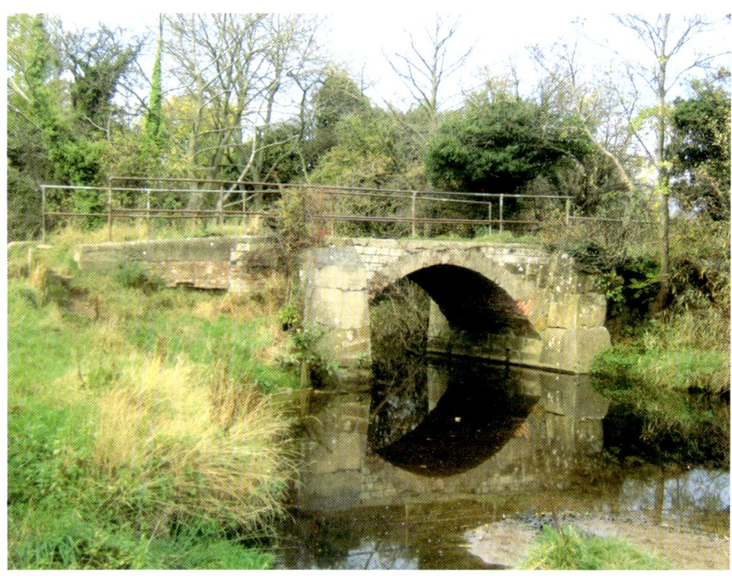

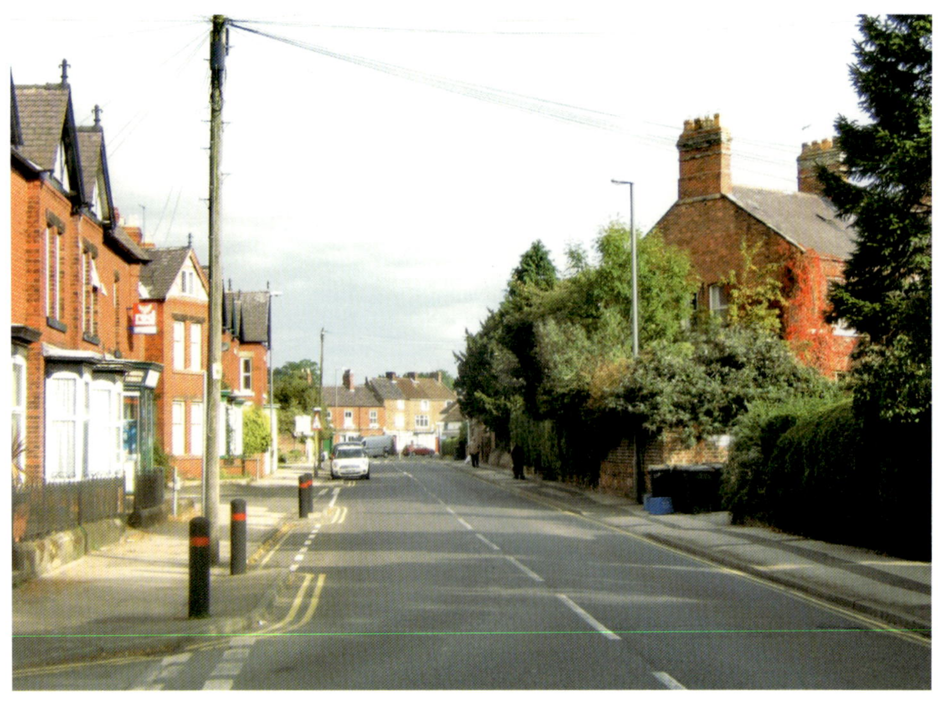

Topcliffe Road

These two photographs show that apart from the road markings and the street furniture, little has changed here. This is a place where Sowerby and Thirsk merge. It was developed in late Victorian times as the growth of industry close to the railway yard brought employment and prosperity.

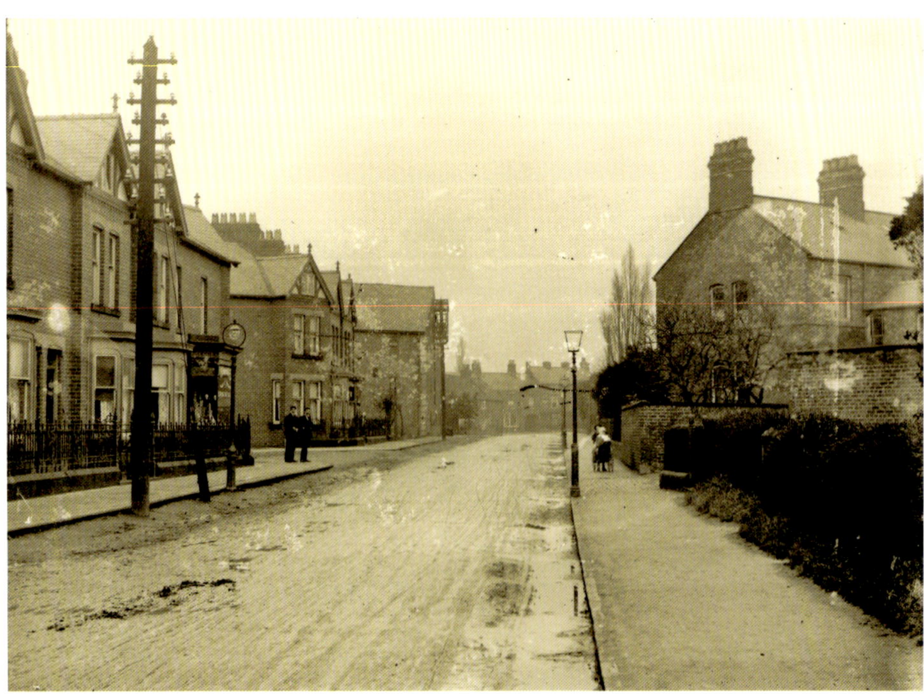

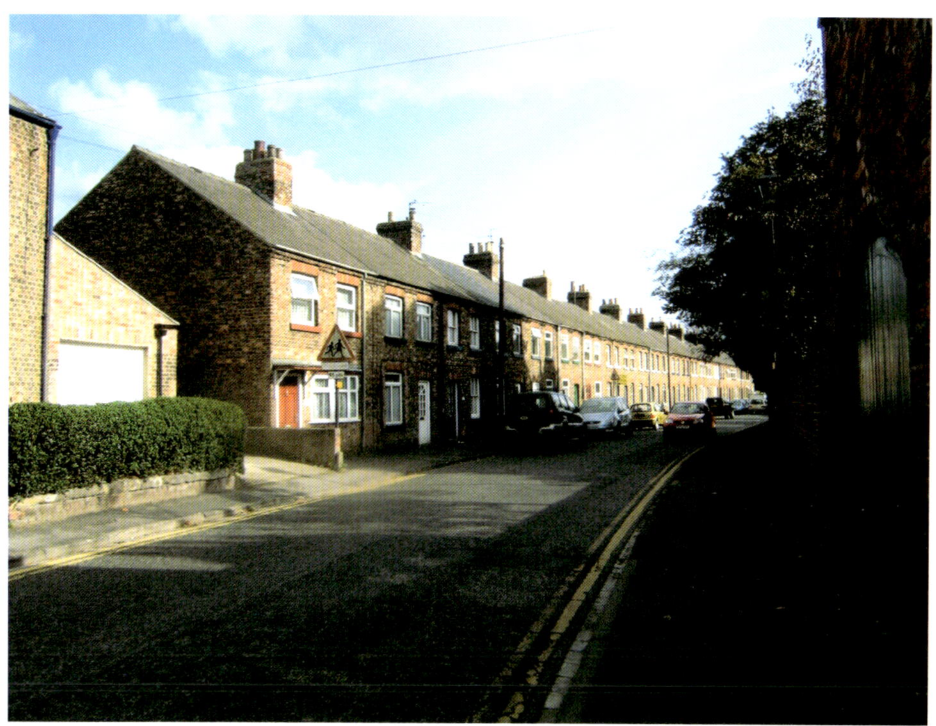

Victory Row

The name of this terrace of cottages goes back to the days when landowners expected their tenants to vote for them or for their candidate in parliamentary elections. Known first as 'Blue Row', this became Victory Row when the 'Blue' party won! The modern picture is a good advertisement for UPVC windows and doors. Note the presence of two postmen in the earlier scene.

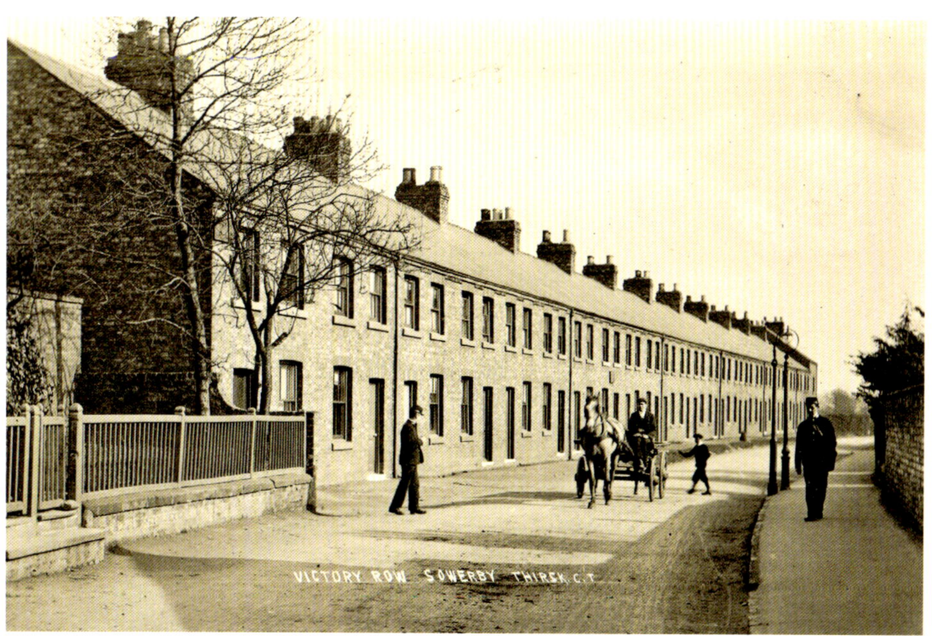

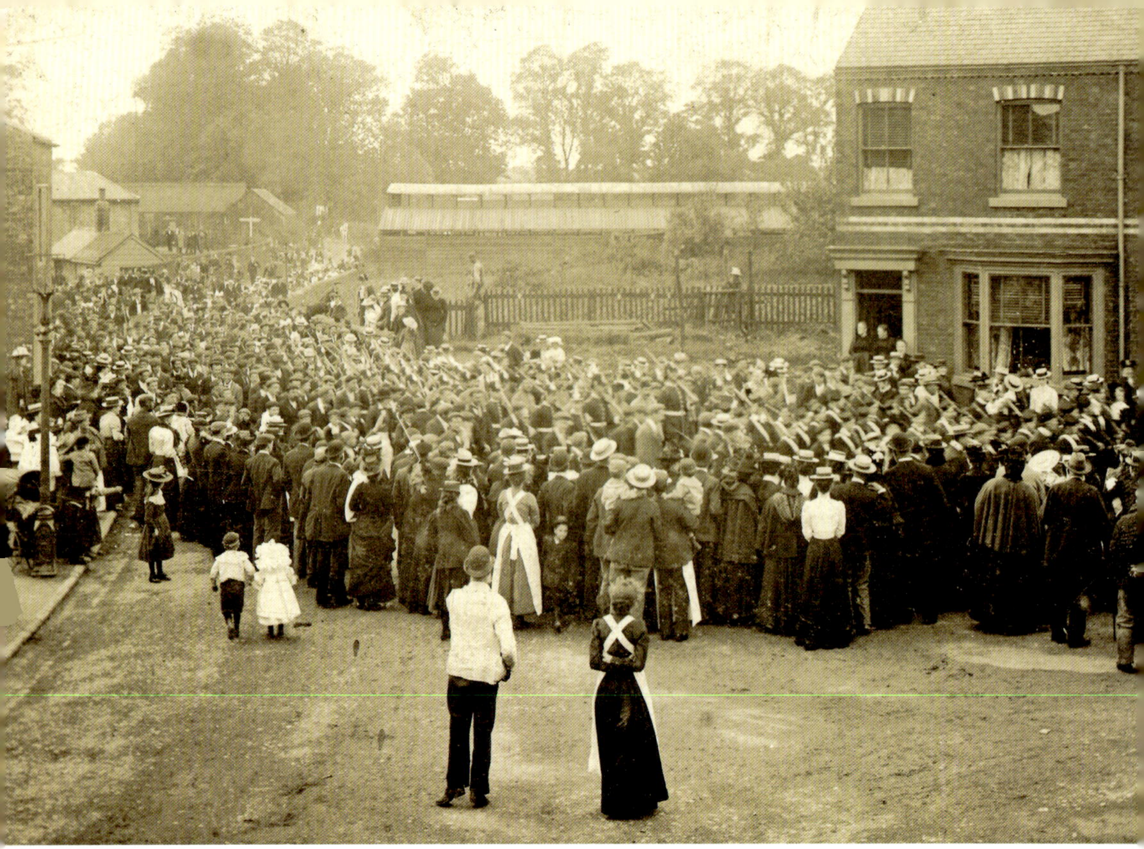

Procession at Town End

It is hard to realise that these two pictures show the same spot at Town End. This junction, where four roads meet, is now a mini-roundabout at the end of Westgate. Most of the buildings seen in the first photo have been removed to open up what was then a blind corner. The long building in the background was a cattle mart, standing where today there is the Tesco filling station. Opposite was the railway goods yard, with Bamlett's engineering works beyond.

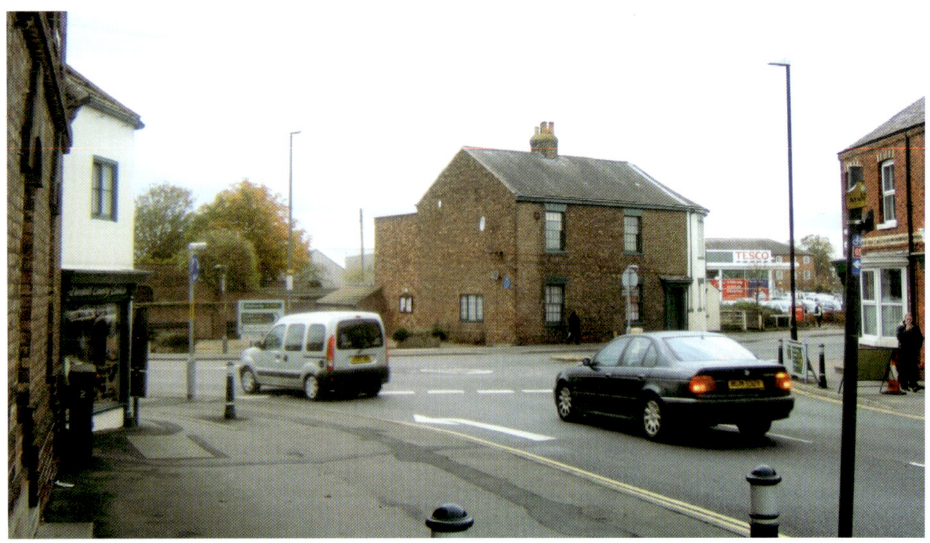

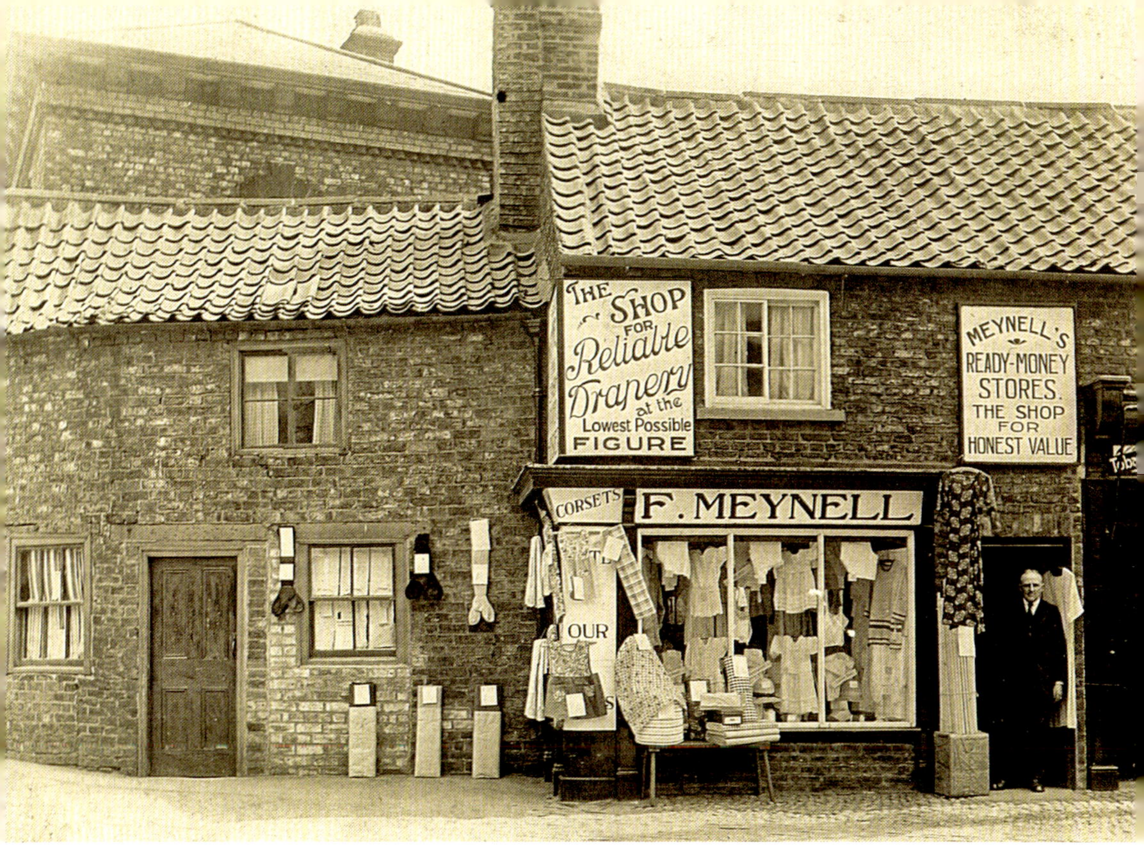

Meynell's Drapery Shop

Fred Meynell stands at the door of his shop on the corner of Westgate. His business is well advertised and his goods are amply displayed both in the window and outside, as was usual in the 1920s. These old premises have had modern shop-fronts fitted, but little has changed above that. The building behind the shop was the town police station but has now been on the market for development.

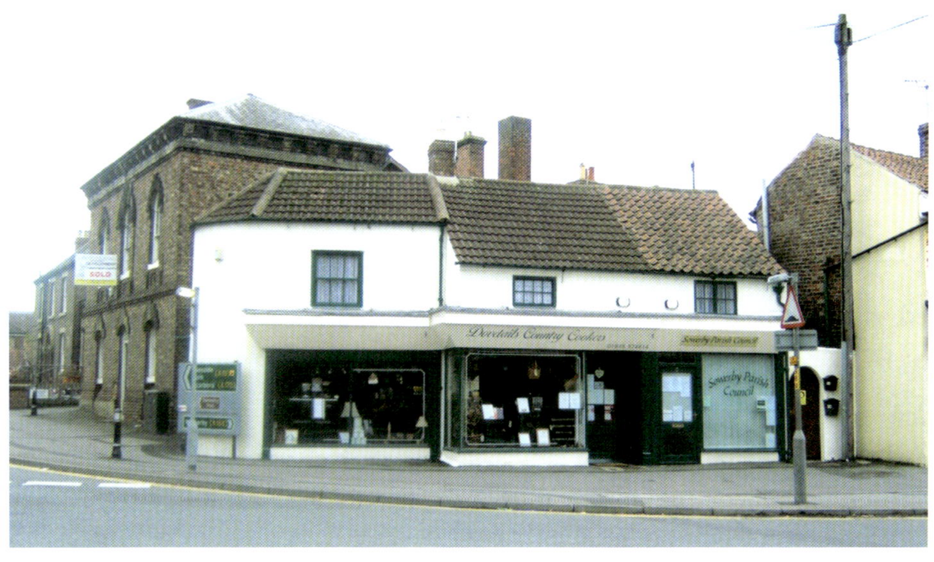

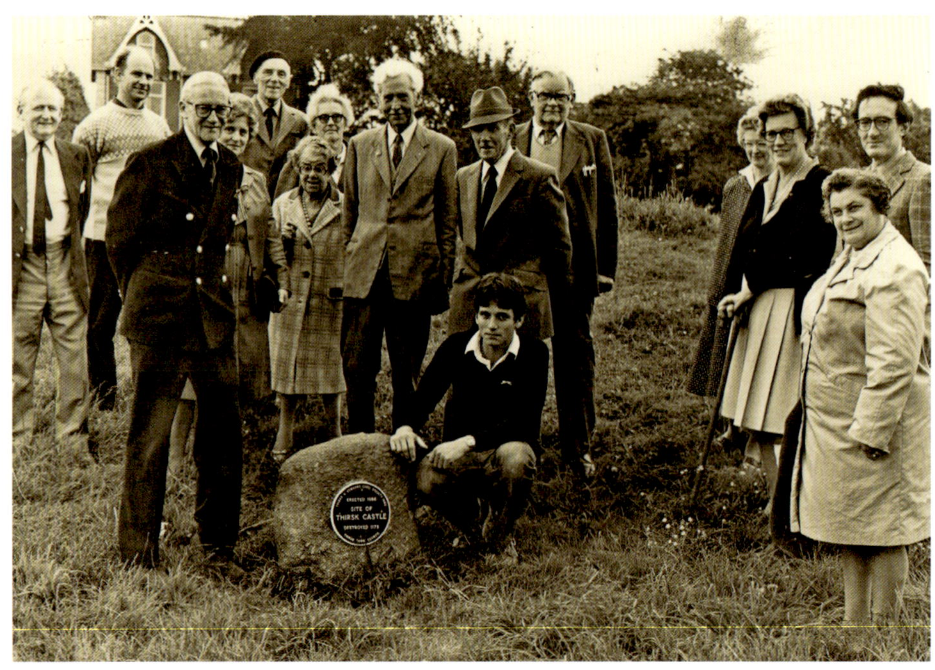

Castle Garth

Castle Garth is the site of a Norman stronghold, which was built in 1086 and destroyed less than a century later. The only remains are part of the castle mound and a section of the ditch and rampart defences. In 1982, the Civic Society marked the spot with a plaque. The late Major Peter Bell, lord of the manor and owner of the land, is the figure on the left in this group of members of the Society. In 1994, a routine dig took place prior to the installation of new switchgear for the electricity company. The discovery of an early Anglo-Saxon burial ground brought further distinction to this area, now set out with information boards.

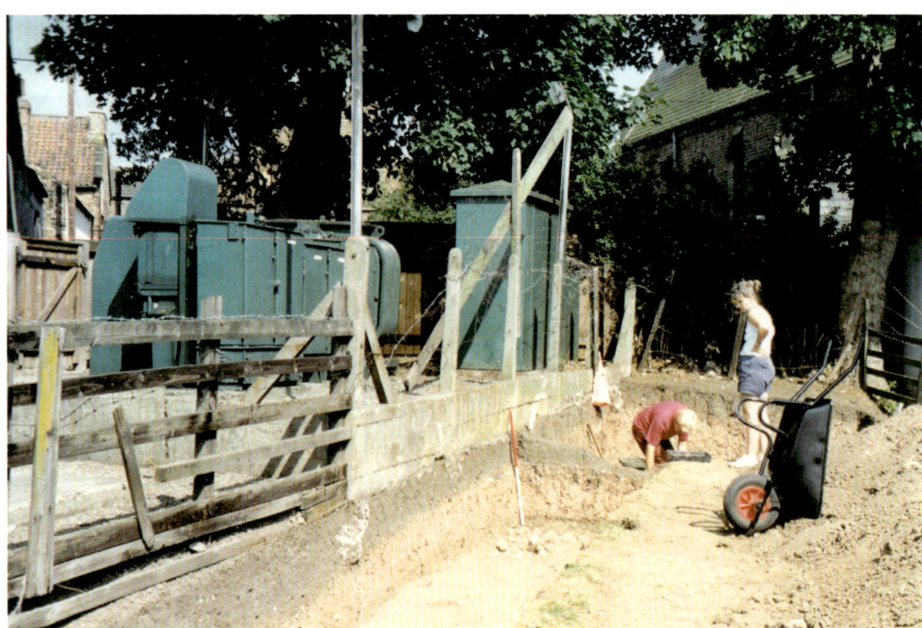

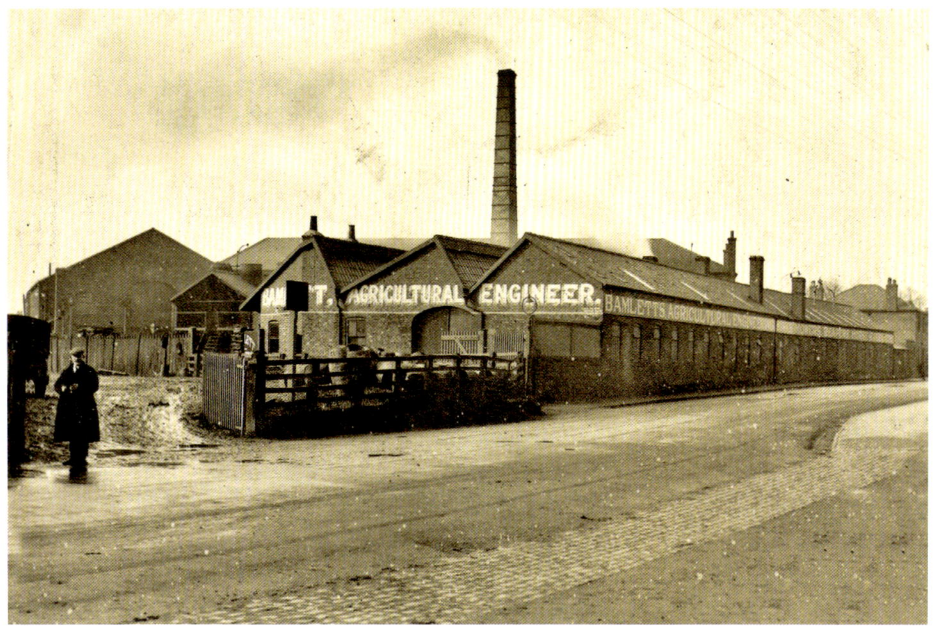

Bamlett's Agricultural Engineering Works

Adam Carlisle Bamlett came to Thirsk in 1860 and set up an engineering works next to the railway goods depot on Station Road. For a century, the grass cutters, reapers and other machines built at Bamlett's went all over the world. Sadly, the company suffered the fate of many British firms in the 1960s, struggled for some years and finally closed in 1985. The site was cleared save for a remaining office block. The rest is Tesco.

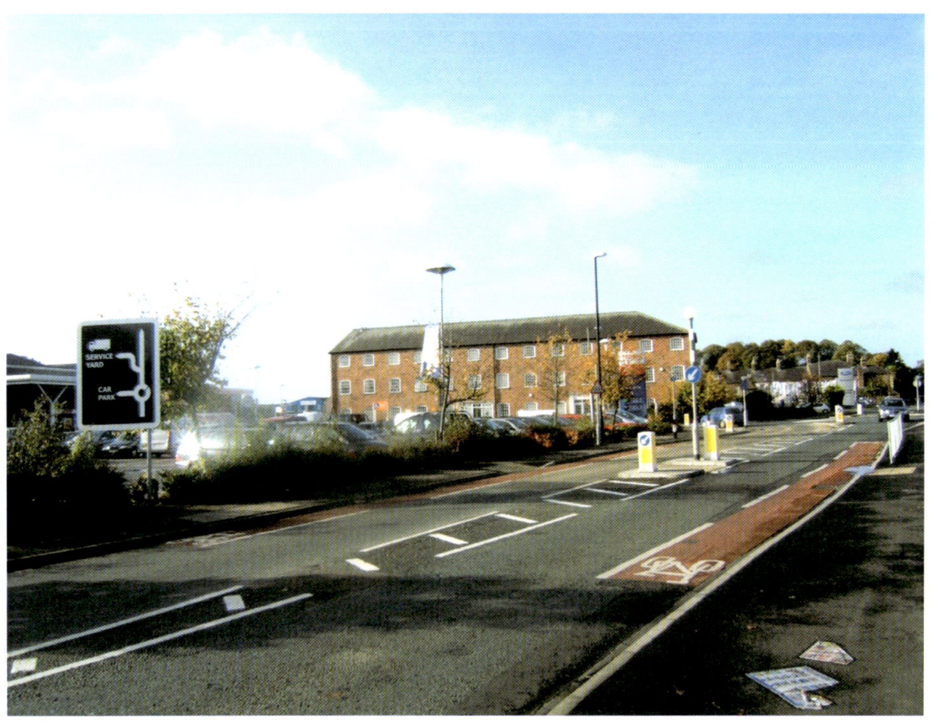

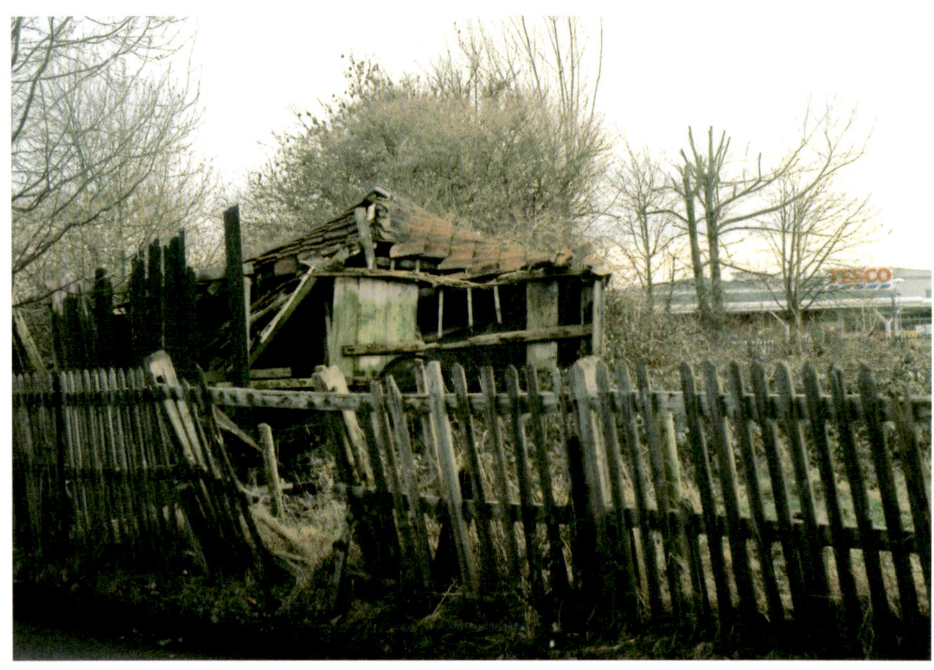

Johnson's Farm

On the corner of Newsham Road and Station Road there was a jumble of derelict farm buildings that were once used to house stock by Johnson's, long-established butchers in Thirsk. Despite its proximity to the racecourse and to development in the area, the old farmyard remained a local eyesore until the site was bought in 2008 by the German trading company Lidl. Their new store now occupies this spot and Johnson's farm is no more.

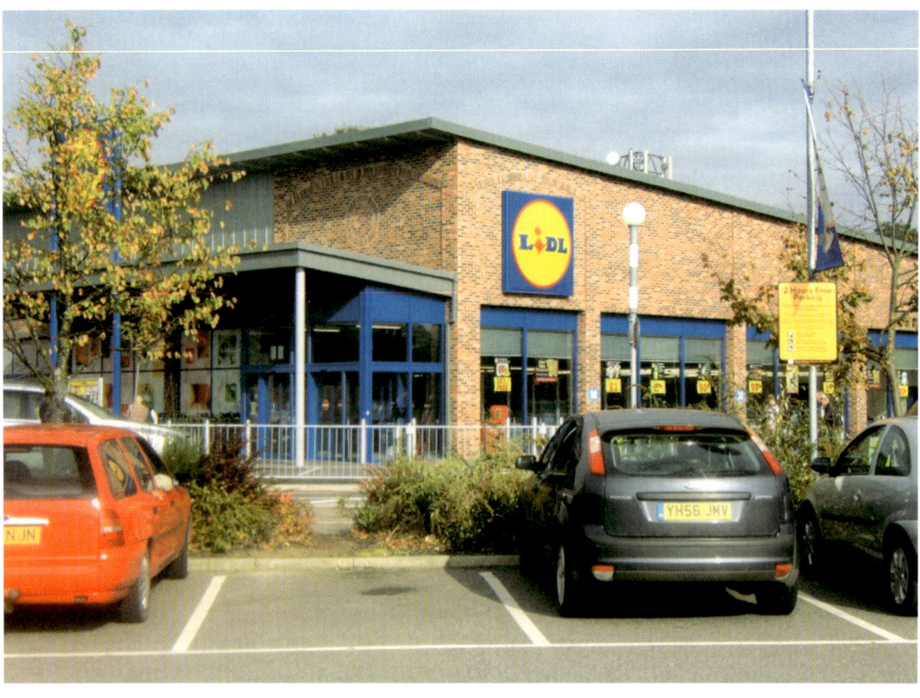

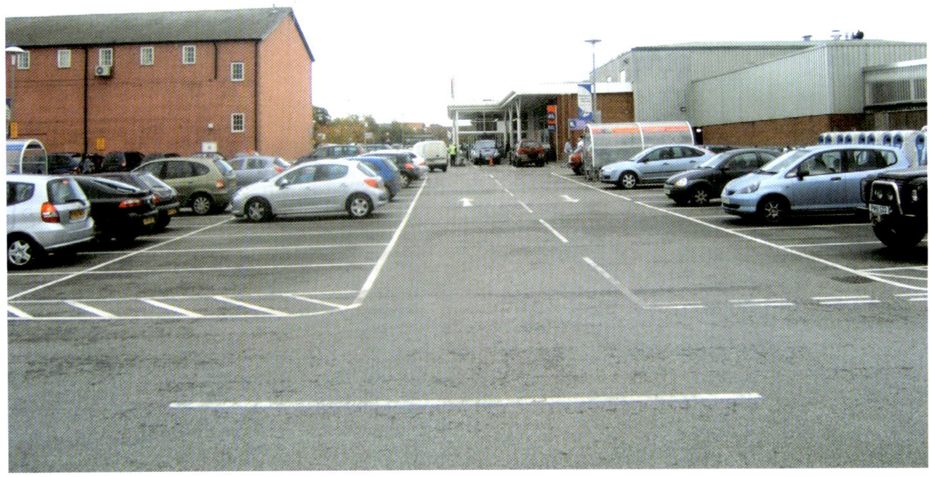

Thirsk Goods Station

How many people who use the Tesco car park realise that fifty years ago the lines here were railway lines? Thirsk goods station was the terminus of the Leeds and Ripon line, which opened in 1848, some years after the passenger station at Carlton Miniott on the North Eastern main line. This goods yard was the centre of an important commercial part of the town, with the coal depot, Bamlett's engineering, the maltings and the cattle mart all adjacent. Like so many branch lines, the goods yard closed with the Beeching cuts and all trace has gone, save for the name of Railway Terrace.

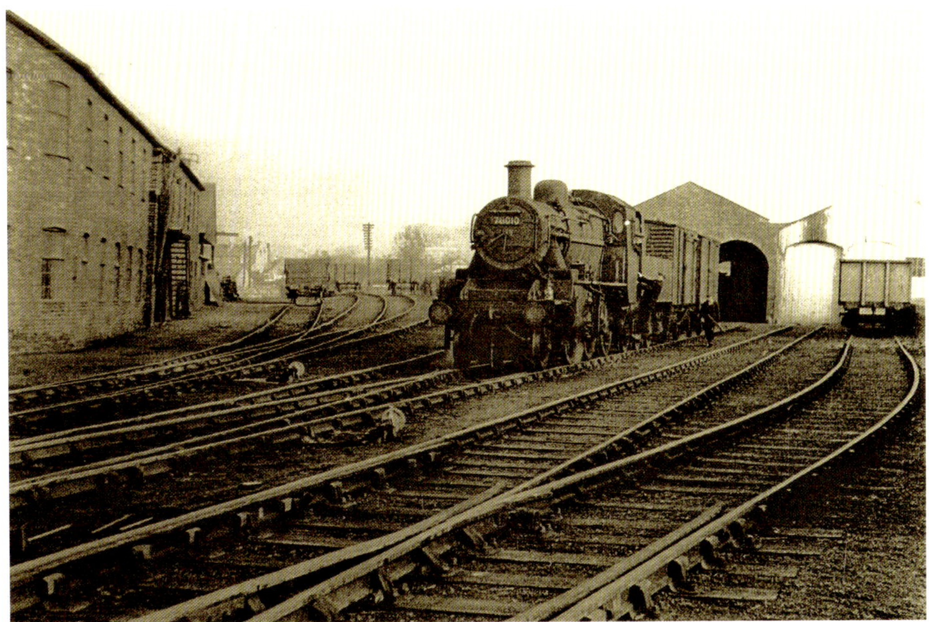

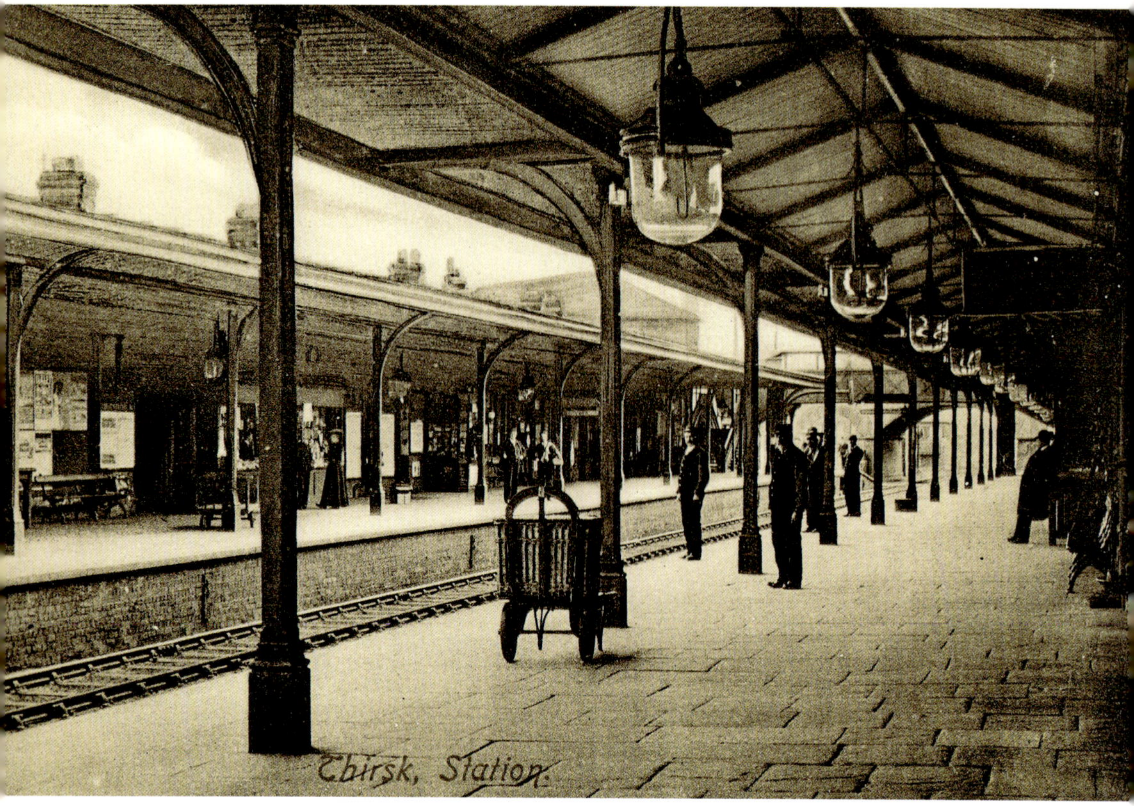

Thirsk, Station.

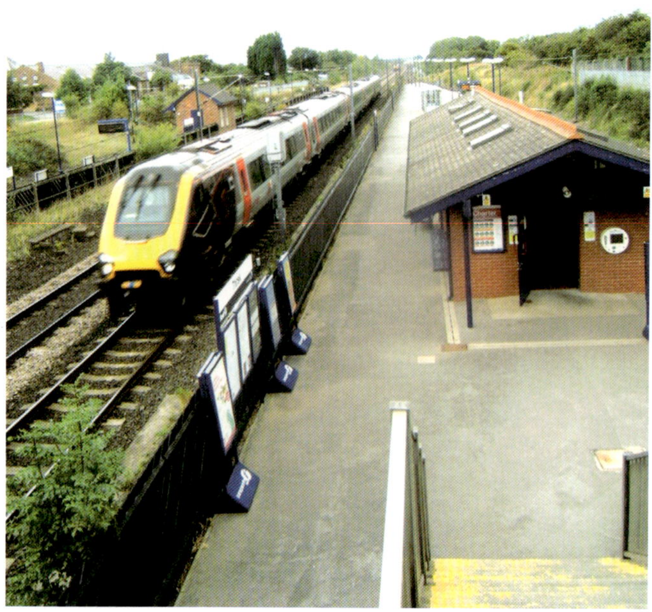

The Main Line Station

The first picture shows porters waiting on both platforms at the main line station. In those days, Thirsk was an important junction, with first- and second-class refreshment rooms on both platforms, ladies' and gents' toilets, booking office, newspaper stall and a tobacco kiosk. Celebrities could often be spotted on the platform, changing for Leeds or the North. The recent photograph shows today's platform amenities as a high-speed train flashes past.

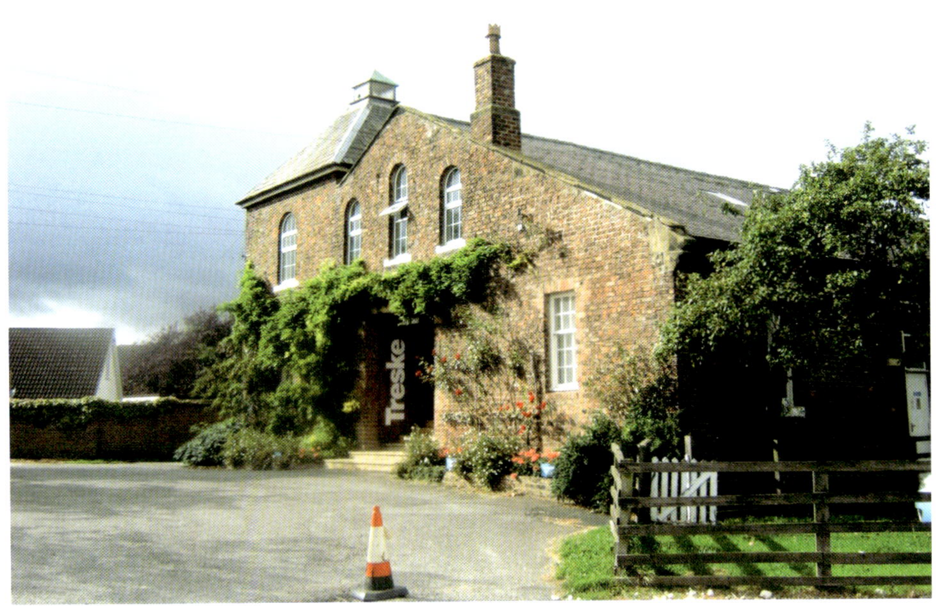

The Maltings

This building next to the station, now Treske furniture makers, was built by Joseph and Edward Milnthorpe, maltsters of Alne. At one time, they owned maltings by the railway in several places, with their own sidings to load and unload both barley and the malt produced from it. There were also maltings next to the goods yard at Town End. The second picture shows a group of maltsters with the wooden shovels, the traditional tool of their trade.

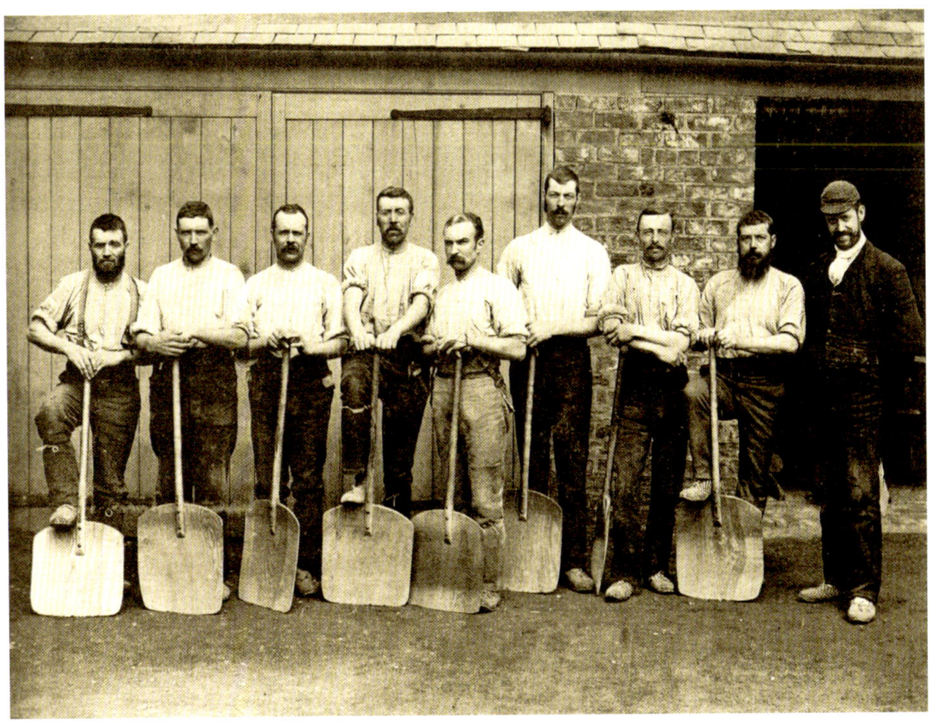

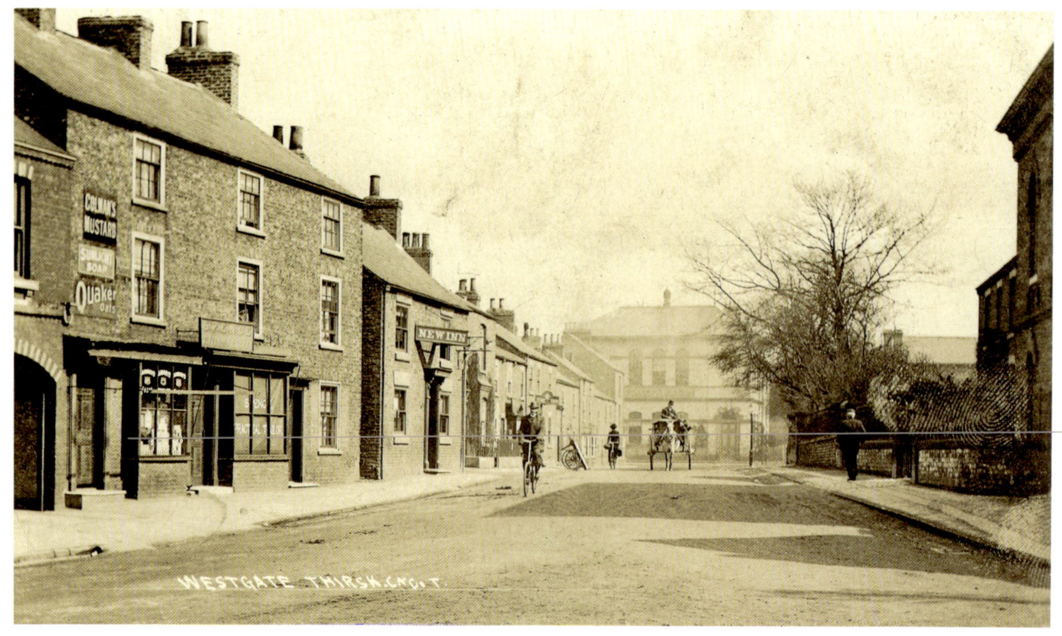

Westgate

This postcard shows Westgate as it was in Edwardian times, the only traffic being two cyclists (both riding on the right-hand side of the road!), together with a horse and cart. The shop on the left was Spence's 'Practical Tailors'. Beyond that are two public houses, the New Inn and the Star. As the modern view shows, all three are now private residences.

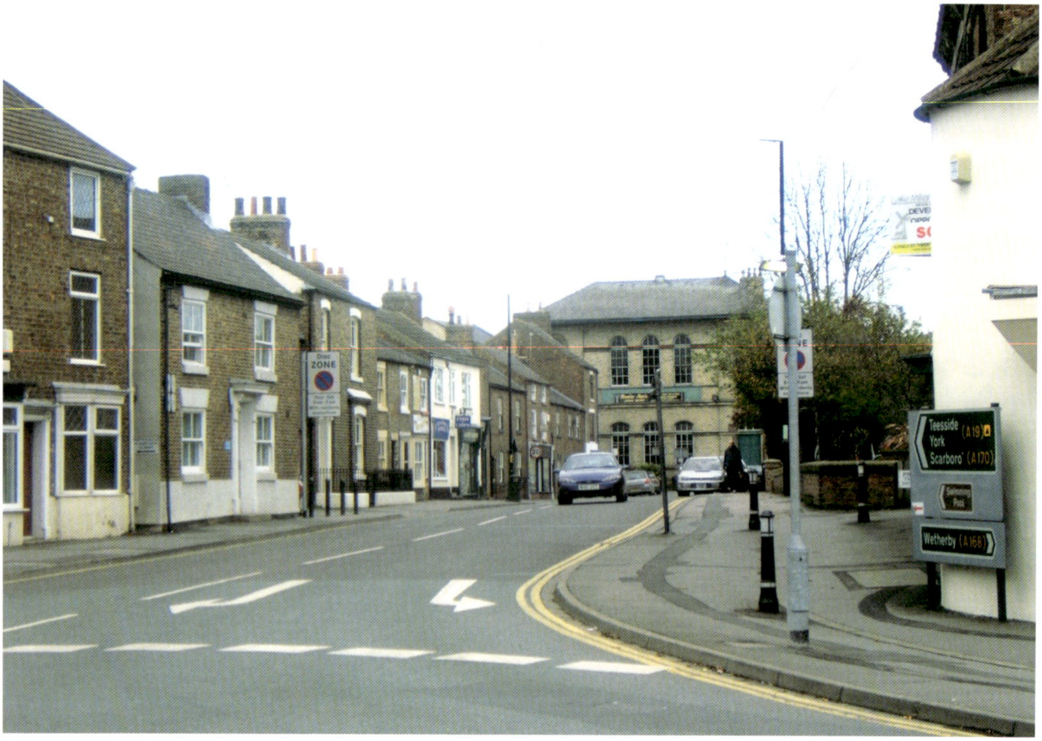

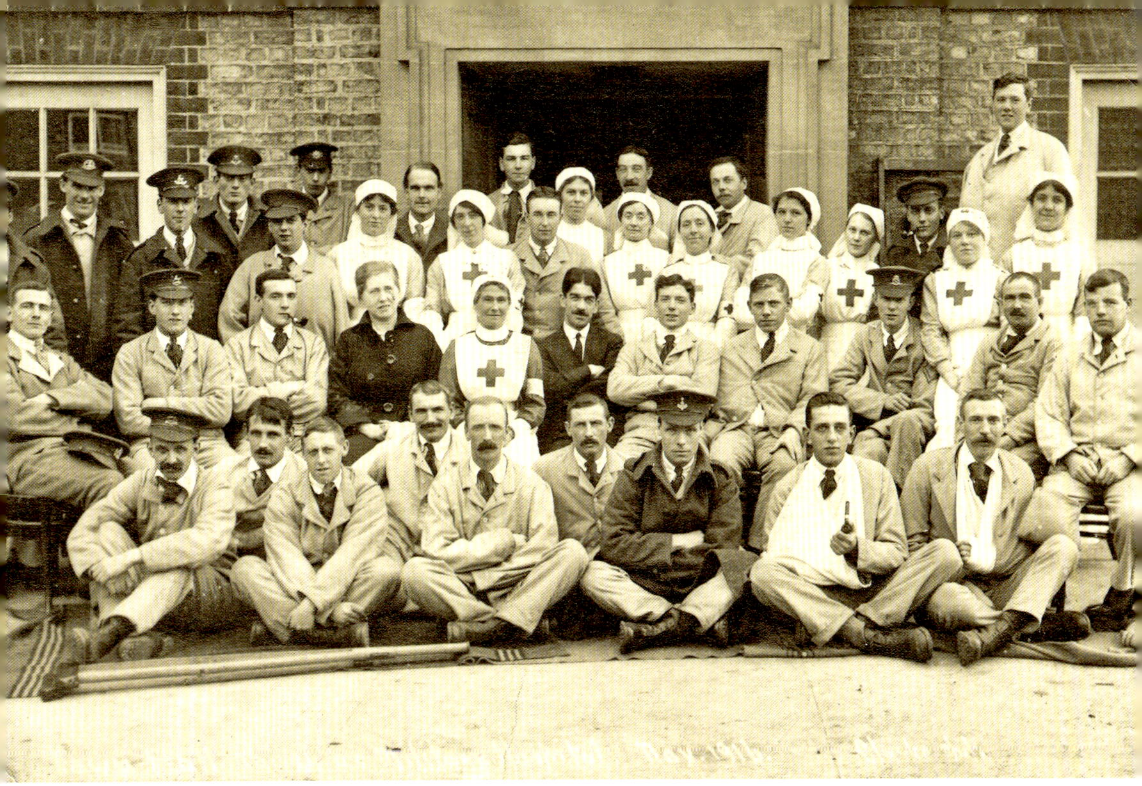

The Ritz Cinema

In 1912, Walter Power leased the former Mechanics Institute in Westgate and turned it into a cinema. With the outbreak of war in 1914, the Town Hall next door became a convalescent hospital for wounded soldiers, staffed by volunteer nurses. Power put on regular free shows for the men. The postcard shows him in the centre of a group of patients and their nurses, his wife is also there, sitting two seats along. Power's cinema is now the Ritz, owned by the town council and run most successfully by volunteer staff.

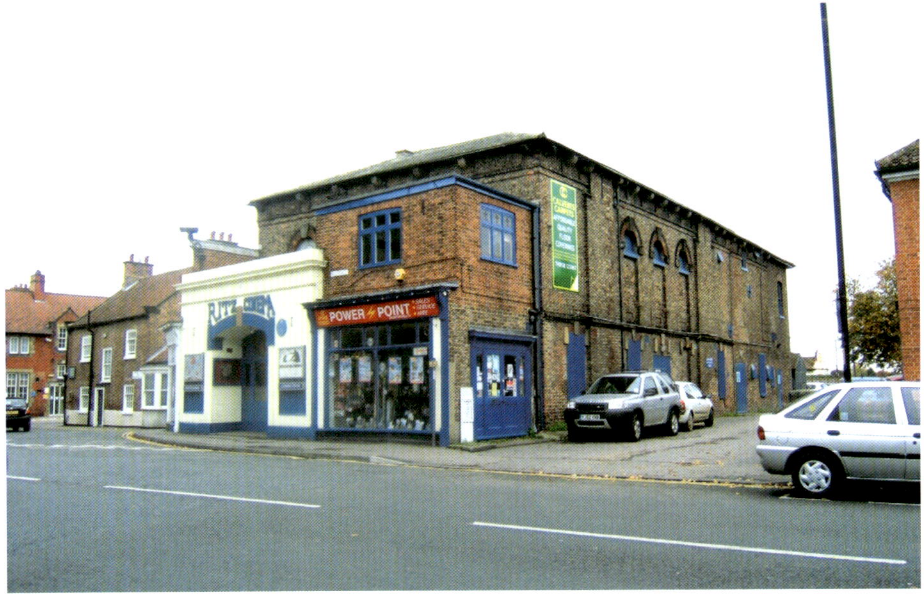

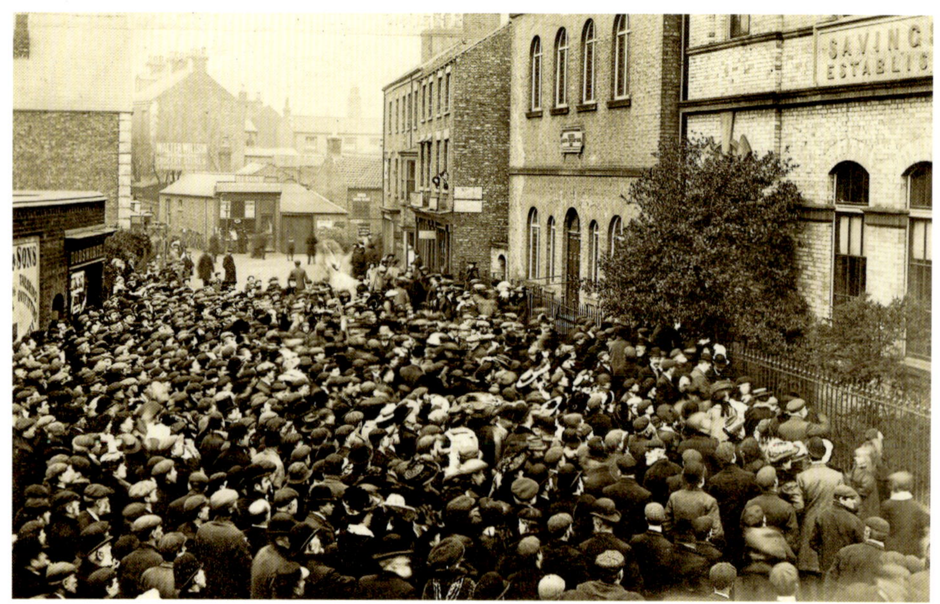

Election Day 1906

The 1906 postcard shows the crowd in Castlegate awaiting the declaration of poll from the window of the Assembly Rooms in the Savings Bank building. The figures show that Lord Helmsley, Conservative, had a majority of 800. The building next to the Savings Bank was the Primitive Methodist Chapel. The single-storey shop in the distance was Dixon's shoe-shop, while the cottages next to it later made way for the Regent Cinema. Today, the bank building awaits development, having been at one time a fitness gym and then a junk store. The chapel is now a carpet shop, while the Regent Cinema has given way to a wine bar and offices.

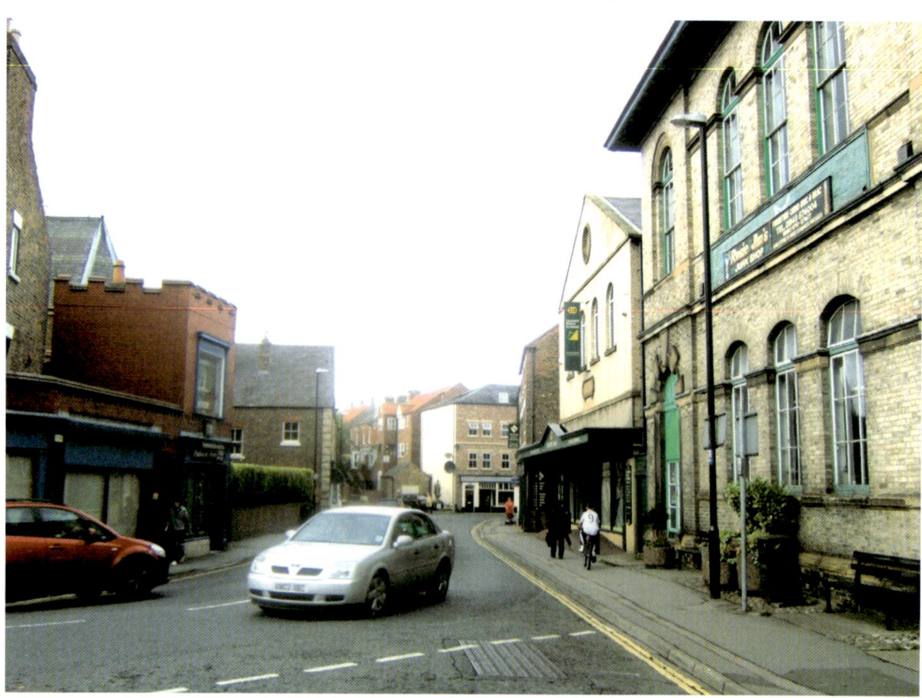

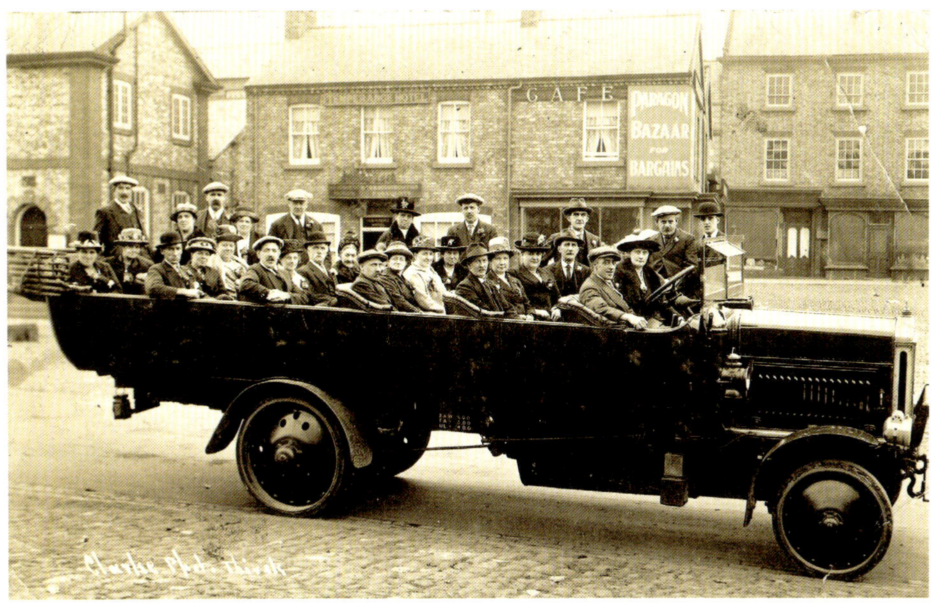

A Grand Day Out!

Lying in the Vale of Mowbray between the North York Moors and the Yorkshire Dales, Thirsk is an ideal starting point for tours of this fine part of the country. The first photo shows a charabanc about to set off from the Market Place on an excursion. The age of the passengers and their rather formal attire suggest that this is perhaps a chapel or social club outing. The modern coach party are nearly all on board, ready for the next stage in their tour of Herriot Country.

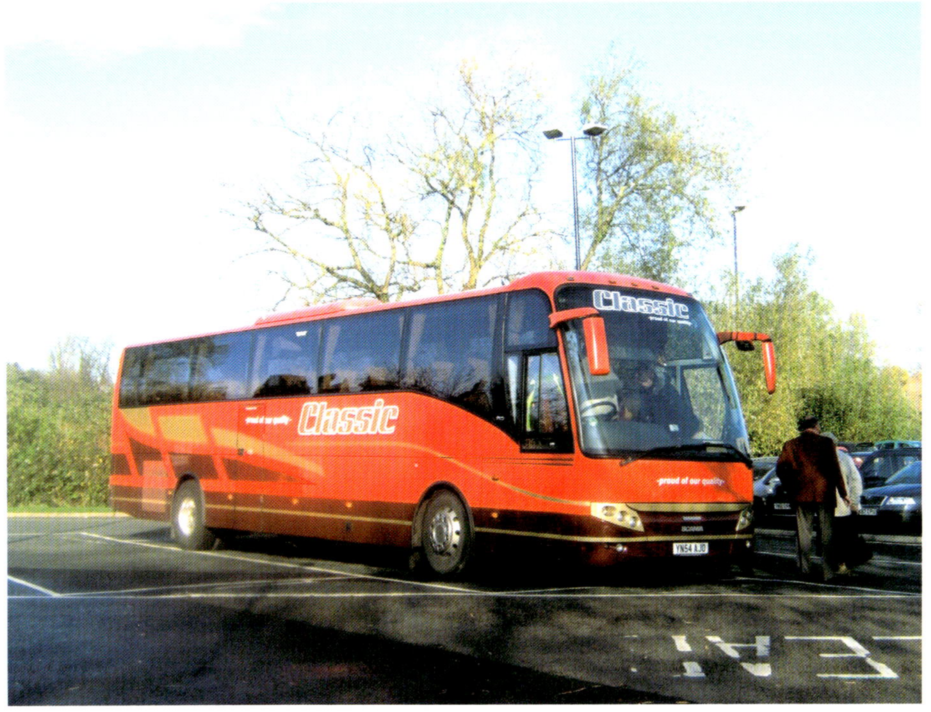

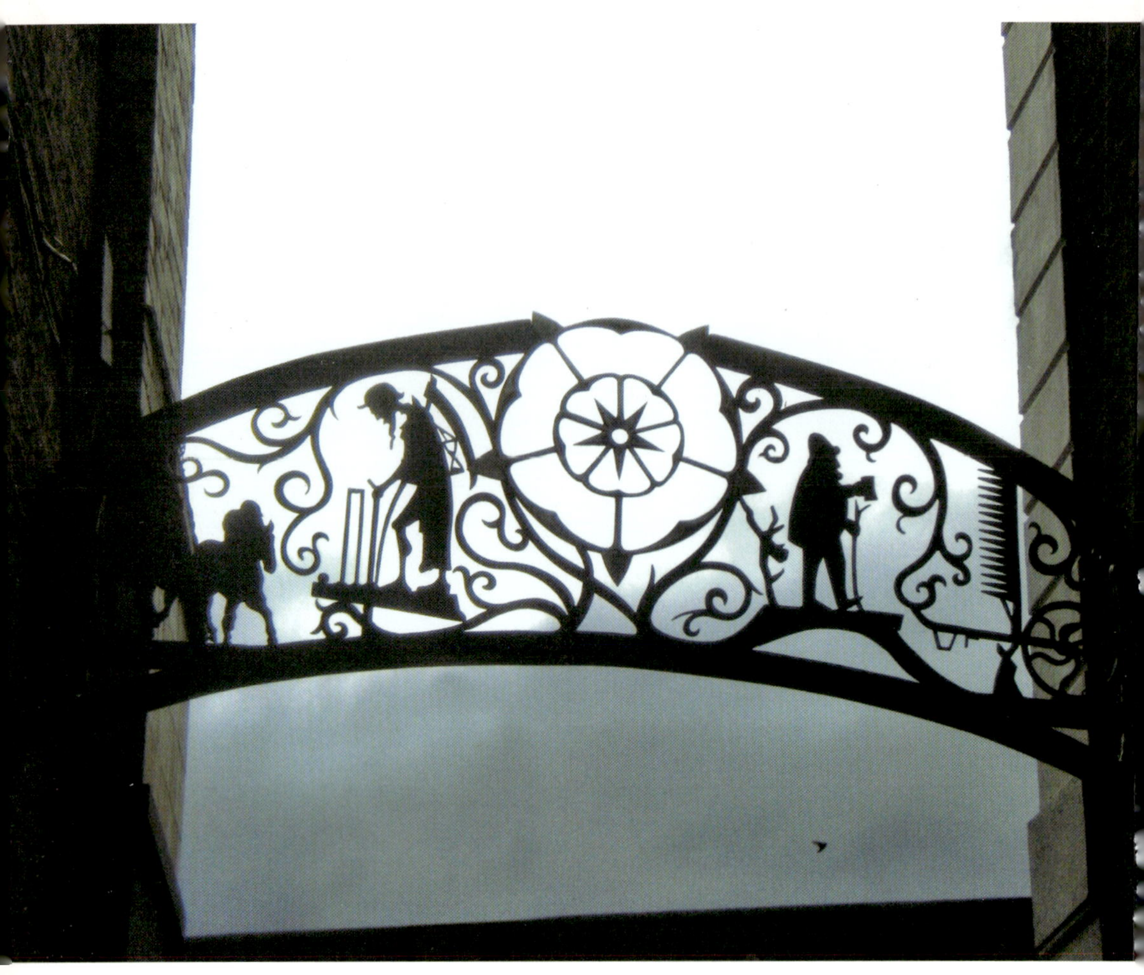

Baker's Alley

This wrought iron arch has recently been put up in Baker's Alley. With the Yorkshire rose at the centre, the other figures symbolise aspects of the town — racing, Lord's cricket ground, the Ingramgate drover and Bamlett's grass-cutter.